Long Live the World! Live with Prosperity!

Vedhathiriam for World Peace

Elaborated by:

Palaniswaamy Velaswamy
Professor- SKY, WCSC, Chennai

Dedicated to Vedathiri Maharishi — the Light of Universal Peace.

Contents

S.No.	Name of the Plan	Page
1	A World Without War	001
2	Equality in the Economic Field	024
3	Justice aligned with Divine Law	049
4	One Governance for the World	072
5	Reformed Culture of Virtue	092
6	Life Guided by the Wise	115
7	Recognizing the Greatness of Women	134
8	Live by the Law of Divine Justice	184
9	Avoiding the (Temple) Car-Festival	214
10	Sports for Children Only	236
11	Education to Realize Cause and Effect	252
12	Explanation of the Bio-Magnetic Principle	274
13	Globalization of Food and Water	300
14	Abolishing the Practice of "Many Religions – Many Gods" and Discern the Single Truth	320

Long Live the World! **Live with Prosperity!**

O Guru, who taught me the art of silencing the mind and being still,
In that state, knowledge remains unmoving, great bliss overflows!
In this vast world, after taking many births, you have granted me A
life of Eternal peace. This is my joyous message!

Preface

Respected Scholars! Throughout human history, divine teachings and religions have arisen through enlightened souls who realized truths beyond the senses. Their noble purpose was to guide humanity toward harmony, morality, and inner peace. Every prophet and saint sought to awaken mankind to one eternal truth - that divinity dwells within all beings, and that love, compassion, and self-realization are the true paths to God.

Over time, linguistic and cultural barriers obscured these truths. The universal message of oneness fragmented into divisions, as people began to believe their religion alone was supreme, leading to conflict and separation.

Among such realized souls, **Vedathiri Maharishi** stands as a beacon of wisdom and practicality. He not only expressed his realizations through prose and poetry but also offered scientific explanations and practical methods to apply them in daily life.

To spread this wisdom globally, he founded the **World Community Service Centre** and trained teachers to help people experience its benefits. His vision transcends all religions and nations, embracing humanity as one family living in peace and divine awareness.

With Guru's divine blessings,

Coimbatore,
20-06-2025

Palaniswaamy Velaswamy
Professor- SKY, WCSC, Chennai

World Peace Through Vedathiriam

Plan One

A World Without War

Bhagavan Vedhathiri Maharishi gifted to humankind an extraordinary, practical philosophy for living; a path of life that integrates both ideals and training. Anyone who contemplates *how to reform this world* will ultimately arrive at **Vedathiriam** as the answer.

It is an epic that begins with individual transformation and culminates in global fulfillment. History has proven time and again: **without individual transformation, societal transformation is impossible.**

To guide such personal change, Maharishi formulated the **Fivefold Code of Discipline.** When individuals attain excellence, world peace naturally follows.

Without personal integrity, the 14 Vedathiriam plans for global peace cannot bear fruit, because the flaws addressed in these 14 plans are **deep-rooted toxic trees**, hidden within society. Uprooting them is no simple task.

Reforming a society that lives by the philosophy: "Each person's wealth is his own; but others' wealth is common property," is extremely challenging.

In individual ethics, two core principles must become universal:

* *Cultivate love that seeks to relieve others' suffering.*

* *Respect and safeguard others' property and freedom as one's own.*

These ideals must begin within the individual and expand to include others as oneself. For this transformation to occur, **compassion must blossom in the heart.**

When one begins to regard others as equal to oneself, love and compassion naturally flow toward relieving their suffering. When this noble quality spreads through society, **world peace becomes possible.**

The **first step** of this mission is to **inform people** about these ideals. Awareness must precede action. A lesson not understood through teaching may strike home when life delivers the blow.

That is the moment when Vedathiriam principles for world peace must be sown into the hearts of society.

The **first principle of Vedathiriam** is: **"A Peaceful World Without War."**

* When did war first arise in human history?

* Why does it persist?

* When, and how, will it cease to exist?

This chapter seeks to answer these questions.

The **root of war is anger**

The root of anger is **desire**

The root of desire is **need**

The root of need lies in **natural law**

And behind natural law is the **Divine Source**.

As poet Kannadasan said:

The sins committed by God are the sorrows we see here

What a mind, what a character, what a form this human has!

What does he mean by *"the sin committed by God"?*

"Is it God's sin we suffer here? No

It is our mind, our tendencies, the masks we wear that cause all this pain."

So, what is this ***sin of God****?*

When the **divine state** surged into dynamic state, **primordial particles** were born. The energy for this creation came from the divine itself.

If one realizes that the merciful Divine is the very state that feeds the embryo in the womb and sustains even the tiny froglet within the rock, world peace will naturally prevail.

At the core of it, all our needs are met by **nature.** Life's prosperity is nothing but the union of **natural resources and human resources.** True prosperity is not having just enough, but **having surplus after need is met.**

Even a plant naturally balances its needs through its instinctive intelligence. When **two-sensed worm** (organism with limited awareness) first appeared, it **lost the ability to produce its own food** and thus became dependent on others for survival.

This dependent state continued up to the **five-sensed birds and animals**, which survive by preying on other life forms for food.

When a tiger is hungry, it chases a deer. The **tiger's anger** arises from its failure to secure food, while the **deer's anxiety** is born of the instinct to preserve life. The struggle between *securing food and preserving life* is what evolves into **hostility**.

Even when human beings emerged, they didn't immediately develop the ability to produce their own food. Thus, animalistic struggles continued among humans as well.

Even after humans developed various means of production and lived through millennia of advancement, the animalistic fight for survival still persists. The **root cause** of this continued warfare is **ignorance about divinity and divine justice.**

Because of the primitive memory patterns centered around bodily survival, humans still ***snatch others' wealth, rights, freedom, relationships, and opportunities;*** *these continue to be the causes of modern war.*

Sometimes a nation invades another to acquire resources it deems necessary. Other times, it annexes foreign territory to expand its influence and impose dominance. This craving for wealth and dominance over others is what leads to war.

Maharishi questions: **Is this truly a necessity?**

History claims that humans have existed for over 2 million years, yet wars have never ceased. After the Twin Tower attacks in the U.S., there has been a slight reduction in global warfare. While this is a positive change, true and lasting peace can only come through a Unified World Government.

So many great intellectuals

In this world, may humankind live in harmony and joy

They compiled, explained, and spread the

Pure path of San Marga (righteous path of truth)

Through the efforts of the noble, many attained

Discipline, virtue, and inner realization

Surpassing all these, now and then,

Doesn't war destroy humanity itself? – *Maharishi*

If we truly wish to embrace the spirit of ***Every place is my home; all people are my kin***, then the path of pure righteous living must be widely spread among the people.

Unfortunately, religions that were meant to carry this responsibility have abandoned this duty.

*If a **Single World Government** is established, **the fear of war will vanish from human life.*** Though the UN Security Council holds the responsibility to prevent wars, there is still no global regulation to disband national militaries.

*After all, can war happen without armies? If **there was no army**, with whom would we wage war?*

The core motives behind war are usually to **conquer territory** or to **seize economic power**. If the value of material things is balanced and if people are educated in **Dharma** that coveting another's property is a sin, *then wars driven by material greed will naturally decline.*

Boundaries between regions were originally set by **nature itself,** with oceans, mountains, and forests serving as natural dividers. These areas were often not suited for habitation or daily use.

If the responsibility of ***maintaining these natural borders*** *is given to the United Nations, border disputes would diminish.*

The ***simplest path*** *to achieve this:* ***One World Government is enough. One governance system is sufficient.***

We have communism, capitalism, and socialism. But what we ***lack is humanism****. When humanism emerges, all other systems will become obsolete.*

Humanism is the true foundation of social life. What more do we need?

When a culture of mutual cooperation and harmony spreads, and when people live without **competition or jealousy**, then **inner peace** will prevail.

By a single world government, the fear of war will vanish

If war ceases, Soldiers and materials will serve noble causes

Poverty will leave the earth, and virtue will flourish,

A reformed way of life will be realized - reflect upon this.

- Vedathiri Maharishi

If a One World Government is established, then the **UN will assume the responsibility of security for all nations**. Individual nations will no longer maintain their own armies, thereby reducing the threat of war. The hard work of soldiers and the vast funds used for military purposes will be redirected toward **public welfare**.

If the billions currently spent on the military efforts, along with the efforts of brave soldiers, are redirected to **social upliftment**, we could: dredge rivers, build dams, repair roads, and undertake many other public improvements.

A large population of **youth with excellent physical and mental potential** is being wasted under the name of war training.

The ***loss of lives in war is unspeakable****. War is* ***illegal by moral standards****, yet it continues.*

If war is eliminated, global poverty will be removed, the quality of life will rise, and culture will flourish. With people helping and supporting one another, humanism will prevail and reach noble heights.

To attentively analyze the pleasure and pain of other living beings using refined intelligence, and to act in a way that alleviates their suffering is compassion; that is selfless love.

Only when such a noble, cultured way of life arises can we say that a reformed living has been achieved. Everyone should reflect on this noble idea`.

Reform means aligning one's thoughts, words, and actions according to the **natural law**, known as harmony.

The lofty plan of a World Common Government

Alone can prevent the rise of war.

Such a system will protect every nation and its people

Without fear or domination.

Any plan lesser than a world common government

Will not bring true benefit.

Science has greatly advanced - in rapid travel,

Communication, and commerce alike.

But without a world common government,

All this will gradually break down over time.

In truth, the people of the world long to live

Safely and free from fear of war

To live and prosper in this world,

Each individual must strive to spread this noble idea

Wave upon waves across the world,

For it is our sacred duty to do so. *- Vedathiri Maharishi*

The idea of One World Government is the only higher-level plan that can protect humanity from war. Any lesser alternative - even the most well-crafted political systems, constitutions, or modes of living - has not, and cannot, offer **complete benefit**.

History has shown this truth across the centuries. Science has reached astonishing heights, especially with the success of research on atomic particles. Discovering the ***atom*** *was a* *triumph for science. If mankind had used this atom for* ***electric power****, it would have been a* ***victory for humanity****. But instead, the* ***manufacture of the atomic bomb*** *became a* ***downfall for science****. Even today, nations continue to threaten one another with nuclear weapons.*

Science has **two directions**:

* One **for upliftment**, and

* The other **for destruction**.

"In understanding dualities - sharpness and righteousness - The world honors those who live with virtue." (Tiruvalluvar)

"Duality" here refers to two qualities:

* **Sharpness** – the power of analysis, observation, and extracting nature's resources for human benefit.

* **Righteousness** – the moral guidance (truth, honesty, discipline, and ethics) that must accompany scientific advancement.

If righteousness is lost, the goal of science is corrupted, and science begins to inflict suffering in various forms.

Indeed, due to scientific progress, fast transportation and efficient commerce have thrived. Internet technology allows people to connect to any corner of the world in seconds.

But what was the ***divine intention*** *behind enabling scientists to develop high-speed travel and instantaneous communication?*

Because the Earth is not uniformly blessed with all resources in every region.

For example, **Arab countries** have petroleum but **lack food**. In contrast, other regions may have abundant food but no petroleum.

To address this **imbalance**, **exchange of goods** became necessary. Transport and communication systems developed rapidly through science to send surplus materials from one place to another.

But without One World Governance, these systems are often disrupted.

If goods are **hoarded**, scarcity causes **price inflation**, allowing some to earn excessive profits. Because **trade** came between **production and consumption**, equitable distribution became a challenge.

Artificial shortages created deliberately cause **confusion and inflation** among the people. If humanity is to live safely and without fear of war, it is our duty to relentlessly spread the noble vision of One World Governance.

The root of this problem lies in the basic thought: "As long as I am safe, that's enough."

Why? Because of the **fear of future need**.

People hoard goods due to **insecurity**. This **same insecurity** is the root of people **seizing others' property**. If people are assured that everything they need **will always be available**, there will be no need for hoarding or rationing resources.

We are **all born on this Earth.** Who has **more right** to it? Who has **less**? Who has **none at all**?

If one group tries to **destroy** another, **who gave them the right to destroy?** Just as **I was born with the right to live freely, so was every other life form.**

We must accept this **truth of nature.** Nature has not given **anyone** the license to destroy the freedom of another. The world must awaken to this truth.

We are ***all born on this Earth****, the same soil*

The ***air that sustains life*** *is one and the same*

The ***Sun that shines its light*** *is one and the same*

The ***oceans*** *are one, the* ***rain*** *is from the same vapor*

Yet none of us ***created*** *any of these*

All who are born must live and one day pass on

If one group of people kills another to survive

And calls it justice, then only murderers remain. *- Maharishi*

When war breaks out, one side kills and overwhelms the other. The one who is killed is declared defeated. The one who kills is proclaimed victorious. But the victor is still a killer. If this killer has a child, what will that child be called?

Jesus said, *"So, you testify against yourselves that you are the descendants of those who murdered the prophets." - Matthew 23:31, NIV.*

This means: the karmic memory of killing, embedded in the genetic center, continues to incite acts of violence in future generations. Everyone has their end; so, why hasten someone else's death? What happened to those emperors who once conquered the whole world?

If we truly understand that and **cultivate the feeling that others have the same right to live as we do**, then and only then can the world be reformed.

Across the world, the World Peace Organization

Serves humanity through many divisions,

Working earnestly in cooperation with governments,

Establish themselves as an international institution.

Honest engineers, doctors, psychologists, and scientists

Their service should reach every village and individual,

Along with this, knowledge will be awakened to wisdom.

- Vedathiri Maharishi

The name **World Community Service Center** carries a deep insight. Had it instead been named **World Peace Service Center**, Maharishi might have received worldwide recognition, wealth, and fame.

But why did he not choose that name?

Because **one day world peace will indeed arrive**. And **when it does**, there must be a **permanent institution** to safeguard it.

That is the role of World Community Service Center (WCSC). It is a perpetual organization to protect peace and serve the people as long as humanity exists.

When humans were born into this world, they **were not born on battlefields.** Then how did war come about?

Just as the animalistic memories embedded in the genetic center continue to rekindle the spirit of conflict, there must be a *protective organization* to prevent such tendencies from resurfacing.

To protect the peace now achieved, branches of the World Community Service Center must be established all around.

Because the primary duty of the World Community Service Center is to preserve individual morality and uphold Dharma, its contributions greatly support the government, particularly in the domains of law enforcement and public safety.

Just as the **administrative system** of One World Governance would be widespread across the globe, so too should the **Peace Organization**, which safeguards and teaches **human morality**, be established **worldwide**.

Honest engineers will undertake the development of safe and ethical urban infrastructure, such as water management through dam construction, roads, and bridges.

With a **corruption-free and bribe-free governance**, engineers will be able to work freely and sincerely. When engineers **lack conscience and honesty**, they **resort to deception**.

If **integrity is missing** in society, governments and officials will act out of self-interest, misusing the **people's tax money**. As a result, both **public amenities and safety** will deteriorate. Moreover, if society becomes obsessed with money, culture and values will begin to collapse.

If honesty disappears from the field of medicine, compassion and humanity will vanish. Even dead patients are sometimes kept in **intensive care** for days, just to extract more money from their families.

Wise intellectuals and spiritual leaders who guide people through **paths of devotion and dharma** still stand as pillars of a virtuous society, through their scripture.

They must consistently reinforce a sense of divine awareness and ethical conduct among the public. As for scientists, they must eventually limit the creation of new inventions meant merely for luxury or indulgence.

Though comforts are necessary, if **newer and newer versions** of the same object are endlessly introduced, the people, being **puppets of desire,** will **never be satisfied**.

When satisfaction can't be attained with one's income, **corruption and bribery** become inevitable.

If, at some point, we decide a product is sufficient and avoid unnecessary additions, even obsession with novelty will gradually fade from human nature.

To explain the philosophy of human life

To all the people of the world,

And to abolish armies everywhere,

All nations must unite under a World Government

With purity of heart and noble intent.

A council of responsible scholars shall arise,

Who, with compassion, will guide the realm of politics

And reform the political parties through their wisdom.

- Vedathiri Maharishi

If comforts and luxuries continue to increase for a few, those who will harbor feel jealousy, resentment, and hatred. This will lead to a rise in cheating, theft, robbery, and even murder, causing the breakdown of social well-being and leading to police action, court cases, and imprisonment.

But do we not all have the same type of human body?

If some demand ever-new comforts while others are left with mere flesh and bones, is that Dharma?

Can we provide all luxuries equally to everyone?

If a person cannot access comforts through honest labor, what kind of situation will that create?

That is what communism tries to do - seize from the haves and give to the have-nots. But if a person can gain without effort, will he be motivated to work at all?

The just way of life is for each person to earn through their intellectual or physical labor. To ensure fair compensation for labor, One World Governance is the only solution.

Once **wages are fairly determined**, economic disparity will gradually reduce, and one day, disappear.

In an office with ten employees, not everyone will have the same level of ability:

* Two may be **highly skilled**,

* Six may have **average abilities**,

* And two may be **lazy or unproductive**.

This is ***natural law****. Why does God give one person* ***more talent than others****? Because he is expected to* ***compensate for the shortcomings of those with lesser ability****.*

If this principle is understood, then one won't complain: "Why am I the only one working harder?"

Instead, one will feel: "I am helping those with less ability," and such a feeling brings **inner satisfaction** and **elevates human compassion**.

Therefore, the duty of administrators is not to **measure productivity alone**, but to ensure:

"Is each person working according to their ability?"

Similarly, while fixing salaries, **human needs** should be the basis; not the false distinction between a **towering mountain** and a **small valley** (i.e., excessive disparity).

Excessive salaries and excessive profits are the real causes of wealth hoarding.

To avoid resentment like: "Why is there no major difference between my high post and his low post?"

We must offer **everyone a clear understanding of life's philosophy and natural law**.

Education must combine:

* **Literacy**,

* **Vocational knowledge**,

* **Philosophical insight**, and

* **Ethical training.**

Only then can a **balanced and just society** be achieved.

To bring about One World Governance, a sacred mindset is essential.

As long as selfishness dominates, such a mindset cannot arise.

Only those with a broad and selfless hearts will actively strive for the welfare of others.

In a world where theft and exploitation are considered cleverness, working for public welfare becomes extremely difficult.

That is why the idea of raising children under the guidance of scholars is an integral part of One World Governance.

Scholars interested in global peace must come together, formulate noble plans, and compassionately take on the task of refining political parties around the world.

Bestowing diverse forms of prosperity to enrich life's joy,

Establishing peace through noble means is the mission

To advance this noble cause, enlightened thinkers of the world,

Filled with enthusiasm, must unite in purpose everywhere.

They should establish a World Common Organization,

So that this ideal may be deeply rooted in the minds of people.

Branches must be spread across nations,

To awaken mind and inspire the quest for understanding.

- Vedathiri Maharishi

The plan that ensures profound welfare to humanity is none other than world peace. Those noble scholars who believe in this vision must come together, engage in sincere dialogue, and with unified will, design a practical, implementable plan.

They must establish both a central headquarters and branches all across the globe. Local branch members should **repeatedly explain this vision to the public**, until it becomes deeply rooted in public consciousness.

Moreover, they must cultivate the habit of inquiry and understanding among people, so that individuals will think clearly and act with discernment.

God is One. The universe is one. The Earth and Moon are one. *The basic needs of all people are also the same:*

Food, water, clothing, shelter, relationships, friendship, education, employment, healthcare, security, happiness, and inner contentment - *these are* ***rights granted by God****, and* ***no one has the authority to deny them****.*

As poet Vaali wrote: *"You have a share, and I have a share; this is assured in the world. Every person's labor contributes to the prosperity of the Earth."*

If the purpose of work becomes firmly rooted, then the desire to exploit or steal will disappear. What is needed is to nurture the thirst for discerning knowledge.

As Thiruvalluvar said: *"Whatever the nature of a thing may be, true knowledge is to perceive its real essence."*

Through such intellectual clarity, the foundations for common welfare and a universal system of governance can be laid and accepted.

If we apply this rational discernment in thought, then the capable may take up **leadership**, and those less capable may, through proper understanding, **accept the capable leader with unity and clarity;** thus, ensuring that only **goodness prevails.**

If conflict is to vanish from among individuals,

The system of ***common ownership*** *must prevail.*

If war is to disappear and peace reigns in the world,

A world governance must be established for all.

- Vedathiri Maharishi

In a society where everyone has equal access to everything, what conflict can remain? Once things are equitably shared, scarcity will vanish.

If such a **peaceful social system** spreads, then war will fade away. To **protect and distribute goods**, a **unified world government** must assume responsibility.

The human energy now spent in warfare

Will, in time, turn toward engineering and creation,

When scientific knowledge flourishes in all,

The order of nature will stand revealed in perfection.

Receiving light and heat from the sun,

Subtle atoms will attain magnetic power.

We shall build instruments to gather that energy

And live with discipline at the pinnacle of wisdom. - Maharishi

The experiences gained by the wise serve as guidance for those who have stumbled in life. Knowledge of **natural resources** grows into **technical expertise**, and both of these evolve into spiritual and scientific wisdom, spreading throughout society.

The Sun's energy becomes the fundamental source for sustainable industries. When one understands the laws of nature, discipline becomes natural.

Food, water, electricity *- all these are natural resources that belong to everyone. But* ***no one has the right*** *to* ***overconsume*** *or* ***waste*** *them. This truth must be understood by all.*

The practical knowledge of how to use each resource efficiently and effectively itself is science. With such **practical insight, scarcity and suffering** can be removed.

The **peak of wisdom** lies in:

* **Clarity of knowledge**

* **Clarity in how to live**

* And **wisdom that relieves the suffering of others**.

What is the inner struggle within each human?

It is the **struggle between needs and possessions**, between **desire and the welfare of others**.

This **inner battle** is the real **battle of life**.

Without winning over oneself, how can one ever conquer the world?

Individual peace is the **seed of world peace**. **Mental peace** is the **foundation of global harmony**.

Only when the mind stands on the side of solutions can world peace become a reality.

Otherwise, man himself becomes a battlefield.

The expansion of morality leads to world peace. Universal brotherhood will rise in dignity.

The land that existed before you were born,

The land that was given for the good of all

Will remain here, even after you are gone

If you call it ownership, it will only laugh at you.

A world without war requires a mind without conflict.

Until the people attain inner fulfillment, our duty is to make righteous living flourish.

Summary:

This chapter is a visionary call for world peace by **Vedathiri Maharishi**, who emphasized that **personal transformation is the foundation for global harmony**.

His approach integrates ethics, meditation, and social responsibility into a unified philosophy known as Vedathiriam. Maharishi identified that **without inner moral discipline, no social reform is sustainable**.

Thus, he introduced the **Fivefold Code of Discipline** to instill values like honesty, compassion, and respect for others' rights and freedoms.

These values must be cultivated within individuals and extended outward to society.

The **root causes of war** - desire, anger, and ignorance - are traced back to **animalistic tendencies** still present in human memory.

Despite scientific and technological advances, **true peace remains elusive** due to the absence of spiritual understanding and ethical governance.

To prevent war and ensure lasting peace, the chapter advocates the establishment of a **One World Government** under a **global peace structure**. This system would:

* Eliminate national militaries

* Redirect defense budgets and manpower toward public welfare

* Foster economic equality

* Promote cooperation across borders

It stresses that **science without ethics becomes destructive**, and only when guided by righteousness can it uplift humanity.

Universal access to basic needs, such as food, shelter, healthcare, and education, is viewed as a **divine right**, not a privilege.

The role of the **World Community Service Center (WCSC)** is highlighted as a permanent institution to **preserve peace and nurture global Dharma**, beyond the arrival of peace itself.

Engineers, doctors, educators, scientists, and spiritual leaders all have vital roles in this vision of service.

The chapter also critiques extremes in luxury and poverty, warning that **unchecked materialism** breeds jealousy, crime, and social breakdown.

Instead, it proposes **fair wages, shared resources, and a system based on merit and need**, guided by compassion and spiritual clarity.

Ultimately, **a peaceful world begins with peaceful minds**.

Each person must reflect on life's purpose, conquer their inner conflicts, and embrace a way of life that aligns with natural law and collective wellbeing.

Plan Two

Equality in the Economic Field

Per Capita Resources:

The second principle of Vedathiriam World Peace Plan is Economic Justice. Though economics is the very foundation of life, people have come to believe that accumulating wealth centered on money is the true sign of economic growth.

The manifestation of the Absolute Reality transforms into the visible material world, perceivable by the senses and measurable through instruments.

Among these manifestations, **land** and **gold** have acquired the status of **valuable assets**.

The true essence of economics lies in the recognition that **natural resources** are the **foundation of life**. It is the resources discovered on Earth that form the basis of our economic life.

If we understand **how money became involved** in this system, the **madness for money** will begin to fade.

Maharishi Vedathiri asks: "As long as the farmer gave goods and received goods in return, in the time of the barter system, where was money? What was called wealth?"

So when, why, and for what purpose was money created?

In the beginning, there existed only **barter system**, focused primarily on **agriculture**. For example, someone who harvested rice would **exchange** it for vegetables. The surplus would be placed at the **village boundary**, and those in need would take what they required.

Thus, the street at the edge of the village where goods were kept was known as ***'mark end street'***. Over time, this practice evolved into the modern custom of going to the **market street** to buy goods.

When someone began to **organize, guard, and give** these goods to those who needed, **trade** was born. As difficulties arose in determining how much wheat for how many vegetables, people sought a simpler method of exchange.

To **ease the barter system**, **money was introduced** as an **exchange value**. Kings took on the responsibility of creating money.

What began as **gold coins** gradually evolved into **paper currency.** Yet, even today, on a global scale, **gold** remains the **universal value to settle trade balance** in export and import.

Money is nothing but a token of labor and the exchange value for necessary.

But once ways were discovered to **obtain money without labor**, society began to face **various complications.**

Within the fortress of money, goods are trapped,

Then released later through a system of gain.

Thus arose the system where wealth breeds wealth

An unworthy administration that has spread everywhere.

To prevent money from becoming a source of evil,

Let us establish cooperative production of goods in all places.

As the need for money gradually decreases day by day,

The working people will gain dignity and rise in prosperity.

- Vedathiri Maharishi

Making money without labor:

1. Land is taxed through lease

2. Homes by rent

3. Business by profit

4. Trade through commission

5. Loans with interest

6. And governance through taxes

These six ways of monetization, become "wealth without virtue", as said by Thiruvalluvar.

What we call **black money** - hidden, untaxed, and unaccounted - is ironically stored and protected in **black bank**. As traders flood the market with **consumer goods**, this gap between the **haves and have-nots** keeps widening.

So, what is **economic justice**? It is the principle that:

Everyone should have access to everything.

A condition must emerge where there is no scarcity.

Let the monopoly of the rich dissolve,

And let common ownership rise in this land. - *Kannadasan*

That is the true **economic equity** we must achieve.

All that Mother Nature gives belongs to everyone. The divisions of 'mine' and 'yours' are just illusions created in between.

In India, among the ***Companies Act 1956*****,** ***Private Companies Act*****,** ***Charities Trust Act 1882****, and* ***Hindu Undivided Family Act 1961****, only the* ***Co-operative Society model*** *truly reflects* ***collective ownership****.*

Some politicians in India claim they own no house yet live in lavish bungalows. When questioned, they say, ***The bungalow belongs to a company***. And when asked, ***Who are the directors of the company***? The reply comes: ***My wife and my son***.

What was the purpose behind enacting company law?

To legally facilitate individuals in converting public money into private property and securing it under lawful protection. It is a joint conspiracy where politics and business clasp hands.

Its core philosophy is: ***The enterprise belongs to the people, but it is under my control.***

If economic equality is to be achieved, in my perspective, the first step must be to **abolish cash transactions in urban areas** and **mandate electronic transfers**.

As poet Kannadasan says: *"When one lives by labor, there is no suffering, no debt, no worry."*

Next, the Companies Act of 1956, Private Companies Act, Charities Act, and Hindu Undivided Family Act must be repealed. **Why?**

Because even when people invest money by buying shares and starting companies, they do get the dividend at the mercy of directors not as rightful share of profits.

In India the stock market is nothing but a legally approved gambling arena, where one person's money is lawfully looted by another.

Because politics and commerce have expanded ways of earning without labor, greedy individuals, unaware that they are being made scapegoats, invest their hard-earned money in the stock market - like houseflies drawn to bait - hoping for profit but ending up with losses.

If such exploitative systems are reformed, India's economy will begin to move toward equality.

"The wise do not engage or encourage, in greed of gain,

Where the capital itself may suffer loss." *(Kural 463)*

Therefore, the **true form of collective ownership,** where all are stakeholders, is the **cooperative society**.

As **Udumalai Narayana Kavi** famously said:

"The farming method suited to our country is cooperative agriculture run by ourselves. The returns will be fair to our efforts. It's wise to abandon outdated practices.

A family cannot till a small bit of land profitably. But ten families working together on ten acres will yield true results." If this **cooperative model**, which begins with **agriculture**, is expanded to **other industries**, **private hoarding of wealth** will decline, and in time, **common ownership** will reach completion.

Homes, factories, farmlands, and trade,

Scientific machines (tools) and seats of governance,

All these must become common to the toiling people,

Through a structured system of cooperation at every level.

By linking each nation's prosperity with that of the world,

And shaping it for the well-being of all,

There must arise a matchless plan

Only such a system will bring welfare to mankind.

- Vedathiri Maharishi

Today, all major sectors - homes, industries, agriculture, trade, scientific tools, and political power - are concentrated in the hands of a few. The benefits of these are not fully reaching the common people. Why?

*Because the **working class is only paid enough** to meet **basic needs**, they **cannot start independent enterprises**.*

This is evident even from a basic example: If prices rise by ₹100, people receive only a ₹20 Dearness Allowance (DA) in compensation. People have become so content with such

meager crumbs; they feel **grateful** for them; and this deeply painful reality has gone unnoticed.

The life of average person is mortgaged into six stages: *Education, job, marriage, children, small savings, and death.*

Young minds are preoccupied only with questions like: "What job should I get? What qualifications are required? How can I develop those skills?"

They lack the **subtle awareness to discover their own true talents**, and sadly, **there's no one to guide them toward that self-discovery**.

"*I was born again and again... worked all my life for others... and remained poor myself!*" **This sums up human life.**

We study for someone else, work for someone else, and survive on the **meager bone-sized salary** we receive; this is what it means to be from a **middle-class family**.

The only solution to this cycle lies in implementing the **cooperative model** across multiple layers and sectors and establishing it as a global system of functioning.

Through this, every nation can attain **self-sufficiency** and connect with the global community.

Through life, our power of thought has steadily grown.

It has flourished greatly, now let us unite together

To enrich life itself through the power of thought.

Let us consciously explore new ways to flourish

To uplift life and free it from its burdens.

Let us gather all the experiences we have gained,

Let us turn them into the capital of our lives,

And live in awareness, knowing our origin and our goal.

- Vedathiri Maharishi

Our quality of life has risen; thanks to the lessons of history. But at the same time, suffering and diseases have also increased. Therefore, the people of the world must unite to investigate the **ways to remove suffering** and work together to find a universal solution.

With the knowledge insight from:

- **Past experience**,
- **Present circumstances**, and
- **Future consequences**

We must recognize these and **sweeten the time we live**.

The land was here before your birth; it nourished all life without claim and shall remain long after you're gone. Claiming ownership of land is nothing but ignorance.

The average human lifespan is just 80 years. With the first 20 years spent on education; we are left with limited time to live meaningfully.

If we don't know how to live the rest of it well, then what's the use of all our education or achievements?

In clarity about our origin and end, we will realize:

A satisfied life is more valuable than a successful life. The true achievement is to be able to say: 'I have lived with fulfillment'.

Let us examine human physiology, mental patterns,

Earth's structure, and everything else, and

From this foundation, let us design a plan

A sacred, all-encompassing, universal solution

That removes suffering from every person's life.

With dignity and compassion, let all humanity unite,

And design this plan with the intention

To fulfill every individual's need. *– Maharishi*

It is a natural truth that bodily structure, mental disposition, and the structure of the Earth are not the same for everyone. Given this reality, scholars must formulate a plan that brings all these elements together and equitably distributes resources so that everyone receives everything they need.

Basic necessities such as:

- Food
- Water
- Clothing
- Shelter

- Family life
- Education
- Employment
- Healthcare.

and arts that bring joy must be **shared equitably** among all.

Just as we calculate **per capita income** (average income per person), we must also define and calculate **PER CAPITA RESOURCES** (average essential resources per person) and ensure fair allocation which are Nature's gifts.

Two meals a day, nutritious and sufficient, are enough for the human body to remain healthy and content.

If **moral discipline** is followed, there will be no crime and hence, **no need for police or courts**. With discerning intellect and rational thinking, any problem can be solved.

Therefore, we must:

** Study human physiology, mental nature, and Earth's structure,

** Create a new global culture, valid across time and geography,

** Design it so that suffering never arises for anyone.

When suffering ends, joy naturally surrounds us. Any action that removes suffering is sacred.

Let us treat the body, knowledge, and energy as common property and let humanity unite with compassion, designing a system that addresses each person's needs with care. Maharishi highlighted:

The foundational tools for generating prosperity, came

Under the control of those who are wealthy on land.

Production, Capital, and Commerce attributed to the rich,

The source to create products never reached laborers

They toiled as wage earners, enslaved to the wealthy.

They had no freedom to sell even what can one produce,

And thus, the working class became impoverished. - Maharishi

To start any business, the first requirement is capital. If capital is obtained through loans, the lender imposes pressure, and the borrower often fails to repay easily.

Established corporations find it easy to borrow, lend, and recover money. Due to natural tendencies, humans fear authority and wealth, so they tend to fear and obey the rich.

Meanwhile, small-scale entrepreneurs suffer hardship and struggle to sustain their livelihood.

In India for a period in the past, politicians acquired wealth primarily through bribery and corruption. But today, many industrial enterprises, educational institutions, and hospitals have all fallen into the hands of political looters.

The worst of all evils is that both wealth and power are now concentrated in the same hands. From such people, who can gain freedom? Is it even possible?

Since **money, industry, and trade** have been monopolized by a few, the rest are **pushed into wage labor**, earning **just enough,** and often not enough for their family needs. As a result, even **middle-class** families are sliding toward **poverty**.

Even if someone bravely starts a small business amid many struggles, **public support is absent**. People consider it **a matter of pride** to be customers of large corporations and show **no enthusiasm** for supporting local or small-scale enterprises.

In such a social mindset, starting a business and becoming successful is nearly a Herculean task.

Thus, people are left with **no option except employment**.

Spend more on employees is the principle in **Western countries**.

Spend more on advertisements is the practice in **India**.

As a result, giving fair wages has become as rare as a **unicorn's horn**.

There's neither **adequate pay for labor**, nor **opportunity to run one's own enterprise**. Trapped in the compulsion to survive, economic crimes become almost **unavoidable**.

Even the most powerful must strive for the prosperity of life

Those who lovingly come forward to serve society

If bribery and corruption seep into their hearts,

Responsibility, duty, and justice will slowly fade away.

As bribe money subtly circulates from hand to hand,

Justice will soon decay, and the human mind will turn toxic

Like a termite-eaten book, human life will lose its essence

Isn't bribery that venomous force that ruins civilization?

– Maharishi

There may be a calculated estimate of what corruption costs. But no such scale exists for bribery. Bribery can seep even where air cannot pass. It is, in truth, a greater evil than corruption itself.

Once caught in its net, both the people and the nation struggle to recover.

If a wealthy person steps forward to start an enterprise with the idea of benefiting society along with personal gain, the so-called political leaders - **true political thieves** - will bargain by saying:

"We will grant you the right only if you agree to give us half the profit."

Responsibility, duty, and justice have all faded, leaving society in turmoil. If the book that offers solutions to these problems is eaten away by termites, what benefit can it possibly give?

Let wealth exist, but let it be a common asset for all people

Let the youth everywhere toil to earn and create it

Let the elders share their wisdom and technical skills

Let governance of wealth, science, and intellect

Be entrusted to those who understand the

True nature of the physical body and life.

Let us affirm that all wealth is for life; Let us reject

The idea that we exist merely to amass wealth. – *Maharishi*

Valluvar, the great sage, has already declared that there is no world for those without wealth. Therefore, all material resources should be made common and accessible to everyone.

Since youth play a major role in productive work, every young person must be given the opportunity to work. The right environment, education, opportunities, and training must be provided to support their efforts.

To achieve this, the elderly, who already possess experience, must take responsibility to impart intellectual and technical skills to the younger generation. A society that combines the experience of the aged with the energy of the youth will excel both economically and culturally.

Only elders who have learned from their own life experiences are qualified to guide others in this way.

Otherwise, irrational superstitions will grow unchecked, and technical skills in professions will not be properly passed down. Unripe elders may insist on unrealistic ideas and create unnecessary complications.

As Valluvar said: "Speak only what is truly useful." If an elder who has not learned from experience tries to teach others, it will only lead to decline. One who understands the nature of wealth, policies, science, mind, and body be the one to rule.

What is Political Wisdom?

It is the capability of a person who:

* Understands the value of money and the means of earning, saving, and utilizing it effectively,

* Possesses administrative skills,

* Has the discernment to assign tasks to the right individuals based on their capabilities,

* Is knowledgeable about innovations in the economics field,

* Is aware of the nature of reasoning and critical thinking,

* Understands the nature of bodily needs, desires, and passions.

When such a person with these noble qualities leads the government, the people will benefit and prosper. Valluvar said: **The capable government is one that can:**

1. **Create** – Turn natural resources into usable comforts through labor
2. **Earn** – Work within one's ability, earn fair wages, and buy needs
3. **Protect** – Prevent the decay of life's resources
4. **Distribute** – Ensure fair distribution to all citizens

A government that functions with awareness in all four domains - **production, acquisition, preservation, and equitable distribution** - is truly powerful.

One who upholds these qualities is a **true statesman**.

Without them, he is merely a political thief.

All material things are meant for life; Life should never become only for the pursuit of material things.

In other words, instead of earning to meet the needs of the body, life itself has tragically turned into a nonstop chase for money.

What shall we call this pitiful state?

If one must spend the entire day only toiling for wealth, when is there time left to actually experience life? Such a way of living, which defies the rhythm of nature, makes **death seem sweeter than life**.

"What is the use of life to those whose tongues know only taste, but ears know not the taste of wisdom?" - Thirukkural (420)

A true human life requires time for reflection, joy, wisdom, and alignment with nature; not just endless labor for wealth.

In a nation where all resources are held in common,

People align their self-interest with public welfare and

Work in unity to create wealth. The teachings of the wise

will easily turn into action. Even those who lack

The ability or knowledge to earn will receive a fair share

To meet their needs. When the economy is built

On shared principles, public service itself becomes

The way of life and righteousness will flourish. – *Maharishi*

This verse explains how wonderful life can be, if we truly understand the laws of nature.

In a nation where all material resources are commonly owned, no one hoards, no one steals, and no one is burdened by the duty of protecting private wealth.

When self-interest is aligned with public welfare, it becomes beneficial. But when **self-interest ignores the common good, it becomes dangerous.**

Every individual must live within society. It is impossible to survive without the cooperation of others. Therefore, society must realize that living with mutual help is the essence of humanity.

Great scholar and noble politician Hon'ble K. Kamaraj once said: "People expect something or other from the government. I have the currency-printing machine. I could print as much money as needed and give each citizen a sack of cash. But what would happen then? No one would work. Industries would shut down. Goods would vanish from the market. What will you do with money when there's nothing to buy? That's why - **labor is the true economy of a nation!**"

Under the leadership of such noble souls, righteous speech held value, and life had meaning.

Even those who cannot earn must be provided for:

* Students have needs during their learning years, but they do not earn.

* The elderly have needs, but they no longer work.

* Those who are ill also require support, though they cannot labor.

* Similarly, children, the physically or mentally challenged, and those lacking comprehension must be cared for.

It is the duty of the able-bodied workers to provide for them. This is essence of a compassionate and balanced society.

At a farmer's market, if you go near closing time, they often give more than what you asked for. But in a retail supermarket, even if you go at any hour of the day, will they ever give extra out of kindness?

The reason is: A working life is touched by compassion. A commercial mindset is not.

In a culture guided by thoughtfulness, frugality, and reform, when a family system structures its needs wisely, the surplus becomes a natural act of charity. When such values are embraced, everyone receives what they need; in just the right measure.

If the **general principles of fair economics** are recognized, then **public service becomes the purpose of life**, and **righteousness (dharma)** will flourish.

As Maharishi said: “In the race between money and morals, character often loses, and people become diminished.” But if compassion blossoms and dharma are upheld, then no one will suffer material want or ruin. **The Earth will become heaven.**

Those who live in a nation without fertile fields

Depend on goods they produce and trade abroad

But if foreign nations refuse to exchange for food

Then how can life be sustained? Think deeply about this.

If food, clothing, and all other essential goods

Were governed under a unified world administration,

Then food distribution to all, regardless of nationality,

Can be made equal and fair for everyone. – *Maharishi*

“*See world unity in a handful of food; Offer the world your labor in return.*” ***Wasting food*** *is not just careless; it is a* ***disrespect to the sweat of laborers***.

The karmic result of dishonoring labor is disease. Whatever food one wastes, that will become **prohibited for eating** due to illness.

If foreign nations refuse to exchange food for our goods, then how can people survive? *Reflect deeply*, says Maharishi.

There is no region on Earth truly without wealth. Even if **food is scarce**, other **valuable resources** will be present.

Through barter, one can exchange and sustain comfort this is the natural design of creation.

To **understand this interdependence** and choose wisely is the essence of intelligent reasoning.

If food, clothing, and other essentials are brought under the system of One World Governance, every country will have access to a balanced and fair distribution of resources.

You can shut down many industries, but you ***cannot shut down agriculture****. The truth is that the entire world survives by begging food from farmers.*

Just because we buy food with money, it does **not mean farmers are inferior.** Money cannot devalue their dignity.

As Thiruvalluvar said: "Only those who till and eat their own food truly live; the rest merely survive by begging behind and following." (Kural 1033).

Only when ***farmers gain access to global markets****, the* ***middlemen who exploit them*** *will disappear. Then, farmers will* ***receive fair prices and proper respect*** *for their labor.*

Economic stability is essential. The continuous **rise in prices** is not just due to **fluctuating production**, but more due to the **greed of traders**.

Out of ***greed****, some* ***artificially restrict supply*** *to drive up prices. This is a* ***sin****. What they accumulate through this is not wealth, but a* ***burden of bad sinful karma****.*

The word **Godown** in English comes from **God + own**. It means **That storage belongs to God**. He is the only owner of everything.

Understanding this, one who acts ***righteously will never fall.*** *But one who acts selfishly will surely fall,* ***Go + down****.*

Often, ***truths and dharma*** *that don't strike us when taught* ***strike deeply when we're harmed****.*

Resources ***belonging to God*** *must* ***reach God's people****; this is the law of* ***divine justice****.*

When you study **why a booming company suddenly collapses**, you'll understand the working of **divine justice**. Sometimes, this happens within one generation; in other cases, it takes place **over future generations**.

If we truly want **economic equality**, we need a **unified administration** that serves **three categories of people**:

1. Those who cannot live on their own,
2. Those who are incapable due to limitations,
3. Those who are capable and active.

Is asking shameful? No. Because in nature, the law is to give and to receive. That is the rhythm of universal balance.

Without the energy of pure black space, the cosmos cannot revolve. Without the energy of life, a human being cannot survive. The transfer of energy is what drives the universe.

As science states: “**Energy can neither be created nor destroyed, but it can be transferred.**” It is **natural law** that **what is in excess** must move to where it is **lacking**.

In the same way, resources meant for human needs must flow from places of abundance to places of scarcity; this is not only natural justice, but also divine justice.

“What is this so-called debt? One who had more gave. One who needed it took and ate. That’s it.” – Maharishi.

If this truth is truly understood, then concepts like debt, loan waivers, and interest will disappear.

Debt itself will become a historical artifact.

It is easy to talk, hear, or read about economic justice. But is it **practically achievable today**? Only when *the Five-Fold Virtuous Culture* (Elaborated in Plan 5) is implemented can the ***World Peace Plan*** become a reality.

Without individual moral reform, there will be no economic justice.

Among the five virtues, **two crucial ones are**:

1. Respect and protect the property and freedom of others, and

2. Cultivate compassion to alleviate others' suffering.

These values of public-centered thinking are the foundation for: **Economic equity**, and **One World Governance**.

Many approach wealthy individuals, for **donations to public causes**. Rich one often responds with irritation: “How much can I keep giving? There must be a limit!”

Why this reluctance? **How did they become wealthy**?

Let's examine:

1. Underpaying employees is one reason.

2. Selling products at prices much higher than procurement cost is another.

3. Tax evasion is the third.

Given all this, how much of the wealth truly **belongs to them**?

Their rightful claim includes only:

- The **capital invested**,
- The **interest for that capital**, and
- The **salary for their leadership** - nothing more.

All wealth accumulated beyond this is fundamentally the people's wealth.

So why the **hesitation in giving back a small fraction** to the very people from whom it came? Actually, it is **theirs**.

Business rooted in dharma will not accumulate excessive wealth. A life rooted in dharma will not accumulate sin.

If someone accumulates great wealth, it is likely that **adharma** has also accumulated. Those who are wealthy often **reject the principle of collective ownership**.

Only when **nature enforces a correction**, and people come to live by the principle of "*Living simply is enough*," will such philosophies be **practically implemented**.

If today's system continues unchanged, **economic justice will remain a dream**. But **nature is bound to bring change**. With that change, *society too will be transformed.*

Maharishi has predicted that this transformation will occur **within a century**. So, it is **inevitable,** a **law of nature** that cannot be altered.

If we understand this truth, we can change without suffering. If not, change will come with suffering. Let us use the intellect gifted by God, honor divine justice, and reap good fortune.

Summary:

This plan emphasizes **Economic Justice** as a cornerstone for world peace. Maharishi Vedathiri challenges conventional ideas of economic growth, urging a shift from money-centered wealth to **resource-based equity**.

True wealth, he states, comes from **natural resources** - not currency, profit, or private property. Originally, economies operated on **barter systems**, exchanging goods without money.

Over time, money was introduced to simplify trade, but it led to profit-driven systems that **monetized basic needs**, enabling wealth without labor (through rent, profit, tax, etc.)

Maharishi proposes that all natural resources must be seen as **common property**. The **cooperative model**, where ownership and benefits are shared, is the only fair system.

He critiques exploitative laws and business practices that legally convert public wealth into private control, especially through corporate structures.

He urges the abolition of black money, cash transactions in cities, and speculative stock markets, advocating instead for **electronic transactions, transparency, and cooperative ownership** across industries, agriculture, trade, and governance.

A new metric, **Per Capita Resources**, must be added with **per capita income**, ensuring fair access to essentials like food, shelter, education, healthcare, and employment for all, especially students, elders, the sick, and the disadvantaged.

Maharishi warns that **economic inequality**, hoarding, and corruption are not just social issues but moral and karmic failures. He calls for a united global effort to:

- Eliminate poverty through shared wealth
- Uplift laborers and youth
- Use elders' wisdom in economic planning
- Respect the balance between production and consumption

Economic systems must align with **natural law, compassion, and dharma**.

A system where **public welfare is the purpose of wealth** will prevent crime, reduce suffering, and bring dignity to life.

In summary, **economic justice is not just a policy goal - it is a moral necessity**.

Plan Three

Justice aligned with Divine Law

What is righteous or honest justice?

Many of us tend to think **honesty** and **justice** are separate concepts:

* **Honesty is Personal conduct**

* **Justice is Legal fairness**

However, they are deeply interconnected. As Thiruvalluvar wrote: *"Greatness lies in those who, with both* ***sharp intellect*** *and unwavering* ***honesty****, live by dharma."*

* Sharp intellect refers to **scientific clarity** and logical reasoning.

* Honesty reflects **moral wisdom**, ethical behavior, and reverence for divine justice.

* It is the **conscious choice to put dharma before desire**.

As poet Aalangudi Somu says: "The soul has no form but without it, nothing moves. Truth is invisible in appearance and honesty can never perish in this world."

Because **honesty is the visible expression of divine justice**, it is indestructible. People who truly desire sweetness in all aspects of life must practice flawless honesty. The foundation of justice lies in individual morality.

The **honesty we expect in courts** must first be initiated at the level of the individual and then made stable within **society**. For in every field, it is individuals who act. So, if we neglect **personal honesty**, we cannot expect **institutional honesty** in any field.

"In a country where people don't know how to live, leadership will always fall into the hands of those who don't know how to govern." - Maharishi.

Isn't this the truth? In the **race between status and wealth, character suffers**, and man loses his moral standing.

So then, **where can we even search for honesty**?

"Neither loss nor gain affects the great; their steadfast

Neutrality is their true adornment." *- (Kural 115)*

"Know a man is doomed the moment his heart strays

From the path of neutrality." *- (Kural 116)*

If one acts without neutrality, at that very moment one must realize, "We are heading toward ruin." The moment one departs from fairness, their action becomes like a bullet fired off-target, causing pain and destruction.

So, to **live a life of comfort, wealth, and respect**, we must abide by the law of just consequence, and live beyond likes and dislikes, aligned with dharma and integrity.

"Even if gain appears good, reject it at once,

If it strays from justice." *- (Kural 113)*

Even if one is promised a **position, luxury, or immense wealth**, if it is gained by **compromising dharma and**

fairness, it must be firmly rejected. Tempted by the bait, the fish loses its very life; remembering this, one must firmly restrain the greedy mind that falls prey to temptation.

If you reach for a **lost object on the street**, pause and realize that object is not just a thing, but also carries the **emotional pain** of the one who lost it.

Say to yourself: "I don't need anything that I did not earn through honest effort." "I will never interfere in another's freedom."

Such a sentiment is a **mark of detachment;** and it is the **true symbol of honesty**.

"If one removes his own faults before seeing those of others,

Which act of his could be against the God?" (Kural 436)

Since the **universe is a divine home**, finding **fault with others** is equal to **accusing the Divine itself**. When you point one finger to accuse someone, three fingers are pointing back at your own faults.

Maharishi asks: "When your duty is to first find your own fault, and correct yourself, what right do you have to place blame on others?"

Life itself is a golden opportunity to remove the impurities within and nurture what is noble. When we realize this, we understand: It takes us years just to correct ourselves; how can we expect others, who know even less, to avoid error? People do not know the truth. How can they avoid making mistakes?

True integrity lies in tolerating the shortcomings of others with compassion. Patience is also integrity; not losing temper, not resorting to arguments or violence, and protecting oneself without falling into legal entanglements.

'If you wish to perish, ignore the wise; if you seek success,

Seek guidance from the capable wise'. - *(Kural 893)*

To live a good and meaningful life, one must follow the advice of the enlightened who have lived and understood life deeply.

Acting impulsively without listening to their wisdom will lead to failure due to lack of experience. One may even completely perish by mocking, dismissing, or trying to destroy those who are guided by knowledge.

Great souls like Adi Shankara, Jesus Christ, Vallalar, Bharathiyar, and Swami Vivekananda did not live beyond the age of 40. Yet their wisdom transformed the world.

The tendency to rob others of their prosperity is an ingrained trait of some, but it can be changed. For that transformation, the friendship and guidance of honest, noble souls is essential to the people, as vital as the air we breathe.

'What use are worldly riches or heavenly rewards if one

Incurs the wrath of the virtuous and the just'. - *(Kural 897)*

The truly *worthy* are those who respect **Dharma** and **justice**. Those who act against these principles are the *unworthy*. Many, in the name of achieving their ambitions, boldly commit wrongs, succeed in those acts, and celebrate that success. This, they think, is hallmark of *distinguished life*.

But what is the real value of the wealth, high positions, or fame gained through such means? It's like fattening a goat only to later sacrifice it. The luxuries and glory one gain now are merely a deceptive shine, like fattening for slaughter.

When the moment of reckoning comes, there may not even be an heir left to enjoy those fruits. *As poet Kannadasan said:* ***Man believes his life is secure through his own will; But God knows that is his illusion.***

Thus, integrity is not just a moral ideal; it is Divine Justice, Cosmic Law, Nature's Order. Whereas *law* is a construct of society, justice is the framework of life designed by thinkers.

Kannadasan also rightly said: ***Law protects the external; Dharma protects the inner self.***

True protection for life comes from **just and honest conduct**. The best legal system is one that aligns with natural law and universal order.

While different nations implement laws shaped by political leaders and enforced by judicial institutions, most of these leaders are not rooted in deep philosophical wisdom or scientific understanding of the universe.

Thus, **a flawless system of justice** and **an impartial, intellect judiciary** are still absent in practice, says Maharishi.

Due to this deep-rooted flaw, the judiciary continues to toil yet remains unable to liberate humanity from suffering.

As Poet Kalyanasundaram said: "The group that steals has planned it thoroughly and keeps stealing. The group that makes laws keeps trying to stop them. But unless a thief reforms, theft can never truly be eradicated."

Criminal law states that **need and greed** are the root causes of all crimes. According to the ***Indian Penal Code*, 576 distinct crimes** have been identified. But in truth, there is ***only one crime in this world*** - the imprint of animalistic instinct that drives one to seize other's wealth.

Need drives it to continue. **Greed** drives it to grow. If a hungry man finds no food, he will naturally be driven to steal or snatch.

*Punishing the one who steals due to hunger is law and justice. But punishing the one **who had food but refused to feed the starving** that is **true justice**, Dharma, fate, divine law.*

As Bharathiyar declared: **If even one person goes hungry, let us destroy the world!**

*Therefore, from a Dharmic perspective, society must feel **ashamed** of such thefts done out of hunger and forgive them with understanding humanity.*

The bitter truth is that **the justice system does not have a clear and adequate definition for THEFT**.

If theft is defined as "taking something without the owner's knowledge," then what do we call it when a school collects funds from students in the name of development and uses that money to build structures under the name of a personal charitable trust?

When a buyer doesn't know the cost price of a product, and a trader sells something bought for ₹10 at ₹50, what do we call this?

If a man who starts a small business becomes a millionaire within five years, what do we call him? And what is the respect he earns in society? In reality, the number of **indirect or invisible thieves** who **cannot be punished by law** is ever increasing. Only direct or visible theft is penalized.

To address such moral chaos, Maharishi Vedathiri proposed the culture of Fivefold Virtues:

1. **Self-reliance** – Everyone must live by the strength of their intellect and physical labor.
2. **Mental discipline** – One must not, through words or actions, hurt the body or mind of others.
3. **Non-violence** – One must not kill any life for the sake of food.
4. **Respect for others** – Uphold and protect the property and freedom of others.
5. **Compassion** – Possess a loving heart that seeks to relieve the suffering of others.

Until this personal, dharmic code of conduct becomes widespread in society, the responsibility of protecting the good lies with the justice system and law enforcement.

As Kannadasan said: ***Law guards the outer life; Dharma guards the inner mind. If both are absent, what remains to guard? And who will guard whom?***

In society today, **personal morality is neither valued nor practiced**. Even the law itself is often not respected. In many cases, **governments that draft the law fail to uphold it**.

What is the result? **Crime is on the rise.** Even though India has a Supreme Court, 23 High Courts, and numerous district judges and subordinate courts, the number of pending cases continues to increase in the justice system. Therefore, the true foundation of a just legal system is **personal integrity**.

When integrity fails, the responsibility lies with the law and its enforcement. The **justice system** and **law enforcement agencies** are tasked with implementation.

Inside the court, the roles of judge, lawyers, plaintiff, defendant, witnesses, and legal procedures must collectively manifest into a verdict rooted in Dharma (righteousness).

Following that, **punishment must lead to correction**, and ultimately, offender must undergo inner transformation.

This alone constitutes a **truly honest and complete system of justice**. The court, judge, lawyers, plaintiff, defendant, witnesses, and police work together to determine a solution for a given issue; that is **justice**, the practical expression of legal principles.

Over time, many past verdicts and judgments on various crimes, disputes, and problems serve as **precedents** for future decisions.

What is the core foundation of a legal code? It is the **rational thinking** of social reformers who were concerned about the **welfare of society**. However, due to the **ambiguity**

in legal clauses, many offenders are acquitted, encouraging **boldness in committing crimes**. Though the principle that *'it is better for ten guilty to go free than for one innocent to be punished'* appears compassionate, ***the rise in crime that follows from it has never been seriously addressed until today.***

A **lawyer** is one who has studied and qualified in legal codes framed by great thinkers. A lawyer argues the case on behalf of the **plaintiff** before the judge. On the opposing side, another lawyer represents the **defendant**.

After hearing arguments from both sides, the **judge** examines the law books, compares the case with existing legal provisions, and if there are relevant past verdicts, uses them as **precedents** to deliver a judgment.

However, like us, lawyers and judges are also human beings, subject to personal desires, biases, and attachments.

Once a position becomes a *job*, the spirit of **service may diminish**. When it becomes about *job and money*, even **justice may falter**.

If honesty falls so low that **justice can be bought with money**, how can the people ever live in peace?

Mistakes *are doing wrong unknowingly.* ***Wrongdoing*** *is committing a known offense. One who makes a mistake should seek to correct himself. One who knowingly commits wrong must feel remorse. - Poet Vaali*

What use are hearts that **refuse to reform**? What use are people born without **remorse**? The one who errs unintentionally should be guided by moral education. The one who commits wrongdoing knowingly must be **corrected through punishment** and inner reflection.

Until true reform is achieved, **punishment must be enforced with appropriate severity**. If punishment is **delayed or avoided**, the **number of criminals will increase**, and society will suffer.

Legal provisions must be made clear, leaving **no loophole** that enables criminals to escape under the protection of law.

A thief may appear virtuous, simply

Because he lacks the opportunity to steal.

Even if he lives solely by stealing, until someone

Uncovering his crime, he may be seen as decent.

An honest man too, may be falsely

Accused of theft due to mere suspicion.

The thief, the captor, the goods, and witness

Stand before the Court, still Justice may fail. *- Maharishi*

In this context, Kannadasan powerfully laments:

Is law something that bends like a reed in the wind?

Must one earn a lawyer's degree just to twist the truth?

Should the children of Dharma blind their own mother?

Should truth be silent and forced to bow its head?

The plaintiff and the defendant are children of Dharma and Adharma. But can justice truly be on both sides? Is Dharma something the other party does not know?

Kannadasan insightfully said:

The thief is praised as a philanthropist,

The one who demolishes temples appears divine,

The corrupt seems respectable,

The conman is seen as noble.

Behind the law stands a troupe manipulating power,

Today power is turned on its head

Many days the thief lives free, but one day in jail;

The sin-doer's curse haunts generations - I witness it all.

What are the qualities of a true judge?

Thiruvalluvar says: "Those who desire admirable civilization will even drink poison with grace when it is offered."

Like ***Socrates****, who gave his life for truth, a judge must be willing to* ***sacrifice even life for justice****.*

Such a judge - a living embodiment of justice - must be ***protected by both the police and the people****. Let us examine the* ***virtues of a true judge*** *through Valluvar's eyes:*

"Like a balance poised with equal weight, unswerving

Neutrality is the ornament of the wise." - *(Kural 118)*

The scale stands still when empty, but once a weight is placed, it tilts. Likewise, a judge must not **tilt judgment toward one side after hearing only one part**. The scale held by Lady Justice reminds us of this sacred duty; **balance and neutrality**.

'Vigilance, learning, and courage - these three,

A ruler must never let flee'. - *(Kural 383)*

The judicial system should operate with protection, compassion, cultural refinement, and conscious awareness. Reform and progress can only be achieved by spreading education widely. Any force that hinders this awakening must be met with firm and fearless resistance.

Thus, the **ornaments of the judiciary** are:

- Constant vigilance
- Clear and unbiased judgment
- Fearless honesty in the face of any threat

"Associate with the virtuous and mature in wisdom,

After discerning their true nature and worth". - *(Kural 441)*

Justice is not mere law enforcement. It is a sacred balance of legal understanding and divine discernment. True judgment arises when one reflects deeply, combining **scriptural wisdom** with **spiritual insight**.

Skill in action may be visible to the eye; but **intentions and inner wisdom** lie hidden beyond sight. Thus, when plaintiffs, lawyers, or witnesses speak, the wise judge must observe: Are they speaking from **conscience**, or merely **for convenience**?

"To act after reflection, without haste, and with devotion,

To God is the only right conduct". - *(Kural 541)*

Just as mustard seeds scatter from a torn sack, an untrained mind, led by desire, runs in many directions. But when it is united with wisdom and governed by Dharma, justice becomes a path of **discernment, reflection, and grace**.

Such justice weighs what is right, not just for the moment, but for the long journey of life. It cares for both **body and soul**, benefitting not only the individual, but society, the future, and even the wrongdoer, by giving them a chance to reform.

"If a ruler governs without faults and upholds justice,

The world protected by Divine will stand by him".- (Kural 547)

For divine justice is impartial and orderly guided not by bias but by the welfare of all. When a judge rules with **equanimity and clarity**, he elevates the very soul of society, its values, its culture, and its conscience.

This is the highest gift a judiciary can offer: Not just **verdicts**, but **virtue**. Not just **law**, but **light**.

"The ruler punishing the wicked and violent, is like

Removing weeds from the tender crop". - *(Kural 550)*

If weeds are not removed from the field, they will drain the nutrients meant for the crop. Likewise, when **evildoers increase in number**, they begin to **steal the rights, wealth, and freedom** of innocent people.

Divine nature expresses itself as both compassionate love and the power to destroy unrighteousness. To reward virtue is God's grace of righteousness. To inflict suffering in response to sin, thereby purifying the soul, is God's grace through justice; his corrective compassion. Likewise, a judge who punishes a wrongdoer does so as an **instrument of divine justice**, offering not cruelty, but discipline born of compassion.

At times, the unrighteous may seem to succeed but that victory is temporary. We must **enlighten people** with the truth: Divine justice will inevitably prevail.

The wrongdoer may escape human courts, but never the **witness of the divine court**.

Therefore, both the judiciary and the state must actively remind society: ***No evil shall stand unpunished.*** It is a moral and social responsibility to ensure that people do not lose faith **in divine justice.**

It is based on this principle that **every legal agreement traditionally requires two witnesses**.

What is the deeper meaning behind this?

"God, whom I serve in my spirit in preaching the gospel of his Son, is my witness how constantly I remember you in my prayers at all times..." (Romans 1:9, NIV).

One witness is one's own **conscience**, and the second is the **witness of Divine**.

But sadly, neither of these two ever appear in court.

The good people have two witnesses

One is the voice of conscience,

The other is the witnessing eye of the Divine.

If you look even at a stone with trust,

God becomes your witness.

That is the witness within the soul,

And the true witness to the truth itself. - *Kannadasan*

Such is the **Divine Court of Justice** which is internal.

In this Divine Court:

* The **plaintiff** is one's own **conscience**.

* The **defendant** is one's **mind**.

* The **judge** is the divine wisdom seated in the **soul**

* **Lawyers and witnesses have no role**.

* Only **one law** - **Consequence that matches the action**.

* There is **no appeal**, and no second trial.

* **No modification** of the verdict.

* Rituals, Poojas, Donations, Reparation Ceremonies - **none of these are considered** in this higher justice.

The purpose of true education must be to awaken the realization and spread the understanding in society that:

"Whether my body trembles, my mind grieves, my wealth diminishes, or my honor fades, no consequence of my actions

can ever touch or disturb the soul or the divine intelligence within me." Maharishi beautifully expresses this in his verse:

In the path of righteous law, O friend

Enduring your memory and proven skill,

The plaintiff, defendant, lawyer, and judge

There is a way that you shall become all four

Caste, religion, nation, language, race, and

Ownership - are these not all forms of injustice?

You, the beginning and end, Seated on the eternal,

Undivided throne must deliver the judgment. – *Maharishi*

Humanity has existed for several hundred thousand years. Across this long history, many experiences and insights into justice and righteous living have accumulated. Some have attained mastery over these truths.

In the highest realization, there is a unique understanding: that the plaintiff, defendant, lawyer, and judge - all these roles are ultimately one.

This is the essence of Advaita (non-duality): Knowledge, the act of knowing, the knower, the known, and the clarity of realization - are all one and the same.

Dualism manifests as distinctions - caste, religion, nationality, language, race, and attachment to property. As long as these are accepted as inherent parts of life, **true unity cannot be attained**, and the barriers will persist.

Therefore, the human being, as a reflection of the Divine, must transcend these divisions and recognize his true Self as the **eternal Atma**, which has neither beginning nor end.

From that state, rising above the body and ego, he must sit in the **seat of Divine Justice that governs the cosmos**, and render judgment. It is the **supreme intelligence of God** that runs the universe with order, balance, and precision.

The laws of society should be structured based on this **divine principle of justice**. But who is truly capable of framing such a law grounded in divine justice?

Even if one lacks the capacity to perceive it fully, it is still possible to **build legal codes** by taking inspiration from the moral and spiritual texts of enlightened beings, such as the **Bhagavad Gita**, **Thirukkural**, the **Bible**, and **Vedathiriam**.

The original Manu Dharma, said to be written before the Mahabharata, is lost. What remains today as Manu Smriti, written much later, is in conflict with true Dharma and therefore, it must be discarded.

The **Gita** clearly states: **"Action, its leadership, and its outcome - none of these are created by the Supreme. It is nature alone that causes them to function."**

This raises the question: **Is God separate from Nature?** Yes; they are distinct. God is that **primordial vastness**, untouched by desire or aversion, beyond emotions, beyond attachment and separation - the **pure infinite space.** From the pure space, when a rise of force occurred within itself, it gave rise to divine particles.

But when these energized particles couldn't express their motion in full accordance with their nature due to the surrounding pressure, they began to spin in response to external constraints.

This spinning under pressure marks the emergence of the Law of Mutation. **If even those original divine particles could not function as per their own will, how can human beings expect to fulfill every desire they wish for?**

Just as particles are governed by natural law, human life is governed by Dharma; the divine law of honesty and justice. To realize this and live accordingly is true spirituality. And recognizing this law and using it to elevate oneself; that is the mark of true rational intelligence.

The principle of "action and consequence", or Divine Justice, operates in the same way both in the cosmos and within the human body.

Blood pressure: 120/80. Body temperature: 98.6°F. Even these bodily constants reflect the universal law of cause and effect.

Since action, its initiator, and its outcome occur within the realm of the universe, they have no direct link to the pure divine space.

Hence, as the Gita says, God did not create action, its leadership, or its outcome; Nature and cosmic law carry them out.

This natural law is what is truly meant by fate, divine justice, and moral righteousness. In the consequences that arise through this law, it is wisdom that helps us eliminate suffering and preserve happiness. When mistakes are made, it is justice, and the judge, that protect the affected. Understanding this delicate distinction and choosing the path of welfare is essential.

If a person who understands such subtle truths causes harm to society, then it is the duty of the judicial system, even up to the level of the International Court of Justice, to protect the people.

Every human being is born with a natural gift from nature; the right to live and the freedom to exist. No one has the authority to deny these rights. The world must be made aware of this truth.

The right to live belongs to all.

Let it serve the welfare of all who live.

Let all who wish to live unite, and design

A plan to live prosperously together! - *Maharishi*

If a person becomes a criminal, the real cause is improper upbringing. There are no born criminals or sinners in this world. The faults lie in the flawed systems of past societies.

A man born to parents, who carry minor faults may become a major offender, shaped by the societal failure. Lack of responsible guidance, and the absence of meaningful employment or income opportunities, have turned many into criminals.

Only a strong foundation of ethical justice can protect humanity and ensure peace. Can the general public alone bring about such reform through reflection? No.

Those who hold positions of social leadership and responsibility, governing authorities, judges, lawyers, writers, and community leaders must come together, reflect deeply, and pave the way for a better path.

That is why Maharishi emphasized: "All leaders of the world must awaken to inner wisdom, the awareness of life-force."

Such life-force awareness is the realization and experiential understanding of God and Divine Justice.

Sculptors' intelligence and skill unite together

And crafted a chariot of immense worth

Offering the chariot for a jasmine creeper to hold onto

That act of ignorance was glorified as charity

Suicides and murders are honored as paths to salvation

Forgetting his learned knowledge, The Chola king

Crushed his own son under the wheels of the chariot

The people praised, 'Manu's justice has prevailed'!- Maharishi

King Paari, the famed philanthropist, gave his chariot to a mere jasmine creeper. Emperor Shibi cut his own flesh for the sake of a dove. King Manu Needhi Cholan offered to give his son under a chariot to console a grieving cow that lost its calf.

If easing the sorrow of a jasmine vine is praised as greatness, ***where is the punishment for insulting*** *the labor and sweat of the artisans who built that chariot?*

If Shibi gave his flesh to match a hunter's claim for a dove, ***did the hunter stop hunting*** *thereafter?*

When man, endowed with discernment, fails to question justice, ***how can a cow,*** *guided only by instinct,* ***ring the bell*** *for justice? The one who killed the calf is a murderer. And the king who killed his son, is he the embodiment of justice?*

Stories like these, which dull people's ability to think clearly, *must be discarded. Through proper education, we must explain in a way that the people understand: living in mutual support and harmony is divine justice.*

Next, how should judgments be delivered?

Although punishments may vary based on the nature of the crime, the fundamental goal of justice should be **the reformation of the offender**.

In a Tamil movie *Neethi* ("Justice"), a man dies in an accident caused by a drunken truck driver, and the punishment given to the driver aligns with Maharishi's view - that justice should be corrective, not merely punitive.

That is, instead of delivering a typical sentence from the law books, the judge assigned a punishment where the offender was made **responsible for financially supporting the victim's family**.

Such reformation must, of course, be rooted in ethical discipline. Until then, it is our duty to ensure that ***righteous living becomes firmly established in this land.***

Summary:

This plan redefines justice not merely as legal fairness but as an expression of divine righteousness (Dharma), rooted in personal integrity.

Maharishi Vedathiri insists that true justice begins with the individual, not the courtroom. If individuals lack honesty, institutions too will fail.

Righteous justice arises when sharp intellect (logical clarity) and moral honesty (conscience) unite in service of Dharma.

The law may govern external actions, but Dharma protects the inner being. Without this foundation, laws become vulnerable to manipulation.

Maharishi and Thirukkural emphasize that:

- Impartiality, patience, and moral courage are the ornaments of true justice.
- Even if great wealth or power is gained unjustly, it must be rejected.
- Accusing others while ignoring one's own faults is a betrayal of divine truth.

Justice must be corrective, not merely punitive. The goal of punishment is inner transformation, not revenge. Courts, judges, and laws must align with natural justice, which reflects cosmic balance and the law of consequences.

Maharishi critiques legal systems where the letter of the law overrides the spirit of justice. Many criminals escape punishment through legal loopholes, while real justice remains elusive.

The increase in white-collar crime, black money, and systemic corruption proves that institutional justice alone is not enough. Thus, he proposes the Fivefold Code of Virtues as a foundation for dharmic justice:

1. Self-reliance
2. Mental discipline
3. Non-violence
4. Respect for others' freedom and property
5. Compassion to alleviate suffering

The Divine Court is internal:

- Plaintiff: One's conscience
- Defendant: The mind
- Judge: The soul's wisdom
- Law: Cause and effect. This higher justice requires no rituals, only realization and transformation.

True reform requires wise, fearless, and dharmic judges. Like Socrates or King Harishchandra, a judge must be willing to sacrifice even his life for truth.

Judicial integrity is vital for societal balance.

When justice is rooted in Dharma, it nurtures not only the individual but society, the future, and even the wrongdoer.

This is the essence of righteous justice: not punishment, but transformation guided by wisdom and compassion.

Plan Four

One Governance for the World

In Vedathiriam World Peace philosophies, the fourth plan is **"One World Governance."** Though there are systems of governance in the world like democracy, capitalism, and communism (collective ownership), when we investigate whether there exists any nation that is entirely free of flaws and crimes, we may find countries with fewer crimes but not a single country that can proudly claim to be crime-free.

Even though scholars and wise people have understood the root cause for this situation, the arrogance and ego of political leaders have prevented the implementation of real solutions. As a result, even after many centuries, the world is still entangled in various forms of crisis and suffering.

Compassionate sages, motivated by universal welfare, have envisioned a just order so that humanity may live in peace and dignity. If the world follows their righteous principles, the Earth can truly become a land of wisdom.

The insight shared by Poet Vali must become a motto:

Even when the truly poor struggle to survive,

There are wealthy people who still say, "I have nothing."

Their houses are full of material wealth, yet

Their minds remain clouded in darkness of greed

Who treats whatever wealth they receive belongs to all

Let us praise such selfless souls with elevated hearts.

Nature's resources are not distributed equally across all regions. Since natural wealth varies from place to place, we need an administrative system that can collect and distribute it fairly to all people.

Currently, people claim ownership over what they have produced through their labor, and this sense of ownership extends to nations as well. *Because of this, resources are not reaching those in need, leading to economic inequality.*

Consequently, like a poor man snatching from the wealthy, one nation invades another, and after victory, loots its resources. Such wars destroy any hope for world peace.

Maharishi, after deep study over time, proposed an actionable plan and strongly emphasized the need for **a single world government** to implement it. Let us now look at the **ten resolutions** that this unified world governance should put into practice.

RESOLUTION 1

A single **World Federation** shall be established through a democratic system that unites all countries under one supreme authority; a world government that ensures **equal rights and representation for all human beings**.

Explanation:
The right to live and be free is a divine gift granted to all humanity. Furthermore, the wealth of the Earth belongs equally to all. To eliminate divisions based on religion, caste, race, language, political systems, or property rights, and to ensure

unbiased and equal representation for all, a **unified global empire** is essential.

For this to work practically, people must be intellectually categorized (based on wisdom, not discrimination). Experts and thinkers should prepare plans, and qualified administrators should be selected to implement them and guide the public.

RESOLUTION 2

A **Global Democratic Parliament** shall be formed, with one representative for every ten million people, elected or nominated through each country's existing government system.

The above parliament will create and enforce laws that protect human rights and individual freedom. It will also establish a **Global Administrative Council** composed of renowned scholars and subject-matter experts as required.

This administrative council will operate under the supervision of the global parliament and will be responsible for implementing its laws and regulations. The authority to **monitor, revise, amend, upgrade, or dissolve** this administrative body shall lie solely with the **World Democratic Parliament**.

RESOLUTION 3

The **World Government** shall be responsible for safeguarding the fundamental rights and freedom of every individual. No individual, group, or national government may deny or suppress a person's birthright or liberty.

RESOLUTION 4

Each government under the world federation must ensure that its citizens are provided with **basic necessities** — food, clothing, shelter, education, employment, marriage opportunities, and access to research and innovation.

RESOLUTION 5

Women shall be granted **equal rights in all fields**, just as men. In addition, necessary facilities that naturally suit women's biological and physical needs shall be provided to ensure their dignity and participation.

RESOLUTION 6

If a group of one crore people within society - whether belonging to a region or a nation - so desire, they have the right to demarcate their own administrative boundary, form their own legislature, and live under it, provided they remain within the framework of world governance and their national collective administration, and uphold the Charter of Human Rights.

RESOLUTION 7

The **entire world belongs to all people**. Every individual has equal rights to reside or travel in any part of the world. However, to ensure public health and pleasant living conditions, only the **World Government** has the authority to impose essential regulations regarding migration and travel.

RESOLUTION 8

If any national government fails to fulfill its responsibilities or proves to be unfit, the **World Government shall take over** the governance of that region. It will uplift the people through qualified leadership and later hand over the administration back to the citizens of that country when they become capable.

RESOLUTION 9

War shall be declared illegal. All armed forces, military weapons factories, and research centers related to warfare anywhere in the world will come under the control of the World Government. These will be repurposed for **productive industries** and to uplift **underdeveloped countries and people**, based on well-planned global programs.

RESOLUTION 10

Under the World Government, a **global service institution** composed of leading scholars from around the world shall be formed. This center will periodically draft **strategies for the betterment of human life** and function as a platform for global social reform.

It will integrate five core domains - **Spirituality, Economy, Health, Science, and Politics** - through expert-led research councils that guide humanity toward constructive transformation.

PHILOSOPHICAL CONCLUSION:

Clarity of knowledge is the solution to all problems. And such clarity is brought about by **spirituality**. The foundation of spirituality is austerity and inner discipline.

As Thiruvalluvar said: *"He who practices penance performs his karmic duty; those who do not will fall into disgrace, bound by desires."* Only a **refined mind** can lead to a **refined life**.

Meditation is the training that refines the mind. When desires are regulated through austerity, they align with **dharma**, resulting in **lasting happiness**. If all people follow spiritual discipline, **economic justice will follow**. Resources are the foundation of livelihood, and they are gifts of nature. If the world accepts the principle that all humans have equal rights to these natural resources, **economic inequality will disappear**.

The art of maintaining the body is **health**. To build a disease-free society, one must maintain balance in food, labor, rest, sexual discipline, and thought. When lived with moderation, this ensures both **health and prosperity**. People must be educated that the **key to well-being** lies in practicing moderation across these five elements.

If the products of science are to truly benefit humanity, they must be guided by love, compassion, and humaneness.

All wealth derived from the earth belongs to all people living on it. To **gather and distribute** this wealth fairly, a **strong world federation** is essential.

Just as the Divine governs the cosmos with perfect order, the governance of humanity must be undertaken by those **endowed with divine virtues**. This principle was beautifully expressed by the sage Thiruvalluvar as the foundation for righteous political philosophy.

In harmony with these **ten resolutions**, Maharishi has also composed **six verses**, offering poetic support and inspiration for this vision.

When narrow thoughts that lead to crime

Are pulled out from their rooted grime,

And wisdom lights the path ahead,

Uniting all under the one world governance

The books of law that once grew vast,

With crimes and punishments amassed,

All legal texts that define and explain crimes

Will shrink into and end with few lines. *– Maharishi*

*While the word **crime** originates from Latin, we may interpret it symbolically as **Cry + Am**.*

*In the Bible, God declares, "I am That I am"- revealing His eternal, unchanging nature. The word **Am** thus signifies **divine order**, **eternal law**, or **the presence of Supreme**.*

*When a person acts **against this divine law**, it leads to inner conflict and sorrow - **the cry**. Hence, a **crime** is not merely a social offense but a **violation of** the universal moral law.*

This interpretation reminds us that **true justice is spiritual**: Every crime disconnects us from our own higher self, and the consequence is not just punishment; but **fall from divinity**.

*What drives a person to commit crime? **Narrow motives** - typically arise from **need and greed**.*

Needs are connected to the **body**, and to fulfill them, **nature has generously provided all essential resources**, along with the **intelligence** to transform them, enhance their quality, and make them suitable for use.

Greed, however, stems from the **mind**, which is shaped by experiences. If experience is refined, **mind becomes pure**.

The mind that seeks the **Infinite Supreme** can never be satisfied with **petty pleasures**. Thus, even in fulfilling basic needs, the mind intervenes and **expands desires into insatiable greed**.

The obsession to be superior in everything leads to a desire for high positions, limitless wealth, and boundless sensual joy; but neither **societal order** nor **natural law** supports this.

Unfulfilled desires agitate the mind like a mad ghost. And from this agitation are born **crimes**. The only way to uproot the narrow motives behind crime is spiritual austerity and inner discipline.

"If one wishes, renunciation is possible; once renounced, many natural benefits follow." This means there is a shortcut to satisfaction. When the mind surrenders and merges with the **source of consciousness**, it experiences **Supreme Bliss**.

After that, the mind seeks nothing more, says Thiruvalluvar. It is **philosophy** that points the way to **restructure desires**.

The **average human life span today is about 70 years**. If we subtract the learning years of childhood, **only about 50 years remain for domestic life**. If we can't even live those 50 years in peace, isn't that a tragedy?

Is a human life meant to wander in confusion from age 20 to 70 - never truly aware, never truly content? *"One who falls into the trap of desire, attachment, and love loses peace. He wanders, suffers, struggles, and perishes. No one gains from it." – Kannadasan.*

This **meaningless cycle of life** can be transformed through conscious thought and awareness. That is the only way to **uproot crime** from humanity.

Under a **common global governance**, where people live with **righteous awareness**, we must undertake research to categorize and analyze crimes thoroughly.

Punishing is easy. But **did the punishment reform the person**? The true purpose of punishment is **reformation**. If the criminal remains unchanged, then the punishment must be **redesigned to enable transformation**.

If the **wealth granted by Mother Earth is shared equally**, and **moral education teaches** that stealing others' possessions leads to suffering, then **a crime-free society is possible**.

Problems in economics and moral conduct

Have led to countless crimes among mankind

Grace and spiritual values were distanced from public life,

Misdirected and scattered knowledge has lost its peace

Most people are bewildered, not knowing what to do

If excess wealth is used to end poverty and kindle learning,

And the wise who dispel darkness lead politics everywhere,

The world shall bloom with grace and a blissful life.

- *Maharishi*

What is the root of today's problems in **economics** and **moral conduct**? Humanity, trapped in **temptations**, tends to commit two major types of crime:

1. **Desire for excessive wealth**
2. **Desire to possess beautiful women**

These two form the **basis for most crimes**. Even devotees are not always free from these desires. Some religious leaders, concealing their emotions, have used **rituals and traditions** to enslave people under the guise of devotion which has allowed crime to spread even within temples. Crimes multiplied as temple management fell into the hands of trustees ignorant of righteousness.

Knowledge was misdirected in such a way that people's minds drifted away from the realm of grace, leaving only a loss of peace. Even those with elevated thinking stand bewildered, not knowing what to do.

To escape from this, one needs:

- **Proper training**
- **Persistent effort**
- **Unshakable patience**

Devotees who seek **instant results** fall into the trap of desire, suffer **financial losses**, and endure **emotional and moral collapse**.

Society is misled by manipulative thinkers with shortcut ideas, leading the people astray from life's true purpose.

Surplus wealth must be used to eradicate poverty and nourish education. Due to social imbalance, wealth accumulates in the hands of a few. This inequality leads to the devaluation of others, treating them as inferior.

On one side, there is suffering from overconsumption; on the other, from hunger. To correct this imbalance, both mental maturity and political integrity are essential.

True spiritual education must be implemented across the world. We must strongly emphasize righteousness grounded in discipline, duty, and compassion. If enlightened thinkers who dispel darkness take up leadership everywhere, the world will attain a life of joy and harmony.

When positions of power are held by good administrators - those who are not slaves to money nor sell themselves for posts - countless benefits will reach the people.

Had today's level of government revenue existed during Hon'ble Kamaraj's administration, Tamil Nadu State in India, would have become a paradise.

Such noble political leadership must emerge from a culture of integrity and service, which should blossom and spread across the nation.

To safeguard both property and populace

Appropriate laws began to emerge from the beginning

Wealth accumulated excessively in the hands of kings

Wars followed one after another, thereafter,

Wealth, the nation, the ruler, power and governance

Wars eventually gave rise to laws to protect these

As wealth shifted into private hands through trade,

New laws emerged to protect the capitalists. - *Maharishi*

The Origin and Corruption of Politics:

When we explore the origin of politics through history, we find that rulers were initially chosen based on physical strength, to protect the people and their property. The **principles of protection** evolved into **laws**, and the system to implement them became **governance** (administration).

To meet the **expenses** of governance, **fines** were introduced - which over time became **taxes**, the means by which wealth was collected by the state.

But what can we say of the present degradation, where governments have **transformed into mere tax-collection agencies**?

Due to excessive income from taxes, **luxury entered politics**, leading to **competition and envy among nations**, and ultimately to **wars**.

To succeed in war, nations devised strategies based on:

- **Increased taxation**
- **Political fragmentation**
- **Abuse of power**
- **Tyrannical laws**

As a result, the world has drifted down a **path of destruction**. No matter how many **forms of government** exist in the world today, the question remains: **Who really rules?**

There is only one answer: **The wealthy rule the world and the nations.** Politicians serve primarily to **protect capitalists**.

In some countries, **wealth and political power** have become concentrated in the hands of a few. This has led to a dangerous situation where **the lawmaker and the beneficiary of the law**

are one and the same, while **the common people are left in poverty**.

Private ownership and commercial enterprises

Division of the nation into states by monarchy

If this situation prolongs any further, mankind will

Realize that life could no longer continue in any way

Many people united for the well-being of all humanity

Yields varied outcomes based on changing situations

Explaining kindly and with a sense of shared ownership

Let us envision a flawless One World Government.

- *Maharishi*

What happens to a world where:

- People **refuse to listen to dharma** (righteousness),
- Have **no fear of committing unrighteous crimes**,
- **Feel no guilt** for deceiving others, and
- **Fell no shame** even in being deceived?

How can the good survive in such world, nation or society?

If private ownership, profit-driven commerce that quickly enriches individuals, nations built upon pride and power, manipulative politics, and the falsehoods that divide people in the name of God continue to persist, then the destruction of humanity will become inevitable.

Realizing this, the righteous must unite and form a compassionate, truth-speaking social movement; one that explains clearly to the people the root of present suffering and the path of moral living.

This movement should establish branches across the world, spreading awareness of the current crisis and the solution grounded in righteousness.

It must emphasize that only unified One World Governance can resolve these issues and must design and implement a clear action plan to bring it into reality.

A unified world government will eliminate the fear of war

If war ceases soldiers and resources will serve noble causes

Across the world poverty will vanish and culture flourish

A reformed life will then be realized, reflect upon this.

- *Maharishi*

Every year, nations allocate billions specifically for war. If that vast funding were redirected toward social welfare, how many benefits will reach the people! And what compensation can truly match the mental illnesses born from the fear of war?

If the great thinkers and leaders of the world reflect on this and ***declare war itself to be illegal, poverty would vanish from the earth, and human civilization would reach its highest virtue.***

War cannot truly end without a One World Government

If ownership does not become common to society

Individuals are classified into groups in multiple ways

Ever widespread, yet at times it sprouts and rises again

With unrest unending, the people of the world face ruin

By elevating thought and acting accordingly with discipline

Removing divisions like castes is impossible, unless,

The government begins with responsible parenting.

- Maharishi

Without establishing a One World Government, no nation can be brought fully under control. If wealth does not become common property, economic struggles will never end. Parties, unions, and factions that arise to address these problems cannot eliminate conflict.

There is only one true solution: implement a global system where children are raised by scholars.

To uproot evils such as religion-based division, caste, poverty, wealth, loss, theft, begging, selfishness, weakness, power, attachment, pride, hatred, and conflict - the only way is for the government to adopt every newborn child and entrust their upbringing to enlightened scholars.

Is there any other path? Reflect deeply.

If the government takes custody of newborns and hands them directly to wise mentors, the emotional attachment of "my child" will not arise. The desire to accumulate wealth for one's offspring will fade. A desireless mind naturally aligns with righteousness, making world peace possible. A child and God are no different in essence. Just as we revere God without attachment, let children also live freely and joyfully, unbound by attachments.

Wise leaders rooted in the noble principles of democracy

True democracy never allows injustice to another nation

One World Governance that cannot be shaken by others

They will dedicate themselves to establish democracy.

- Maharishi

Democracy is a system where the people, by the people, elect their own leaders to govern. When such a model spreads across the world, where people govern themselves, no system will attempt to destroy another.

No single administration will hold absolute power. Only a One World Government will have the capacity to oversee and regulate all and thus will become a strong and just form of governance.

If the current United Nations General Assembly were to include representatives at the ratio of one per crore (ten million) people from every country, it would truly reflect the welfare and voice of all humanity.

Likewise, if the UN Security Council takes full responsibility for the defense of all nations, then no country would need its own military. Border disputes would vanish. The arms race would come to an end.

In a world without war, governed by the awareness of divinity and the guidance of dharma, all people would live in fulfillment under One World Governance.

As humanity evolves into a state of divine consciousness, let us fulfill the Supreme's evolutionary purpose and experience a life free from suffering, filled with bliss.

Summary:

Establishment of a **single democratic world government** will eradicate war, injustice, and inequality. While existing systems like democracy, capitalism, and communism have failed to eliminate crime and suffering, this plan envisions a globally united administration rooted in **divine justice, equality, and compassion**.

Core Premises:

- No country is crime-free; ego and power prevent true solutions.
- Nature's wealth is unequally spread and should be equitably redistributed.
- Wars arise from national greed; peace demands collective ownership and governance.

TEN RESOLUTIONS:

1. **World Federation**: A democratic, unified global government ensuring equal rights and representation.
2. **Global Parliament**: One representative per ten million people; guided by intellectuals and experts.

3. **Rights Protection**: Safeguarding individual freedom and birthrights globally.
4. **Basic Necessities**: Universal access to food, shelter, education, and employment.
5. **Women's Rights**: Equal rights and biological sensitivity to ensure dignity.
6. **Regional Autonomy**: Allowed under world law and human rights.
7. **Free Migration**: Universal right to travel and settle, regulated only for health and well-being.
8. **Intervention**: The world government can step in if national governments fail.
9. **End of War**: Declaring war illegal; disarmament and redirection to development.
10. **Global Reform Body**: A scholarly institution guiding progress in spirituality, health, science, economy, and politics.

PHILOSOPHICAL FOUNDATION:

- True justice is **spiritual** - violations are crimes against one's higher self.
- Crime arises from **need and greed**; solution lies in **spiritual austerity and inner discipline**.
- **Greed blinds**, and competition for power distorts society. Austerity aligns desire with dharma.

Practical Reforms & Reflections:

- Redirect war budgets to social welfare.
- Prevent corruption by rooting governance in ethics and humility.
- Wealth and leadership must not coexist in the hands of a few.
- Raise children under the guidance of **wise scholars**, removing caste, property, and power divisions from early life.
- Reconstruct politics based on spiritual wisdom and shared resources.

Ultimate Vision:

- A crime-free, war-free, spiritually awakened world governed by enlightened leaders.
- True democracy thrives only when **selfless leadership** aligns with **divine order**.
- United Nations could evolve into this system, ensuring defense and equality for all.
- Humanity's goal: To live with **bliss, awareness, and dignity**, fulfilling the Supreme's purpose.

Plan Five

Reformed Culture of Virtue

'Reformed Culture' means a way of life rooted in divine order and understanding.

* *'Order'* refers to harmonious functioning of natural law, divine justice, cosmic order, and intellectual clarity.

* *'Understanding'* means refinement, disciplined life, culture aligned with divine justice, and wisdom.

Essential Questions:

- What did that exist before?
- What must be reformed?
- Why must it be reformed?
- Who will do the reforming?
- Who will be reformed?
- How will reform happen?

What did that exist before?

Since the time of early humans, the tendency to **seize others' wealth for survival** has persisted and remains widespread even today.

What must be reformed?

Ignorance of human nature; **desire**, **ego**, and the **mind** must be refined.

Why must we reform?

Out of 8.2 billion people in the world, how many live a truly joyful, fulfilled, and peaceful life? Very few. According to **divine law**, *bliss* exists everywhere and always in nature for our enjoyment.

But when our sense *of joy* becomes distorted, we experience an emotional disharmony, which manifests as **suffering**. To eliminate this suffering, reform is necessary.

Who will reform?

Those who are capable of **reflection**; those who seek the **causes behind pleasure and pain**; those who explore natural law and divine order; those who discover that **wisdom is divinity**; those who live what they preach, like Bhagavan Vedathiri Maharishi; and those who see that **everyone can live this way** and are ready to **teach it to the world**.

Who will be reformed?

The ones who, for over 2500 years, **refused to change**. Even if someone suffers deeply, they may **not listen** to a wise person who speaks to help them.

Then who will listen? **Only those who come to the Temple of Consciousness** are likely to seek reform.

How will reform happen?

Through:

- **Explanation**
- **Training**

- **Social effort**
- **Political law**
- **One World Governance**

When all people gain equal access to basic needs and opportunities, reform will naturally follow.

How culture evolves?

Just as a **single human being** gave rise to human society, individual character, when cultivated, gradually spreads and transforms into **culture**.

When **culture becomes corrupted**, it is the responsibility of great intellects to restore it - just as **God, metaphorically, became the devil** and then returned to reestablish order.

Restoring Dharma through Culture:

When God becomes a **realized sage**, He undertakes the task of **removing social decay**, reestablishing **Dharma**, and upholding **Justice**.

In this lineage of sages, Bhagavan Vedathiri Maharishi designed a system of **fivefold discipline** to restore society. Later, he simplifies it into the **two-fold discipline.**

One attains awareness of the feelings of other beings

Perceiving the measure of pleasure and pain,

By forming a bond and sensing with the heart,

One compassionately stepping down to offer help

A noble turning point in intellect and reflection

The dawn of awakening begins in this world

Righteousness arose, and that became religion over time

By the names of sages who nurtured it, it grew into many.

- Maharishi

The act of removing the suffering of other beings, known as **charity**, can be performed in three ways: ***through wealth, through labor, and through wise counsel.***

On the other side of this virtue is discipline: the resolve that no living being should suffer because of us.

To practice both - helping others and avoiding harm - is the essence of **Karma Yoga**, the highest refinement of character.

To be refined is to be cultured; and that refinement is what we call virtue. Among all virtues, the highest is noble excellence. Those who guide society with such grace are called nobly distinguished.

Just as barren land must be tilled and cultivated for agriculture, a raw, unrefined mind must be disciplined to make life fruitful. **To refine the mind is like hunting a magical deer; it requires patience, skill, and awareness.**

In the Ramayana, when Sita saw the golden deer adorned with silvery spots, she was instantly captivated by its beauty. Unable to catch it herself, she asked Rama to capture it alive for her. Although Lakshmana warned them that the creature was a magical illusion, neither Sita nor Rama heeded his words.

That illusory deer led Rama far away and was eventually killed by his arrow. *What is the inner meaning of this magical deer, the enchanted deer hunt?*

With the advancement of science, new and attractive things constantly emerge. Even without considering whether we truly need them, our mind tends to desire them. The mind, by nature, longs for the new, without questioning its necessity.

Yet, the mind lacks the power to acquire these by itself. So, it turns to the intellect for help. It is the role of wisdom to remain alert and regulate desire.

If, instead, the intellect becomes a puppet of desire, ego arises, and ego has the power to imprison the soul.

This is symbolized in the Ramayana when Ravana abducts Sita **in the absence of Ram (Awareness) and Lakshman (Guru).**

Furthermore, there are **three key truths** embedded in this:

1. **A magical deer cannot be captured alive** – illusions cannot be possessed; they vanish when chased.
2. **Only wisdom (intellect) has the power to destroy illusion** – it is the arrow of discernment that ends delusion.
3. **With the guidance of a Guru, one can escape the traps of illusion** – the Guru's presence helps the seeker avoid being ensnared by maya.

Thus, **the guidance of the wise is essential for society.** Their insight protects individuals from falling prey to delusion and keeps the collective consciousness aligned with truth.

When the fire of desire rises and begins to burn,

Using the active organs of the body guided by intellect,

It can be extinguished only by experiencing it without fear

There is no other way to overcome it. Therefore,

To let not the mind give rise to poisonous desires

I established a path of noble discipline for a virtuous life.

- *Maharishi*

How can we identify this illusion?

* It begins with thoughts like: "All the wealth of nature must be available to me in whatever measure I desire."

* "Others must obey my word, but I will never submit to anyone else's."

* "Crowds must gather to praise me. No one should ever be above me in any way."

The dice in this game are **ego and selfishness**. This kind of thinking is the key to recognizing maya, illusion.

When a person demands to enjoy **wealth, fame, influence, and sensory pleasures without limit or resistance**, can nature ever truly cooperate? Not at all.

Even this resource-rich Earth is not sufficient to satisfy the endless desires of **a single man**, let alone the needs of **8.2** billion people. This **ignorance** of the self, of society, and of nature's laws **is maya - illusion**. To overcome this illusion is the true **hunt for the golden deer**. And only the **true hunters** - the wise ones, the *Veda Vyas*, the *Vedantic sages*, and above all, **Vedathiri Maharishi** - *can teach the subtle art of that hunt.*

To undertake this inner battle, we must seek the guidance of such noble Gurus.

The authority to decide whether the Tamil New Year begins in Chithirai or Thai does not belong to corrupt politician, but only to realized sages.

According to historical era, place, time, and need

Countless rituals have arisen according to the situation

If that ritual action or that belief inflicts suffering upon

Intellectual thought or experience, it is wise to avoid it.

– Maharishi

Since culture itself is subject to change, the Five-fold Culture outlined by Maharishi has also undergone revision twice.

A new culture is needed for the world

Let eliminate intoxication, war, and falsehood,

And implement righteous living with responsibility.

It is not too great a burden, for everyone to live by

The strength of their intellect and physical labor.

Let's not a derailed intellect harm another's mind or body.

Righteous conduct and the vow of non-killing...

Devotees asked, “Swamiji! When we spray pesticides on plants, living beings die. We kill mosquitoes, we squash bugs. If we don't do these things, won't they harm or even kill us? What should we do?"

Maharishi immediately replied, “Is that so? Fine, then we can modify it,” he said, and revised the line to say: “A vow not to kill for the sake of food.”

He clarified: “It may be impossible to completely avoid killing life. But we can at least refrain from killing for food. In farmers’ markets, vegetables are available in plenty. Grocery stores sell a wide variety of rice and lentils. There is no difficulty in obtaining and eating these instead.”

He then continued: “Smoke is a major toxin. A person who drinks alcohol may only destroy himself. But cigarette smoke also harms the lungs of people nearby. Both the smoker and those around him suffer. Therefore, smoking must also be eliminated.”

Thus, Maharishi revised the earlier verse once again, adding smoking to the list: “Let us eliminate intoxication, war, falsehood, and smoking, and implement the right values with responsibility.”

In this way, adapting actions according to the time and ensuring that they lead to complete well-being is what defines *culture*. **Though many cultures have come and gone, since problems and illnesses remain unresolved** even in individual households, there arises a need for a new culture to get rid of such suffering.

A new culture is needed for the world

Let us abolish intoxication, war, falsehood, and smoking,

And implement righteous living with responsibility.

"A drunkard, while sober, on seeing another drunkard,

Will he not think the misery of drink." – *Kural 930*

When one lies unconscious in a drunken state, he has no self-awareness and therefore cannot know what is happening. But even if he has the habit of drinking, when he is sober and sees another person lying senseless in intoxication, should he not realize, "I too must have fallen like this when I was drunk"?

Shouldn't such a disgusting sight at least inspire him to correct himself? This realization must arise. At the very least, seeing this pitiful state, should he not feel compelled to correct himself? Thus, Thiruvalluvar expresses deep concern.

Alcohol, which clouds the intellect, must be avoided and eradicated. By doing so, one can escape numerous undesirable consequences: losses, sorrows, illnesses, confusion, and social complications.

Is there not intoxication in fame?

Is there not intoxication in a child's prattle?

Is there not intoxication in love?

Is there not intoxication in the compassion of the heart?

Can liquor grant the bliss that the mind,

Wisdom, virtue, and the moral path bestow.

The high you seek will come, just try doing something good

If you stand in search of peace, try speaking the truth

Some are intoxicated by songs,

Some are intoxicated by the (liquor) bottle. – *Kannadasan*

Next comes war:

"A true nation is one free from factionalism, internal

Conflict and corruption in governance." - *(Kural 735)*

Many groups - caste-based associations, political parties, fan clubs, service organizations, temple committees, and charitable trusts - ***all claim to exist for the welfare of people.***

But if that is truly their purpose, why do they generate differences of opinion, disputes, clashes, and even murders?

If killing one another is accepted as justice, then murderers would outnumber all others in the world.

Self-serving politicians, corrupt officials, and ignorant masses are trapped in blind loyalty. When will the dawn ever come?

We live on a wondrous planet, filled with immeasurable wealth, inhabited by a highly capable human race; and yet everything is being destroyed.

An arrow may be beautiful, but it is still a weapon of death. When violence and mischief prevail, divine justice and the bliss of nature are destroyed.

A land free from such evils is a true nation; if not, it is merely a cremation ground. War is not a path to glory, but a fall from human dignity; this is the message Valluvar conveys.

Next comes falsehood…

"If falsehood can bring about faultless good in a situation,

Then that falsehood may be deemed as truthful." (Kural 292)

A lie that produces unblemished good is equal to truth. Why does Valluvar say, *"falsehood in the place of truth"* instead of saying *"falsehood becomes truth".* The distinction is subtle but profound.

To understand this, we must reflect on the true essence of the word **Truth**. It goes beyond mere factual correctness. The deeper meaning of *"Truth"* lies in its etymology: which means **the inner reality** or **the divine essence within**.

As Bharathiyar beautifully said: "The Divine itself is Truth."

We declare Truth as the supreme God

Other gods chanted by, we see as false.

Truths alone are the real Vedas (scriptures)

The rest of the sacred texts, we see as mere tales.

- Subramanya Bharati

If a thought, word, or deed brings good, for the present and the future, for oneself and others, for both body and mind, that is truthfulness. A thought, word, or deed that causes **harm or sorrow is false.**

"Speak not falsehood which your conscience knows; if you

Do so, your conscience will scorch you." *(Kural 293)*

Conscience is a divine court of justice. It draws in the waves of thoughts, words, and actions, compresses, records, and stores them within, and delivers just consequences at the appropriate time.

The saying ***'A good heart never sleeps'*** is no exaggeration; it is a timeless truth. In wakefulness, these inner waves appear as thoughts; in sleep, they continue as dreams. Beyond dreams lies a deep state, where intellect merges with its divine source.

Hence, instead of simply advising us *not to lie*, Valluvar subtly warns us: ***do not lie to your own conscience****, because the* ***punishment from within is inescapable***. One may lie without detection, but never without inner consequence.

There is no escape from the suffering dealt out by the conscience in response to falsehood.

The reason Valluvar did not write about smoking is because it did not exist in his time. Tobacco was one of the poisons later introduced in India by British colonial rule.

Among the evils that should be eliminated from society are **intoxication, war, falsehood, and smoking**. Only in a society free from these four poisons can sweet, meaningful living becomes possible.

For that, a culture of **five-fold discipline** is essential.

First Discipline: Every person must live by the strength of their **intellect and physical labor**. Labor skills and the wealth one produces are lasting and permanent. Without work, one cannot transform nature's resources into usable conveniences.

There is a share for you and for me, in this world. When each person contributes their labor, the world prospers. **The highest way to live** is to work righteously, with spiritual awareness, and in harmony with dharma. He who lives by the nobility of his mind and by the sweat of his toil is indeed **Divine**.

There are two types of labor:

1. **Physical labor**
2. **Intellectual labor**

But even physical labor must be guided properly by intelligence. Therefore, people should live by the wealth earned through union of **bodily effort and mental skill**.

There are **four ways** for people to live **without labor**:

1. **Begging** – but dignity does not permit this.
2. **Stealing** – People think this only means breaking into houses and taking things. But the definition of theft is misunderstood.
3. **Looting/Robbery**
4. **Suicide** - There is only one way to be born; but a thousand ways to die.

To overcome this each individual must affirm, 'I shall earn everything I need through my own labor'. Such a culture will uphold the truth that: ***God alone is the Master of the world, and all of humanity are His laborers.***

The laborer who turns the soil into fruit (Farmer)

Will one day regain attention; and in that,

A new society where the noble people live

Will surely blossom one day.

In this journey called life,

Many will come and go on this Earth.

A few will shine like the moon in the sky,

And leading that line stands the laborer. - *Kannadasan*

Second Discipline: Even if one does no good, refraining from causing harm to others is itself a great virtue. When intellect falters, arrogance arises, and with arrogance comes trouble. The mind is the seat of arrogance, the stronghold of the devil, and the throne of Satan.

As Thiruvalluvar says: *True virtue is that which avoids the four: envy, greed, anger, and harsh speech.*

The cause of the clouded intellect is **desire**, and from desire arises **jealousy**. Their consequences are **anger and cruel words**. Who has not experienced the pain, mental or physical, caused by someone's anger?

When one lives under the intoxication of the mind instead of the guidance of reason, **ethics, duty, and compassion disappear from action**, leading to suffering for one and all.

He who lives without causing pain to anyone; he alone is the true sage, the righteous Brahmin.

Third Discipline: A Life of non-killing for food - in nature, one living-being becomes food for another. For humans, plants are the natural food. Even the human body is designed to accept plant-based nourishment.

Yet, when plant food is unavailable - or due to habitual consumption - people begin eating meat; not for the meat itself, but for the **flavors of spices** rubbed over it. It is time to awaken widespread awareness that **meat is not essential**.

When a human dies, we call the body a **corpse**. But when animals are killed, we call it **meat** or **flesh**, not *corpse,* to make it more palatable and acceptable.

If someone said, "**Chicken corpse for sale**," or "**Goat corpse available**," would anyone feel comfortable buying or eating it? The word *meat* masks the reality of **death, corpse and decay**.

Why should we avoid flesh? Valluvar gives two clear reasons:

"He who eats another creature's flesh to nourish his body

How can he ever attain divine grace?" *(Kural 251)*

A person who kills and eats another being for self-gain cannot awaken to **divine grace**. True **humaneness** is found in relieving another's suffering, not in increasing it for selfish pleasure. Therefore, meat consumption **blinds us to the divinity within** and must be renounced.

Valluvar further declares:

"For him who lives by the vow of non-killing,

Death that consumes life shall never prevail." *(Kural 326)*

For those who live with the **firm resolve** not to kill or harm other living beings, even unexpected accidents or major surgeries often do not occur. Such a person becomes a **witness and guide** to others in life.

If we study the karmic history of someone who suffers in an accident, we may see how divine justice operates; even beyond temple offerings and donation. *Nothing deceives the **divine justice**.*

Fourth Discipline: The highest moral path is to ***respect and protect the wealth and freedom of others***. Freedom is not something that can be given by one person to another. It is a **natural endowment;** a gift granted by nature to every living being. It is enough **not to take away** the freedom and rights.

Even though the literal slave trade is abolished, subtle forms of **submission to power and authority** are still widely prevalent. ***Exploiting others' benefits is praised as administrative skill*** nowadays.

We must rise to a noble mindset: *"What is given to me is from God; it is my duty to preserve and protect it with care and gratitude."* One must develop the quality to safeguard others' belongings as one's own.

For example, in India, if a government officer uses an office phone to speak monthly with his daughter in London and his son in the U.S., spending ₹25,000 of public funds; this is not just unethical; it is punishable.

Officials must not misuse their authority. They must develop a sense of ownership and care: *"This is my office, my society, my country."*

Likewise, as citizens, we must protect public resources built through **our tax money**. ***Treat public property as your own; but do not treat it as private property to be carried home.***

"Wealth not gained through compassion and love is

Unworthy of pursuit or possession." *(Kural 755)*

If people gain wealth through exploitation and manipulation, without grace or compassion, such wealth will only bring misery both to the one who gains it and to the one who is used in its making.

If humanity had acted wisely the moment the **atomic bomb** was discovered and **avoided producing it out of fear of destruction**, then perhaps such weapons would never have existed today. The practice of **protecting others' property and freedom** would have flourished.

Fifth Discipline: Cultivate Love that Relieves the Suffering of Others. Suffering arises in countless ways for living beings. We need a heart that asks: *"What can I do to ease their pain?"*

Human life is deeply connected to society. If we do not live with mutual support and cooperation, there can be no lasting prosperity in society. Therefore, we must develop **a love that relieves the pain of others**.

We must possess the nature to see others as ourselves.

To have that grace, compassion must awaken in the heart.

If one's mind shines like gold, no other wealth is needed.

There is no god than the one who understands this truth.

- Kannadasan

Compassion is love that eases others' suffering through:

- a compassionate look,
- compassionate words,
- and compassionate actions.

When the negative imprints (karmic residues) within a person begin to dissolve, the **innate love and compassion** buried deep inside emerge naturally.

In that state, love, gratitude, and compassion manifest in human form and that human becomes divine.

"Through the supreme compassion called graceful vision, the

World comes into being and continues to exist." *(Kural 571)*

Just as **water flows beneath the earth**, and **air flows above the earth**, **love must flow through society;** only then can sweet life be sustained.

FIVEFOLD MORAL DISIPLINE:

1. **To live by physical and intellectual labor.**
2. **To not harm the body or mind of others.**
3. **To not kill any living being for food.**
4. **To protect others' property and natural freedom.**
5. **To help alleviate the suffering of other living beings.**

These five can be summarized in **two essential disciplines**:

- **One**: Do not cause suffering to yourself or to others through your thoughts, words, or actions.
- **Two**: If others suffer for no fault of yours, ease their pain as much as you can, without harming yourself.

"Moderation of the body's needs, and abstaining from

Harm to anyone is the true outcome of penance." (Kural 261)

"To share the pain of others": Every being naturally experiences bodily suffering. Hunger is painful. Thirst is pain. Even the inability to relieve bodily waste for a day causes pain. Nature has gifted us **intelligence and resources** to remove these basic sufferings. Helping to remove such natural sufferings is true compassion.

"To not cause harm to life": One must not cause pain; not even to oneself, through thought, word, or deed.

For example, **the ghee in a sweet dish** may later become **cholesterol** ($C_{27}H_{46}O$), leading to a heart attack; a truth not fully understood by many.

"Do not harm life" doesn't apply only to others; it includes *not harming your own life* as well.

*Many believe **sin is only what we do to others,** but we must also recognize the **sins we commit against ourselves too**.*

The root cause of most diseases is food.

To Live Rightly, One Must Undergo Austerity:

Without inner discipline, moral living is not possible. Austerity expresses itself as **love and compassion**.

Devotion without an understanding of austerity yields no lasting good. History proves this. People have cut themselves with blades and offered their blood to God, claiming it as devotion believing the wounds won't hurt.

But once the truth is understood, one questions: *"Does God need blood?"* And the answer becomes clear: **No. God needs love and compassion, not blood.** Some say walking through fire after 48 days of strict fasting is devotion, and if one doesn't, the fire will burn them.

But wearing sandals in the scorching sun, lighting fire pits, and walking across them thinking ***God wants us to suffer is mere ignorance.*** If God is pleased by bodily harm, ***what is the difference between God and a villain?***

The True Meaning of Rituals and Vows:

In ancient times, rituals were introduced to cultivate goodness. If one follows 48 days of disciplined living, avoids harm, and does good deeds, then naturally they develop compassion and moral sensitivity.

But if people forget the purpose and keep practicing rituals mechanically, the **true meaning is lost.**

The divine nature we seek must shine through truth and love. Without understanding this, rituals and ceremonies are of no use and **history proves this beyond doubt.** No further evidence is needed.

Only through **true austerity** can we awaken divine awareness. Then we can live without bringing pain to ourselves or others; fulfilling Valluvar's ideal.

These two declarations **contain all five disciplines**. They are simple to remember; yet profound to practice. Maharishi further instructs: After finishing your austerity, **recite these two vows aloud**.

Also, visualize the face of the person you may have hurt and firmly resolve: "I will never do this again." A ***calm mind*** *carries greater power in thoughts.*

If you put these two principles into practice, you live the ideal: *"Wherever and in whatever way good deeds can be done, One must tirelessly pursue them without ceasing."(Kural 33)* Such a transformation naturally leads toward **realization of the Divine**. Valluvar said: *True joy arises only from righteousness.*

How Dharma Lifts Like an Escalator: Once you step firmly onto **the path of dharma**, it lifts you like an escalator. Just stand firmly, it elevates you to the higher realm.

When saints awaken these values in society?

When people follow the guidance of nobles with faith, this moral culture spreads from self, to family, to society, and to the world. Thus, the **Fivefold Moral Discipline**, conceived in the mind of Maharishi, has begun to spread among the people.

If every person lives by these principles, there will be no scarcity. Through intelligence and reflection, one can understand nature and transform them into well-being and harmony.

On Selfish Hoarding and Divine Ownership:

When people hoard wealth selfishly and deny its use to others, it becomes the **greatest sin**. If one remembers that everything in the warehouse (godown) is truly **God's own**, as the word suggests, *God + own,* they will treat it as a sacred opportunity to serve society. Trade done with dharma brings **abundance to life and future generations**.

But if one arrogantly claims ownership, one day, the family may perish in a car crash, and all that property returns to being **God's own.** If we do not give willingly, **He will take it back.** Let us be aware that **nature governs silently.**

The Role of Reflection and Satsang:

When we reflect often on these truths, our mind begins to listen to the voice of wisdom. Practice at home without attending Satsang will not sustain spiritual growth.

Without regular participation - even once a week - **austerity will not develop**, and **practice will fade**. **Satsang** is the space that completes life. This connection should last **a lifetime**. Maharishi says,

Another's wealth, another's life, another's freedom

The great greed wrongly seizes them all; And also,

The joy gained by causing sorrow to another's heart

To realize the formless Absolute through inner austerity,

Within others, within oneself, as vast universe, and also

Supreme intellect - all within divine justice; let us realize

It cannot be attained by merely speaking to, and hearing from,

It can be truly gained only through the art of mind enrichment.

Summary:

A *reformed culture* is a way of life based on **natural order**, **divine justice**, and **moral understanding**. It fosters inner refinement, compassion, and discipline.

Why Reform is Needed: Most people suffer due to ignorance, uncontrolled desires, and ego. True happiness lies in living a disciplined life aligned with nature and Dharma.

How Reform Happens: Through explanation, education, politics, and One World Governance, culture can be uplifted. Reform begins with the individual and spreads to society.

Five-fold Moral Disciplines:

1. **Live by physical and intellectual labor** – No living without contribution.
2. **Avoid harming others' body or mind** – Refrain from anger, jealousy, and harsh words.
3. **Do not kill for food** – Adopt a compassionate, plant-based lifestyle.
4. **Protect others' property and freedom** – Respect public and private resources.
5. **Relieve the suffering of others** – Cultivate love, compassion, and service.

Thirukkural and Maharishi's teachings emphasize **living without causing harm** and actively **helping those in need**. This will lead to the rise of a new world of harmony, health, and joy.

Plan Six

Life Guided by the Wise

It is the path shown by thinkers that truly governs the world. People and party cadres tend to believe whatever political leaders say. It is these political leaders who initiate wars.

People buy products based on the words of economic leaders. Even today, many still purchase sunflower oil believing the advertisement that it contains no fat and is good for the heart.

But how many acres of sunflower are actually cultivated in India to meet this demand? Hardly anyone pauses to reflect. Similarly, religious leaders influence prayer rituals, worship methods, riots, physical assaults, and even acts of terrorism.

Thus, life proceeds under the directions of so-called **thinkers**.

"*But no one thinks about the fact that it is these very people who are the cause of growing problems and suffering.*"

If one begins to think deeply, they will realize that all three of these types of leaders - political, economic, and religious - are driven by selfish motives.

Once this truth is understood, the world will recognize that true thinkers are only those sages like Valluvar, Jesus, Buddha, and Vedathiri Maharishi.

(Soul, Reflection, and Noble-thinker) - Mind, thought, and the act of thinking. To observe keenly, to penetrate deeply, and to unite, i.e. to unite with nature, with God, and with Dharma.

O Guru, who taught me to restrain my mind and remain still,

In that state, when knowledge remains unwavering, great

Bliss overflows. In this vast world, through many births, the

Final fruit of constant awareness and peace you bestowed

This is my message of joy. — *Vethathiri Maharishi*

What is this 'joyful message'?

The word *joy* can often be deceptive. What does this mean? According to natural law and karma, true joy arises only when good comes to us without force; through divine grace.

But when one pursues good through unrighteous means simply out of desire, even if it appears pleasurable at the moment, it leaves a stain, **a karmic flaw** on the soul.

"True joy comes only through virtue; all else is

Naught and without praise." *(Kural 39)*

Only the joy that comes through dharma should be accepted. Other forms of pleasure that we chase ourselves may go against righteousness. One may earn great wealth or fame through adharma, but such glory is impermanent.

Behind that fleeting fame lies the pit of disgrace. Wealth and honor gained through unrighteous means may **elevate a person temporarily, only to throw them down into ruin.**

This stone, if it falls on someone, it will crush them; but if someone falls on it, they will shatter. – Luke 20.18

The craving for luxuries beyond what is righteously earned stems from selfish leadership. *Valluvar states:*

"Even begging water for a cow brings disgrace to the tongue;

There is nothing more degrading than begging." (Kural 1066)

Even if someone requests leftover gruel to feed a cow, it is still seen as begging. That was the moral standard of ancient Tamil Nadu. But today, in India, people are made to beg for freebies and money; a degradation taught by corrupt political leaders.

This dire situation was foreseen and righteously addressed by Valluvar, who emphasized **just and moral governance** through his Kural. (Ch. 55.The Right Scepter)

Righteousness refers to refined and orderly governance; an evolved leadership rooted in divine intellect.

Since the Supreme Intelligence (God) is the source and sustainer of all things through law and order, the essence of true leadership, rule, and authority stems from **Divinity**.

The governance of God is primary and all-encompassing. In human society, **governance by rulers and systems is secondary.** From this arises delegated authorities who handle various responsibilities in **different sectors.**

Next are the **heads of families** who manage their households. And finally, the power of action and moral order emerges in the form of **individual leadership;** the way of living guided by thoughtful beings.

Thus, from the **divine down to man**, the progressive order of conscious functioning is what defines 'The Right Scepter.'

Even though the great cosmic sphere is vast,

I perceive it as a single movement, your very body.

All wondrous movements are awe-inspiring thoughts,

Who else but You commands this grand universe? *- Maharishi*

"Divine Law stands as source for the scriptures

Of the Sages and the path of virtue." *(Kural 543)*

The **Brahmins** here represent not a caste, but all who live with divine awareness, love, and compassion. Their path of life (scripture) is rooted in divine justice. Even before thinkers composed ethical codes, the primal divine intelligence existed.

In primitive societies, when natural resources were scarce or needed safeguarding, people chose the strongest among them to lead and protect.

From this tribal structure evolved monarchies, autocracy, and eventually, democracy. Only when people's lives and properties are protected can virtue thrive and be respected. Hence, the divine leadership rooted in wisdom is the foremost governing force.

"All living beings depend on the sky for their life; likewise, the

People depend on the king for justice and order." *(Kural 542)*

Without the sun's heat and rain from the sky, life on earth cannot exist. The functioning of the planets, solar influence, and rainfall form the basis for life.

Though natural resources may be abundant, their protection, regulation, and fair distribution are the responsibilities of the state. Therefore, people are dependent on their government not just to feed their hunger, but to nourish their intellect.

"When a king rules justly and cherishes his people, the

World will gladly stand under his rule." (Kural 544)

When a ruler dedicates himself to the welfare of his people, even neighboring nations will desire to have such a king. The world will naturally incline toward a united rule under such wise leadership.

If multiple national rulers dissolve into a single **world government**, corruption, bribery, and administrative inefficiencies will decline.

When citizens' lives are based on knowledge, peace and prosperity will follow. As a great thinker once said:

"Dictatorship with intelligence and kindness is better than capitalism, communism, and idiotic socialism."

"If a ruler governs without faults and upholds justice,

The world protected by divine will stand by him." (Kural 547)

Just as all planets must function in harmony without colliding or disturbing each other, human governance too must function with justice. Divine law maintains order in the cosmos with repulsive and attractive forces, ensuring precision and harmony. Similarly, if governance is inspired by divine awareness and order, it will uplift maintenance, culture, traditions, and moral practices. This is the **greatest service** a government can offer to its citizens – not freebies, but *virtuous leadership*.

"The ruler who fails to act by wise counsel will ruin,

Though his land be rich and fertile." *(Kural 548)*

In monarchy, a divine counselor called **Royal Guru** will advise the king. Since a ruler faces many pressures, his judgment may sometimes falter. Thus, critical decisions were taken only after consulting a wise spiritual advisor.

In democracy, however, elected representatives (MLAs) are often not experts in their assigned ministries. A minister, lacking knowledge, may make poor decisions, damaging the sector and its outcomes.

To prevent this, **Upper House** (MLC – Member of Legislative Council) were created to include qualified scholars whose advice would guide policy.

But because these councils often opposed populist 'freebie schemes', arrogant politicians abolished them. By rejecting the wisdom of the learned, the government weakened itself, and with it, the welfare of its citizens also declined.

"For preserving citizens and their welfare, punishing

Evil is not a cruelty but a duty of the ruler." *(Kural 549)*

One king may rule with justice and virtue. But the next may indulge excessively in state resources for personal pleasure. Seeing this, people's morality declines. A person accustomed to plundering will prevent the righteous from ascending power and will do everything to retain control.

To confront such corruption, candidates must possess true capability. They need loyal supporters. Those who plunder the wealth of the people must be punished. Punishing the wicked to protect the innocent is not a sin; it is the *moral duty* of citizens. It is meaningless to say, "I accepted his money, so I must vote for him," and call it dharma.

Next comes Religion leadership:

In *Chapter 28 -Thirukkural*, Valluvar speaks about hypocritical religious figures who exploit faith for personal gain.

Grace may dwell in the eyes,

A thousand meanings in words,

But if the heart is filled with falsehood,

It poisons even the unborn kin. – *Kannadasan*

People who claim to have renounced everything - family, sensuality, material comforts - pretend to be miraculous spiritual beings.

Valluvar uncovers the inner battles of these false renunciates. One must transcend sensual cravings through sincere austerity and serve with divine awareness.

Otherwise, the mind, accustomed to power, wealth, and pleasures, will continue to crave them in secret. Among the five senses, **sensual pleasures** have the strongest pull. And to experience these, one needs **wealth, fame, and authority**.

Taste has a natural limit; beyond a point, the body resists with nausea and discomfort. Smell and sound are subtle, and most prefer music over meaningful words. Sight enjoys natural beauty but seeks tangible pleasures.

The human body craves only two things: **hunger** and **lust**.

Sexual attraction, governed by natural law, manifests as the biological urge to reproduce. Hence, society established **marriage** as a regulated outlet.

"When a deceitful mind pretends to renounce,

The five senses within mock at him." *(Kural 271)*

To reach divine consciousness through austerity, one needs patience, methodical training, and grace from a Guru. But the false ascetic, with hidden intentions, may present himself as a divine soul who has transcended desire. Yet inwardly, his conscience mocks his hidden cravings.

"Deceit, devoid of divine strength yet feigning it,

Is like a cow grazing in a tiger's skin." *(Kural 273)*

One without the maturity to live a dharmic family life will fall prey to wealth, fame, and sensuality. To fulfill these desires, he will portray himself as a great spiritual master, claiming to have conquered the senses and act as a representative of God. He proclaims he is worthy of leading others.

Imagine: a cow wearing a tiger's skin enters a field. The guard doesn't approach due to fear. Thinking it's a tiger that won't eat grass, he assumes no harm. But in reality, the cow disguised as a tiger freely grazes the crops.

In the same way, this *social predator*, masked as a renunciate, exploits his appearance to receive honor, wealth, and prestige. Secretly, he indulges in the very pleasures he condemns, devastating society like the grazing cow destroying the crop.

"Hiding behind asceticism, the deceit commits evil,

Like hunters hide in bushes to snare the birds." *(Kural 274)*

Vedathiri Maharishi once said: *"Let me dissolve into you and let You shine within me."*

Arunagirinathar declared: *"O Muruga, tell me of the grace that dissolved even my ego."* That is the divine state attained in true austerity.

But when austerity is forgotten, the opposite occurs. The impostor, like a hunter hidden in foliage, kills truth under the disguise of devotion.

"Who say, 'We renounced,' yet live in false discipline, will

In many ways bring blame upon themselves." *(Kural 275)*

'We have renounced everything' - with this claim, they had been deceiving the people for generations. But the time and circumstances changed. Their true nature was exposed, and all the hidden truths came out in the newspapers, bringing disgrace to that very tradition they belonged to.

After escaping scrutiny for so long, they were finally caught easily, and now they lamented: ***"Our name is ruined, our honor is lost, and the 600-year-old glory of our monastery has faded."*** Because of such hypocrisy, some monasteries lost their following of devotees and became mere shelters for bats.

"An arrow is cruel; the lyre's string is cruel in disguise,

So, judge by the result, not by appearance." *(Kural 279)*

Just as a beautifully crafted arrow kills life, the grandeur, publicity, and spectacles of false spiritual leaders destroy public wealth and women's honor.

In contrast, the crooked string of a harp, though imperfect, produces sweet, soothing music. Similarly, the teachings and gentle practices of realized sages like **Vedathiri Maharishi**, though subtle, bring peace and joy to both body and soul.

One who truly embraces spirituality must shun hypocrisy and follow a life of ethical discipline. By doing so, they not only elevate themselves but also serve as guiding lights for society.

The righteous path shown by such thinkers purifies the mind, and the fivefold codes of conduct can transform the world into a heaven. If rulers and religious heads come under the influence of humanistic thinkers, even those in charge of the economy will eventually return to the right path.

Hence, at all times, the only true way for the three ruling powers of society - **politics, religion, and economy** - to ensure public welfare is through the moral integrity of individuals.

Even though many enlightened sages have taught virtue through the ages, the peaceful world they envisioned has not materialized.

The reason, as discovered by Maharishi, lies in the fact that the three commanders of society referred above have become self-centered. Only when these leaders realize **conscious awareness** - the inner divinity - and use their position and power for the good of people, understanding that fame should arise from **sacrifice**, not corruption, will this world truly transform into paradise. Being remembered as a **corrupt**

historical figure is not honor, but shame. There is no shortage of the powerful in the world; it is the good who are scarce.

Just as the exile of the righteous Pandavas led to Duryodhana ascending the throne and bringing sorrow to the people, when knowledge lacks humility, arrogance rises to the top, and by then, it becomes too late even to explain. True freedom vanishes.

Will all the thoughts of the learned reach the assembly?

Will the views of the wealthy ever be ignored?

Be it learned or wealthy, whoever it may be,

Can neither stand equal to one who holds power? Kannadasan

Of the two - **strength and wisdom** - only **wisdom** can guide strength correctly. Power without understanding is a waste. That's why the wise always valued **wisdom above might**.

"For those who live by noble duty, doing good

In all things comes naturally." *(Kural 981)*

The word 'due' becomes 'duty'. A true thinker or a virtuous person is one who fulfills their responsibilities in five spheres: self, family, community, nation, and the world.

They live with awareness, doing what must be done in each domain. This defines a person of wisdom and integrity.

"Virtue alone is the true excellence of the noble; all other

Forms of goodness are of no equal worth." *(Kural 982)*

Human experience evolves through ten progressive stages:

1. Feeling, 2. Need, 3. Effort, 4. Action, 5. Result,

6. Enjoyment, 7. Experience, 8. Reflection, 9. Clarity,

10. Conclusion.

The desires that arise from emotions lead to enjoyment, which become imprinted in the subconscious as **traits**.

Even after being born as a human, traits acquired over generations - especially the primitive instinct to seize others' wealth -linger due to inherited experiences. This deviation from virtue reflects a regression to animal nature.

"Love, modesty, benevolence, forbearance, and truth

These five are the firm pillars of virtue." *(Kural 983)*

Just as pillars support a strong structure, **five key virtues** form the foundation of a virtuous life:

1. **Love** – Boundless and divine, transforms into affection when bounded by relationships.
2. **Modesty** – The moral sensitivity to feel shame for wrongdoing.
3. **Consent (Empathy/Support)** – Willingness to help and cooperate.
4. **Compassionate Perspective** – A broader vision rooted in service and understanding.
5. **Truthfulness** – A consistent commitment to righteousness.

These qualities are natural to a true **thinker or sage**. Their love is infused with divine awareness. Their compassion compels them to serve. Their truthfulness ensures their every act is for the good. This is why people are drawn to the guidance of such noble souls.

"Humility is the strength of the truly strong; it is the

Weapon by which the wise conquer his foes." *(Kural 985)*

True strength lies not in aggression but in unwavering, refined conduct, consistent across all situations. The truly great display **humility** and **gentleness**, not out of weakness, but from the realization that **Divinity pervades all**. Such inner grace builds bonds and turns even adversaries into allies. Valluvar calls this gentle strength the weapon of wise.

"Though worlds may fall and ages fade,

The steadfast never sways." *(Kural 989)*

Just as the **shoreline resists the pull of the sea**, protecting life on land, so too do the truly virtuous hold firmly to righteousness, even when fate or nature turns turbulent. They are deeply rooted in a selfless life of **commitment to social good**, never swayed by external change.

"If the steadfast virtue of the noble happens to fall,

The earth could bear the patience no more." *(Kural 990)*

All living beings possess the intelligence to sense a coming storm. Natural calamities are not destruction but physical transformations due to internal imbalance.

When **impure thoughts rise**, Earth's magnetic field is disturbed, causing more turmoil. As the number of righteous beings diminishes, nature's balance weakens. The **elders in wisdom** are the ones who once upheld that balance.

Like today's religious fanatics, those who lack maturity but attempt to guide the masses often lead people into suffering. In all times, there has existed a divide between those who **know how to live well** and those who don't.

It is the **duty and responsibility** of the wise to guide the ignorant. Likewise, those who do not yet know the way of peaceful living must develop a **sense of responsibility** to seek and accept such guidance.

They reject the Guru who can remove their blindness,

Yet accept the one who cannot.

The blind lead the blind in their aimless life

And all fall together into the pit. - *Thirumoolar*

If one does not neglect experience and reflects deeply, they can learn to preserve true happiness. Only a **few great souls** have lived through life's truths, analyzed their experiences, and developed true wisdom. **Not everyone in saffron robes is a sage.**

"Associate with the virtuous and mature in wisdom,

After discerning their true nature and worth." *(Kural 441)*

A true Mahaan does not speak from theory alone, but with the accumulated wisdom of past sages. Knowledge transcends time. We must honor such people and **evaluate the depth of their insights**, not merely their words. Maharishi said: *"If one sincerely practices philosophical training, deep experiences will arise. From these, clarity of expression comes, and words carry real weight."*

Shallow advice cannot guide real life. We must discern and adopt the thoughts of those who **speak from true realization** and live by their guidance to reap real benefit.

"Revere and follow those who remove afflictions

And protect you in advance from suffering." *(Kural 442)*

Those who help remove the pain we've already endured, and more importantly, **guide us to avoid such suffering again**, are thinkers and wise guides. They must be honored and their wisdom followed with sincerity for lasting well-being.

"Among all rare things, the rarest of all is to

Cherish the wise and make them one's own." *(Kural 443)*

People often **chase pleasure and wealth**, listening to agencies, brokers, and superficial advisors. But very few seek out truly enlightened thinkers or sages who can lead them on the path of dharma. This neglect of wisdom, **lamented by Valluvar centuries ago**, still continues today.

"To revere as one's owned those noble in wisdom is

The highest of all strengths." *(Kural 444)*

Even if someone is younger in age, if they are wiser, one must have the maturity to **recognize the strength of their thought** and respectfully accept their guidance. Such humility is a sign of true greatness.

"None can ruin a ruler, who is advised by loyal

And fearless counsellors." *(Kural 447)*

Baseless arguments, arrogance, and refusal to seek advice from subordinates can bring down even the strongest institutions. When a leader makes a wrong decision, those close to them must have the courage to speak up and insist on what's right. Sometimes, it may even require risking one's position to uphold the truth; but very few have that kind of boldness.

Most people prefer to stay quiet, "Why get involved?" But a **genuine friend and good supporter**, who boldly says, "This won't work," in times of poor judgment; such a person cannot be brought down by anyone, no matter the situation.

"The poor have no capital to earn a wage

The friendless have no firmness to stand." *(Kural 449)*

Just as one may invest money or use knowledge as capital to earn income, the true wealth of life is the guidance of the wise. Those who do not live by dharma, and who fail to align with enlightened thinkers, fade into history without significance.

Even in the eras of many kings and wealthy men, only a few are remembered; those who selflessly worked for the welfare of society.

"To forsake the friendship of the noble is ten times

Worse than earning the enmity of many." *(Kural 450)*

What happens when we ignore or abandon the wise? Losing their friendship causes ten times more harm than earning the enmity of the powerful. The present crisis in society is due to this very neglect; the voice of the thinker is not heard, and the voice of the learned does not reach the halls of power. Had Maharishi's ideas been implemented, the world would already be half paradise.

If my ideas don't suit your way of life,

This world is vast; I'll quietly go my own way

I will continue to spread my vision and ideals

Mockery or jealousy cannot stand in my way

If your ideas don't suit my life,

The wide world is open to you as well

I shall walk my path, and you walk yours

And the Divine will bless us both. – *Vedathiri Maharishi*

"Is the body a vessel made to bear suffering for one

Who hides the faults of his family?" *(Kural 1029)*

This is the kind of *recognition* a true thinker often receives. Looking back over 2,500 years of history, we see that most individuals who **dedicated their lives to the welfare of humanity** met with untimely deaths by poison, the cross, imprisonment, stoning, or betrayal.

The world has repeatedly inflicted suffering upon those who sought its good. Valluvar painfully questions: *Is the body of such a noble soul, who worked selflessly for others, nothing but a vessel meant to endure sorrow?* From animal life to today's societies, group living is natural, and leadership within a group is unavoidable. Valluvar, who begins the section on virtue with praise of God, opens the section on wealth by upholding just leadership as divine. A ruler who protects justice and guides the people rightly is considered godlike.

Since only one group becomes a leader, power is concentrated but how that power is used determines the fate of all. Hence, everyone must grow in thinking and embrace dharma, so collective well-being may flourish.

Socrates said: "Do not accept anything simply because someone said it. Whoever says it, weigh it with your own natural reason."

Valluvar echoed: "Whatever truth you hear, from whomever it may be, recognize it with discernment."

Vedathiri Maharishi insisted: "Do not believe words alone; reflect deeply and arrive at clarity on your own."

2,000 years later, Maharishi remains the only sage who boldly declared: '*Think for yourself*'. Thought is the path that removes suffering. But one thinker is not enough; everyone must become a thinker. Let change begin with us; let us guide others not by force; by example.

Acceptance or rejection is their choice. Ripened fruit has taste; artificially ripened ones do not. Maharishi never said, "Let wise people be counted"; he said, "Let them multiply." Until that happens, let our duty flourish in the land of righteousness.

Summary:

In society, the paths taken by people are largely influenced by political, economic, and religious leaders. However, most of these leaders today act out of selfish motives, causing harm instead of guiding people toward peace and well-being.

True thinkers like Thiruvalluvar, Buddha, Jesus, and Vedathiri Maharishi guide through wisdom, integrity, and spiritual clarity. They emphasize **virtue**, **inner discipline**, and **service to humanity** as the highest values.

According to Vedathiri Maharishi and Thiruvalluvar:

* Real joy comes only from righteous actions.

* Leadership is divine when rooted in justice and wisdom.

* Governance must prioritize moral clarity over freebies.

* False religious leaders, who hide selfish desires behind holy robes, are like tigers in disguise, deceiving and destroying all.

Key Teachings:

* Power without wisdom leads to destruction.

* Hypocrisy in religion erodes public faith.

* Virtue alone ensures lasting strength and societal peace.

* Wisdom, even in the young, must be respected and followed.

Ultimately, only when political, religious, and economic powers are influenced by **noble thinkers** will society progress. Maharishi calls for **each person to become a thinker**, living by reflection and righteousness.

Plan Seven

Recognizing the Greatness of Women

Pleasure and love are part of nature's justice. Social inequalities, however, are man-made injustices. The world created by nature is harmonious, but human beings have divided it into many ways.

As a result, we have lost health, happiness, and peace. To restore this harmony and experience a fulfilled life, we must understand nature's laws, proper ways of living, and the divine purpose of creation.

For a noble life, the value of women must be universally recognized. In most societies, very few truly accept and respect both women and men as equals.

In youth, a woman may feel proud of being an 'attractive figure'; in early marriage, she may believe 'life is heaven'; yet in old age, many women regret, 'Alas, I was born a woman'.

Poet Kannadasan reflects this pain: *"Even princesses of royal clans are brought to tears. Is this the fate destined for all women in this world?"*

Such emotional suffering arises from ignorance. Therefore, society must foster mental maturity to accept the birth of a girl child with equal joy and pride. Whether it is a boy or a girl, both are equally our children. A sense of balance must prevail.

Poet Desika Vinayagam Pillai said, *"To be born as a woman, one must have performed great penance!"* Mahakavi

Bharathiyar declared, *"A wife who truly loves is divine! Through her, one may attain even Godhood!"* And Kannadasan observed, *"Of all debts, the greatest is the service of a noble wife. To repay that fortune, many lifetimes may be needed."*

What is the divine will of the boundless, all-powerful God?

To give rise to every life, He wondrously shaped womanhood

As the sacred channel of creation. Among the living,

How many truly realize this treasure? *- Maharishi*

Thus, laments Maharishi, urging the world to awaken to the supreme value of womanhood.

Among the 8.2 billion people on this planet, how many truly understand and realize the greatness of woman? This is the sorrowful question raised by Maharishi.

Notably, he asks not about "men" but "people" - indicating a deeper truth: even women often fail to understand the worth of womanhood.

In a land where womanhood is glorified in art,

Will you not let real women live with dignity?

You elder who hails her as mother and goddess

Is divine sweetness only honey on sacred texts? – Kannadasan

Vedathiri Maharishi firmly declares:

You were formed in a woman's womb,

Fed by a woman's milk,

Living your life with a woman's support

So, realize the greatness of woman!"

Even though a man is born through a woman and lives with a woman, how many respect a woman as an equal being?

Kannadasan questions:

Though born of a woman, though living because of her,

Who honors the woman as dearly as their own eyes?

When she is with us, she is used; when absent, forgotten

If this is humanity, even Nature would cease to function!

When humanity violates nature, calamities follow - tsunamis, floods, earthquakes, volcanic eruptions. Where evil deeds prevail, especially where women are wronged, nature's fury intensifies.

Negative thoughts create destructive forces. When society, culture, and living patterns deviate from nature's path, imbalance arises, and natural disasters become frequent.

Maharishi emphasizes that when human thought becomes severally imbalanced, nature, the supreme force, responds by restoring balance.

Wherever women are suppressed or mistreated, nature's wrath increases. Maharishi declares boldly: *"When women are denied their rightful power or subjected to suffering, their sorrow transforms into a curse. The consequences of such sins manifest disasters, murders, or suicides."*

Hence, the first step is for women to recognize their own dignity and power. Men too must respect and affirm the value of women. All life begins from a woman: *"Man is born of a woman and ends in the earth."*

Traditionally, it's said "half the world is men, and half are women." But Maharishi corrects this: ***Half the world is made up of women; the other half is the children they have borne.***

A powerful tribute to womanhood.

People may ask: *'Are women lesser than men?'* Certainly not. *'Are women equal to men?'* Still, no. *'Then are women superior to men?'* Again, no. So, what is the truth?

Maharishi answers with divine clarity: *"There is no superiority, no inferiority, not even equality. Man or woman - each is unique and precious in their own place."*

Such is the enlightened perspective that the world must awaken to - the sacred, balanced vision of woman as an essential and exalted expression of nature and divinity.

Kannadasan once remarked: *"The snake on Lord Shiva's neck asked, 'Garuda, are you doing well?' Garuda replied, 'As long as one stays within one's own place, all is well.'"* This seemingly simple example holds profound meaning.

Similarly, the **Bhagavad Gita** says: *"Whatever is most excellent among any group or kind, that am I." "Among flowers, I am the Parijata."*

The Parijata flower is not used by people; it is offered exclusively to God.

Nowhere does Krishna say, *"the Parijata tree is higher than other trees"* but rather *"among flowers, it is Parijata; among trees, the wish-fulfilling Kalpaka tree."*

This shows that **within each category, excellence is defined uniquely**.

Likewise, you may say, *"This woman is the best among ten women,"* or *"This man is the finest among ten men."*

But comparing man and woman directly is fundamentally wrong, says Vyasa. It is **null and void**, because each is supreme in his or her own role. Together, they form a complete unit called *family*.

If we start arguing *who is greater*, man or woman; what happens? Life is like a cart journey. If one wheel is smaller than the other, how can the cart move forward? It will simply spin in circles. But even here, observe this subtle truth:

The smaller wheel stays at the center, while the larger wheel revolves around it. So however, you analyze it - **woman is the axis of life**.

Kannadasan says it poetic: *"For a cart to run, two wheels are needed. If one of the two wheels is smaller, which cart runs?"*

In a marriage, if there's no balance between husband and wife, the ups and downs of ego and dominance cause the family cart to tip and crash. Hence, both must *recognize and preserve each other's unique greatness.*

In both society and family, every living being has a natural right to freedom, needs, and dignity. These are gifts from nature; not granted by society or law. Therefore, no one has the right to infringe upon another's freedom.

People argue: *"Let's give women freedom, let's end female slavery."* In truth, **no one needs to grant women freedom** - only to avoid **taking away the freedom nature has already given**. *And if we forget this, what will be the result?*

Maharishi said:

Those who belittled women to glorify themselves,

Bore the burden of sin and suffering; the world knows it well

Those who reflected and honored woman's greatness

Lived joyfully and remain eternal, divine like God himself.

To speak further, in most families, it is women who tend to care for their parents till the very end. As the saying goes: **'A daughter remains daughter for life.'** But: **'A son remains a son only until he gets his wife.'**

This statement often proves to be true. Even if a son doesn't care for his own aging parents, he might still take care of his in-laws. In the end, it is still a *son* - one by birth, the other by law.

If today elders are able to live in peace, it is often because, even if their own son has moved away after marriage, their son-in-law steps in and takes care of them.

But if both daughter and son-in-law abandon their duties, old age homes become the only refuge. Hence, if one understands both the laws of society and nature and lives accordingly, **a son**

will care for us - and so will a son-in-law. But it all depends on our **own way of behavior** and fulfilling our duties.

Human duties can be viewed in three stages:

1. **Before marriage – childhood and student life**
2. **After marriage – family and work responsibilities**
3. **Old age – detachment and reflection**

During student life, even though parents raise their children with love and responsibility, if the child lacks the maturity to understand what is being taught, what use is all the effort?

Even if the parents teach constantly, it won't bear fruit unless the child's intelligence awakens and accepts what is taught.

Only when children combine what they learn from their parents, teachers, society, and nature, and apply it wisely, can their life be considered successful.

As a school student, one must stay awake late to prepare for exams. In college, it's the same. Even in the working world, there's barely time to sleep after a tiring day.

For married women, the load is heavier; they must work outside, manage the house, take care of their husband, and later, children. Every stage brings further **sleeplessness**.

Yet, such **an intelligent, capable, and wonder-working woman** - how much penance must her parents have done to receive her as a daughter?

When her in-laws see her excellence, they should marvel, and in that wonder **she repays her parental family.**

To shape and raise such a daughter, the parents must also be good human beings. A **hybrid seed produces good fruit only with proper** nurturing.

If a woman begins to see all these responsibilities as burdens, how can the world survive?

This entire sacrificial life of a woman was beautifully summarized by ***Kannadasan in a lullaby:***

For one born as a woman, restful sleep comes only twice,

One at birth, and another in death. (So, in the life)

If you miss the sleep now, you may never sleep again.

My precious little girl, sleep now, sleep now...

That's the refrain of the song. After listing all the moments where a woman loses her sleep, he concludes:

Hands tremble, eyes fade, and time comes seeking

All the lost sleep will come back on its own.

This final sleep - **the only peaceful rest after childhood - comes with death**. Such is the life of a woman, built on ***selfless sacrifice***, as even Kannadasan testifies.

It is time the world not only acknowledges this truth but honors it in thought, words, and action.

At the root, foundation, and culmination of everything lies the *Divine Cosmic Power.* The motion of the universe is governed within this supreme force.

Masculinity represents consciousness and the ability to lead.

Femininity represents the principle that yields and flows with that leadership.

Yet, Lord Shiva, the embodiment of the Supreme, gave half of His form to Shakti, manifesting as *Ardhanarishvara* - the perfect union of Shiva and Shakti.

So even in human life, it is wrong to think men are superior and women inferior just because women often consent or submit in speech or action. Male dominance cannot be taken as a mark of true superiority.

Literature and epics exist to highlight the unique greatness of each being in nature, and the cultural values of their time. In the **Mahabharata**, Vyasa illustrates the social setting of that period through a striking scene:

Devayani, daughter of Shukracharya, the Guru of the Asuras, enters into a dispute with a princess over who is superior. In a moment of anger, the princess pushes Devayani into a well and leaves.

Devayani cries out for help, and a passing king, **Yayati**, rescues her. She takes him to her father and narrates all that happened.

She then expresses her wish to marry Yayati, since he was the first man who touched her hand, symbolizing purity and the strict moral code in that era.

During those times, if a man even touched a woman's hand, it was seen as a breach of chastity. Shukracharya agreed and arranged their marriage. This episode reveals that ***women had the freedom to express their will and choose their life partner***, even in ancient times. Vyasa thus emphasizes that such autonomy for women was once honored.

Similarly, in history, kings would conduct a grand ceremonial gathering (Swayamvar) for their daughters. Invitations were sent to all rulers; as the kings assembled, their virtues were announced, and the princess would choose her groom according to her own desire.

Such a practice showed that ***recognition and freedom for women were once embedded*** in society.

*But **when and how did this noble tradition change**?*

Over time, as more kingdoms emerged, greed among rulers grew. Kings began invading neighboring lands, not merely for territory, but for **wealth**.

It was no longer land that mattered, but **treasure** - the riches of another kingdom. Armies would plunder the treasury, load it into carts, and along with natural wealth like cattle and horses, they would also **capture women**, especially beautiful ones.

*Thus, began a dark shift in social values. What was once **freedom and dignity** became **objectification and possession**.*

*The plundering of kingdoms included the violation of womanhood, and this led to the **decline of the status and independence** once held by women.*

The cause lies in this: the sixth sense, unique to humans, gives the ability to ***appreciate beauty, desire it, and attempt to***

possess it. Among thousands of birds, people admire the peacock's vibrant feathers. Among countless birds sounds, the koel's sweet voice captures the heart. Since natural sexual awareness is driven by aesthetic appreciation, ***when men began admiring women for their beauty, they also desired to possess them***.

Kannadasan captures this truth poignantly:

God who created the mind, placed memory within it.

He gave the wisdom to understand fellow humans.

The God who gave wisdom also adorned body with beauty.

Man, seeing that beauty, enslaved the woman.

Though women possess equal intellect as men, *male dominance,* driven by the desire to own beauty, turned women into *objects of control.*

During the historical periods of *conquest*, when women were abducted along with wealth, their *protection became the responsibility of strong men.*

To protect women from abduction during invasions, they were increasingly *confined to the home,* while men went out to earn.

Over time, ***dependency*** *on men for survival became* ***misinterpreted as inferiority*** *solidifying the* ***structure of patriarchy***.

Due to this restricted, domestic life, ***women were denied real-world experience***. Men, being out in the world, gained varied experiences. If a husband made moral errors outside, and the wife questioned him, he could not justify them logically. Unable to answer her valid and ethical questions, he would retort: *"Why do you care? I earn for you; just be quiet."*

This became the veil for his *selfishness,* using his earning power as a *shield* to hide moral flaws, and converting a woman's *protected existence into enslaved dependence.*

Over generations, women were kept **uneducated**, unexposed to the world, and conditioned into silent obedience.

As a result, their feelings were ignored, their thinking stifled, and their potential wasted. That is why **Bharathiyar** powerfully advocated for **women's education**; not just to read and write, but to **awaken thinking**, build **independence**, and experience the world.

He foresaw that only through education would a woman gain the courage to live by her own earnings and principles. Only when she no longer depends on a man will true freedom begin.

Even from her parental home, a girl lives a life of **sacrifice**, adjusting to her parents, siblings, and environment. After marriage, she must adjust again **embracing her in-laws** and their ways. Then, she sacrifices yet again for her **children**, and even for the **grandchildren** born.

This unending life of sacrifice, hardship, and service ***without recognition*** *is what moved* ***Vedathiri Maharishi*** *to deeply reflect:*

'Though a woman manages the family, serves the world silently, and dedicates her life, does she still receive any acknowledgement from society?'

Thus, **'Wife Appreciation Day'** was born - not merely as a celebration, but as a philosophical reminder to the world: *behind every stable home, every peaceful elder, and every growing child stands the* ***unacknowledged strength of a woman.***

She deserves not just love, but respect, equality, and the space to realize her full self.

1. BEFORE MARRIAGE:

After puberty the girl is shaped into a virtuous and responsible person, especially through the observance of the Maiden Vow (a ritualistic vow) that subtly prepares a girl for righteous family life.

We refrained from ghee and milk, bathed at dawn

Adorned ourselves with kohl, placed flowers on our hair,

We avoided sinful acts, refrain from talking ill of others.

This is the essence of Maiden vow. It involves waking up early, bathing, worshipping God, avoiding artificial beauty, abstaining from indulgent foods, refraining from immoral thoughts, words, or actions, and setting aside immoral ideas.

Its goal is to **nurture clarity, self-restraint, and readiness for family life** in young women.

"What use is a prison's guard for women? Guarding their

Virtue within is the truest safeguard." *(Kural 57)*

Poet Ramaiah Dass affirms the ideal:

It was woman who claims back her husband's life

It was woman who commanded time, 'Stop right there'

It was woman who declared justice that shook a king

If you assess their value, their chastity alone stands.

What dowry should a bride bring?

'A flawless smile with mature character,

And more natural beauty of form is here, O dear one,

What more do the poor need, tell me?' - Kannadasan

Just as a plant, grown in a nursery with rich nutrients, is carefully transplanted into a field where it is nurtured with water, manure, and protection, and eventually yields a good harvest, marriage is a sacred ceremony in which a mature girl, raised well in her *parental home (the nursery),* is entrusted to *her marital home (the field).*

Before beginning family life, both the bride and groom must have a clear understanding of life. To ensure this, just as the tradition of the Maiden Vow *(Pavai Nombu)* was established to prepare young girls, the system of *Brahmacharya* was prescribed for boys.

In the 250 Kural poems of the Section on Love, the hero and heroine explore the joys of conjugal life.

To guide that journey, **Thiruvalluvar the great** laid out a preparatory path to marital bliss through the chapter titled "The Worth of a Wife" (Chapter 6) *for the woman.*

"What greater wealth can a woman possess,

Than steadfast chastity - her firm resolve?" (Kural 54)

And for the man, in Chapter 3, he declares:

"He who with discipline guards the five senses, becomes a

Noble seed through which good lineage thrives." (Kural 24)

Thus, Valluvar codified a model of virtue-based marital readiness for both genders, rooted in chastity and moral strength.

Though the word 'chastity' is generally used to describe the relationship between a man and a woman, in essence, it denotes **mental firmness;** the strength of will to live by chosen values. Among these values, the relationship between husband and wife is just one aspect.

To desire everything without discernment is like **Kamadhenu**, the wish-fulfilling cow. But to desire only what is necessary with inner resolve and to reject what is unnecessary is like **Kalpaka tree**, the tree of discernment. To remain firm in such resolve and attain inner greatness is **Chintamani**, the gem of wisdom.

"One who has mastered the five senses is the true seed of prosperity in family life." Just as a well-matured grain, when sown through skilled farming, grows into many fruitful harvests, so too, when a man gains fulfillment in sensory pleasures through restraint, refines his negative traits, and cultivates virtue, he prepares himself to merge with the formless Divine; the true goal of rebirth.

In this spiritual journey, the man's **virile seed** becomes matured over **16 years**, and when infused with discipline and devotion, gains the power to **create a divine child**. Such a man is called ***Varan*** *- a worthy groom.*

On the other hand, one who lives aimlessly, without measure or restraint in sensual pleasures, is called ***Uran*** - *merely a being of flesh.*

The excellence of a **Varan**, who lives with self-restraint, becomes the **seed** - not just for biological succession, but for the transmission of:

- Good health
- Mental fulfillment
- Success
- And ultimately, self-realization (**Atma Jnana**)

Cooking transforms raw ingredients into nourishing meal for the body and mind. Just like that when a girl or boy reaches puberty, natural desires begin to awaken.

Yet, there is no one greater than a woman who resolves in her heart to enjoy love and intimacy only with her rightful life partner.

Likewise, there is no treasure more valuable for a bride than a groom who, with foresight, discipline, and a commitment to righteous living, prepares himself to lead a virtuous family life.

2. MARITAL LIFE:

This is called ***Grihastha*** - householder life, which is not just a social role; it reflects a universal law. It is nature's law for life to unite with its kind for protection, nurturing, and reproduction. That is why a **life companion** is called a partner for life.

So, when a young man comes of age, it becomes the **responsibility of his parents to find him a good woman** and arrange a marriage. No parent or youth ever says, "I want a bride who brings misfortune." No one seeks **Satan**; they seek ***Mahalakshmi*** - the embodiment of beauty, prosperity, and virtue.

But ultimately, **what one receives depends not just on desire, but on the unseen forces of karma** - the records of one's past actions, both good and bad.

Wife is not merely a life partner; she is a divine blessing. Who is meant to walk with whom in life is not decided by caste, horoscope, status, education, salary, or company name.

By the law of karma, Nature determines who is destined to be whose companion. As the Tamil saying goes, 'The match was written by God long ago'.

Yet, in practice, most people marry within their own caste. They claim **God** brings the life partner, but only after checking ***nakshatra***, ***gotra***, and a dozen other boxes.

Even when a boy and girl feel an instant connection on first sight which could be the real divine sign, we often delay that moment, by filtering it through the lens of horoscopes, charts, and background checks.

This has turned into a **checklist-style selection** process, rather than an intuitive connection.

True divine pairing happens when two people **meet with no expectations, no predictions; just a deep acceptance**. That's how the right life partner is found.

Valluvar's Example:

If we truly understand how the great sage **Valluvar chose his wife**, our view of marriage would change completely. **Valluvar wandered with a sack of sand on his shoulder**, saying: "I am seeking a woman who can cook rice from this sand. She will be my wife." One after another, women turned him away, laughing. One day, tired, he rested at the open corridor of a home. The family asked him his purpose. He told the same reply.

Inside the house, a girl named **Vasuki** overheard. She stepped forward and told her father: **"Give me the sand. I will turn it into rice."**

Valluvar handed her the sack. Vasuki took it to the backyard and **quietly used real rice to cook a meal and served him.** He ate the meal, and they got married.

Until the end of their lives, ***Valluvar never asked, "How did you make rice from sand?" And Vasuki also never told what she did with the sand.*** They understood each other without words.

Such was the wisdom they shared, and the silence they honored. ***Accepting that one cannot cook rice from sand and choosing not to even attempt it - that is wisdom.***

Marriage is often viewed as something arranged by elders, based on "compatibility," and assumed to be a guaranteed path to heaven. But in reality, it can become the heaven one hoped for; or turn into a hell no one saw coming.

In both outcomes, be it joy or sorrow, the truth remains: ***"Who is destined for whom" is a divine arrangement, written by fate and granted by God.***

Problems arise when expectations rise too high, and tolerance runs too low. Despite education, social status, a good job, and strong income, newly married couples struggle to live in harmony. Why? Because **no one explains what marriage truly means.**

As a result, even couples blessed with many individual strengths fail to fully enjoy the joys of marriage. Instead, they lose peace, derail their own future, and bring sorrow to their parents as well.

*At its core, **married life requires maturity - the willingness to accept each other's flaws**. Reducing expectations, increasing mutual adjustment, and nurturing patience are essential for a lasting, fulfilling marriage.*

***Love is not just romance and sweet words; it is cooperation, compromise, and understanding.** The modern trend - "Love at first sight; Divorce at first fight" - only reflects **immaturity and irresponsibility**.*

This is a **cultural decline** of recent times.

What about the past?

In earlier generations, people entered marriage **with understanding, duty, and a sense of sacrifice**. They embraced the reality of shared life, rather than chasing illusions. And that gave strength, not only to the marriage, but to families and society itself.

They wore the wedding garland and lived in true union

With unwavering hearts, they enjoyed life together for years

This was once the culture of Tamil Nadu - but

The present Tamil Nadu of yours doesn't know it. -Kannadasan

If one's **karma record** is good, then the **life partner** too will be a blessing. If negative karma dominates, then fate will assign a partner who will **help wash away** those karmic residues, sometimes painfully, but purposefully.

If the wife aligns with the husband's fate and vow,

They will live together forever.

But if there's even a small mismatch in nature,

Then without telling, take silent renunciation. *- Avvaiyar*

This does not imply literally abandoning a difficult marriage. It refers to the inner clarity one gains from understanding the truth of the relationship.

If partners differ in nature, it calls for patience, sacrifice, and compromise - not escapism or running away. The true meaning is that couples must live together with balance, rooted in tolerance, mutual understanding, and selfless giving.

Speak to her with kind words.

Cherish your wonderful wife with love.

Teach her the lesson of love (then)

Is Kashi any holier than wife? - *Kannadasan*

Kannika Dhan:

Let us now explore the next noble thought; the sacred act of Kannika danam: the offering of one's daughter, raised like ***Mahalakshmi***, as a wife to a groom, sometimes even without knowing fully about his past or future.

This ancient custom is considered one of the **greatest forms of charity**. Many noble-hearted individuals, blessed with wealth and goodwill, perform various charitable acts for the welfare of society, such as:

- **Donating Food**
- **Donating cows**
- **Donating land**
- **Donating Blood**
- **Donating Books, Fees, etc. for education**
- **Donating for Healthcare**,
- **Donating for building temples**, **monasteries**, etc.

Among these, the great poet **Bharathiyar** said: *"Feeding a hungry person is a sacred deed but teaching an unlettered soul to read; that is a greater virtue, a crore-fold."*

Yet even greater than all these noble offerings are one that stands matchless and supreme: **Kannika Dhan** - the **sacred offering of a daughter as bride.**

One may wonder, *"What makes this offering so elevated?"* This message must reach everyone.

* **Annadhanam** fills the stomach for a time.

* **Godhanam** is greater; because a cow, considered **living wealth**, contributes over and over again. Even if the owner does not feed it, the cow finds its own food and still returns to offer milk, supporting the livelihood of the person.

Thus, each form of charity indeed benefits the recipient in some way. But **Kannika Dhan is the only gift that combines the virtues of all these** and offers them through the form of a virtuous, well-raised woman entering a family. How?

Today, from poor households to affluent families, **wives contribute economically by working and earning**. This contribution is **Annadhanam** - feeding the family.

A well-educated and skilled wife, who earns a good income, becomes a partner in accumulating wealth - **buying land, property, building homes**, and securing the family's future.

Her earnings also contribute toward Cow donation, Land donation, Free education, Healthcare, Temple donations, etc.

*With so many blessings stemming from a single person - **isn't the Kannika Dhan** the very source that made all this possible?*

*To raise a daughter, to **nurture her, educate her, instill values, teach her skills like cooking, childcare, and family***

***management** and to prepare her to harmoniously blend into another family...*

*Is this not, in itself, a massive act of lifelong **selfless giving** on the part of the parents? What words could ever fully express the greatness of such a **gift**?*

And this is not all. Even if one plants a powerful seed, provides water, manure, fencing and care; yet, it is **the fertility of soil that ultimately determines the harvest**.

Likewise, even when a child is born from a strong father, it is **the mother - with her mind, her energy, and her womb - who becomes the foundation for the child's future**.

As Maharishi said: "A husband's education helps elevate the family, but a wife's education nourishes not just one child but generations to come, like a spring of wisdom and wealth."

"If the wife is virtuous, what can be lacking?

If she lacks virtue, what good could remain?" *(Kural 53)*

Valluvar declares that when a woman of intelligence, grace, and character becomes a man's wife, *his household is complete. If not, life turns toward emptiness and despair.*

Receiving such a wife is not a mere blessing; **it is a rare fortune, a divine gift**. To forget that, and to treat one's wife with neglect or disrespect, is nothing but **ingratitude and ignorance**.

Household life, as Maharishi said, is not merely a social contract. It is a divine bond that purifies karma.

In a dharmic marriage, husband and wife cleanse the karmic records of six previous generations, and by their union, enable future generations to be born and thrive.

To make this possible, in the parental home, a daughter is raised with care, values, and skills; and finally offered in marriage, as a gift, Kannika Dhan, to a man, as his life partner.

Is this not one of the greatest acts of giving? Realizing this, **a husband must treat his wife as his equal** and uphold the sanctity of the home.

His family too must **embrace her with the same love and dignity** they would offer their own daughter – without distinction. But society often makes the tragic mistake of saying: 'Now that she's married, she has no ties with her parents.' 'No matter how the husband is, she must remain submissive.'

Maharishi rejected such ignorant and outdated views. *He questioned:* ***How does marrying a woman give a man the right to mistreat her?***

Does a wedding ritual dissolve the sacred bond between a parent and daughter? *These toxic beliefs, Maharishi said, must be removed from society.*

Maharishi also condemned a cruel custom: Where the bride's parents pour water into the groom's parents' hands, symbolically transferring their daughter as if she's **being adopted**.

"This act of a parent giving their daughter as though she no longer belongs to them, must be abolished," said Maharishi.

At the time of marriage, parents stand before all,

And hand over their daughter to a man they call 'husband',

Pouring water into his hands, giving her away with money,

In the presence of many, as if she is no longer theirs.

Even those who understand character and virtue

Do not reflect on this as cruelty. - *Vethathiri Maharishi*

Though there's no denying that the rigid traditions of the past have begun to shift, **this transformation must spread across all sections of society from the underprivileged to the elite.**

*At the foundation of any household is not wealth or ritual, but a **sacred and divine bond between husband and wife.***

As Kannadasan wrote:

*Like the **aerial roots** of a banyan tree,*

What is the use of a thousand passing ties?

*You were my **taproot**; because of that, I did not fall.*

Just as the taproot anchors a tree, a couple's bond must anchor their home. The **true sign of one's spiritual merit** is not found in religious displays but in having a noble, virtuous life partner.

"When love and virtue dwell in family life,

It yields both noble character and true benefit." *(Kural 45)*

Usually, human love functions within the boundaries of personal affection; caring for family, children, and close ones.

But true love, the kind that resembles divine compassion, expands beyond boundaries, embracing neighbors and strangers alike.

Since the divine itself operates through the principles of love and compassion, those who live with such expansive love are truly liberated. Just as fertile soil yields abundant crops, a cultured mind rooted in virtue bears fruits of goodness and benefit for all.

"Domestic life itself is virtue, that too,

Speaks no ill of others is praiseworthy." *(Kural 49)*

But to say, "If a married couple simply avoids blame from others, they are virtuous," reflects an incomplete understanding of virtue.

Can anyone just criticize a **righteous couple** who live with morality, duty, and selfless giving? Even if such words are spoken, **do they hold any truth**?

As Prophet Muhammad said: "If what you say about someone is true, it is backbiting. If false, it is slander."

Whether true or false, speaking behind others' backs is neither noble nor righteous and especially unbecoming of a virtuous couple.

Thus, while true householder life involves fulfilling fivefold duties through noble thoughts, truthful words, and selfless deeds that uplift all, the highest form of righteousness is to live without criticizing or condemning others.

A woman who understands what is needed, when it is needed, and how much is needed, and lives accordingly with intelligence and grace; such a woman is truly worthy of reverence and respect.

No matter how she may have lived or grown up in her **birth home**, once she enters her **marital home**, the woman who adapts herself to the situation, the financial conditions, and the needs of her husband; becomes an unmatched blessing in her husband's life.

Shanthi Muhurtham (Sacred Consummation Ceremony):

What is the right time to conduct **Shanthi Muhurtham**?

In common custom, it usually takes place **after 10 PM** on the wedding night. But in some traditional households, it is performed only after **a series of Vedic rituals**, chants, and purifications that continue through the night, and the couple is sent to the sanctified room only after **3 AM**, during **Brahma Muhurtham**.

What, then, is the **deeper benefit** of this timing?

Surprisingly, no one has yet explained this spiritually or scientifically. But if we think deeply, the answer is clear:

The act of consummation is a sacred union; one that creates life. For such a holy act, the mental and energetic state of the couple is of utmost importance. Is it not?

What, then, does nature offer to support this?

It is during the Brahma Muhurtham (approx. 3:00–4:30 AM) that two key planetary forces align:

* **Venus** – the planet of reproduction, vitality, and semen

* **Earth** – the receiving force, representing feminine energy and fertility

According to spiritual and astronomical insights, these two forces interact during Brahma Muhurtham. Puranic stories poetically describe how **Venus blossoms in the sky** during this hour, indicating the fertilizing energy of Venus beaming toward Earth's face. *This **timing** is not just merely symbolic – it corresponds with **cosmic rhythms that influence fertility and vitality.***

Hence, conducting the sacred union during this time aligns human activity with **cosmic rhythm**, thereby promoting not only physical health and fertility, but also spiritual sanctity.

At around 3 AM, in the early hours of dawn, as the earth turns toward the sun, the atmosphere begins to shift. The calm, oxygen-rich air, combined with subtle electro-magnetic changes, creates a naturally refreshed environment - ideal for vitality and mental clarity.

*When a man and woman **unite during this powerful window**, with a **rested body** and a **tranquil, focused mind**, it creates **a fulfilling and harmonious experience of intimacy**.*

A **fulfilling experience of Shanthi Muhurtham** strengthens the emotional bond between the couple. If conception occurs at such a time, the resulting child is more likely to be healthy, mentally sharp, and spiritually attuned.

Hence, it is beneficial for couples to make it a practice to unite after restful sleep, in the Brahma Muhurtham hours, when the body is **energetically renewed** and the mind is **free from mental clutter**; this increases the chance of giving birth to **a** noble, healthy, and spiritually attuned offspring.

In contrast, when intimacy happens **at night under fatigue**, after an entire day of physical labor, emotional strain, and social distractions, the **seed may carry the imprint of that exhaustion**. If conception occurs in such a state, it can result in a child whose **physical and emotional well-being** may be affected.

Even if a woman feels inner desire, as Thiruvalluvar noted, she does **not express it fully**. In reality, during the sacred moment, she stands with shy reserve, her silence reflecting its sanctity.

Like a newlywed bride on the first night,

Must I still hide my face?

In front of my husband I married by tradition,

Should ancestral shyness still arise? - *Kannadasan*

Both are true. The **natural shyness and modesty** that appear during *Shanthi Muhurtham* (first night) are genuine and meaningful. But such modesty is **not necessary in day-to-day married life**.

Youth, both physical and mental, is a stage full of vitality and excitement. As one ages, this intensity begins to diminish, and the body's changes must be accompanied by mental maturity and adaptation.

In human memory, whatever is experienced intensely and repeatedly, the mind forms a pattern of recall. So, the way couples begin their intimate life - the quality, frequency, and emotional tone - becomes the foundation for how intimacy is imprinted and revisited in the mind throughout life.

Hence, it becomes the shared duty and responsibility of husband and wife to experience, manage, and preserve intimacy with calmness, mutual joy, and awareness. Right from the beginning, couples should set a healthy rhythm - balancing desire with restraint. If, in the early phase of marriage, the couple **overindulges in physical pleasure** without moderation, later dissatisfaction and imbalance are unavoidable.

The mind's craving may persist, but the body's energy cannot always rise to meet the mind's desire. That's why it is vital to train the mind, which is naturally restless and always seeking fulfillment, to act in harmony with the body's capacity, not beyond it.

Only when the body, life-force, and mind are all aligned can true fulfillment in married life be achieved. Keeping this in mind, physical union must be guided by moderation, mutual respect, and inner awareness.

True spirituality does not oppose marital intimacy; rather it sanctifies and elevates it.

At the peak of physical union, the **mind transcends thought**, lost in deep sensation and stillness. No worldly idea arises at that moment.

It is in this state, when the couple reaches the sacred silence of union, that the fluid is released. This is why sexual union is considered holy, because divinity expresses itself at the climax of intimacy.

This sacred journey from human passion to divine connection, begins with the first night - a gateway to the journey from desire to divinity. When this continues over time with bodily peace, mental calm, and spiritual stillness, the couple eventually arrive at the inner realization: ***"We have lived this life fully, in body, mind and spirit."*** This is the true fulfillment of human birth.

So far, we have reflected on **Kannika danam** and **Shanthi Muhurtham.** Not as mere ceremonies, but as deeply meaningful transitions.

When the bride becomes a wife, and steps into the role of managing the household and nurturing the family, she rises to a place of great honor and responsibility - a subject worthy of deep reflection.

She comes from her **parental home,** the **nursery** where she was raised, into the **field** that is her **marital home**, stepping forward with her **right foot**, as tradition signifies.

In that field of family life, when she receives a single living cell from her husband, she merges it with her own life force and creates a beautiful child.

This mysterious and miraculous power is what makes **womanhood sacred**. Just like **a single seed planted in fertile soil yields countless sheaves of grain**, her womb, her will, and her love give rise to **new life**; generation after generation.

In married life, when a woman's heart fully unites with,

Her soul begins to long, each day, for motherhood.

Without understanding the true secret of life,

For desire that keeps growing, where is the limit?

-Poet Suradha

The natural attraction in a marital relationship is fundamentally rooted in the drive to create offspring. For a man, divine, egoless pleasure is experienced only at the moment when he releases his semen, beyond thought, beyond self.

But for the woman, who receives that seed and ***carries the divine potential of new life***, she continues to experience a ***profound, sacred joy throughout the pregnancy.*** Glowing with a beauty and fulfillment that radiates from within.

It is more than physical pleasure – it is the bliss of creation, a joy that only a soul prepared to nurture life can truly experience – a joy rooted in selfishness.

That is why Bharathiyar declared: "A loving wife is divine, my friends; Through her, even realization of God becomes possible."

This verse carries two profound truths:

1. A woman herself can attain **divinity through her own love and compassion**.
2. A **husband, too, may reach the divine state through his wife's grace**.

Many great souls, such as Sri Ramakrishna Paramahamsa and Vedathiri Maharishi acknowledged the significant role of their wives in their spiritual evolution.

Once, a devotee asked Vedathiri Maharishi: ‘Swamiji, it appears that women rarely seen as spiritually inclined. Only a few like Karaikal Ammaiyar or Avvaiyar became saints.’

‘But among men, we see many, from **Veda Vyasa** to **yourself**, who embraced renunciation. Doesn’t this show that men have greater interest in spirituality?’

Swamiji smiled and replied gently:

‘Tell me, what is renunciation?’

The devotee answered,

‘Renunciation means giving up everything.’

Swamiji then asked,

‘Are you married?’

‘Yes, Swamiji. I am,’ he said.

Swamiji continued,

‘And do you live in your father-in-law’s house, or does your wife live in yours?’

The man replied,

‘My wife lives with me, in my home.’

At this, Swamiji calmly observed:

‘Then you haven’t renounced anything. But your wife - she left her family, her home, her identity, and came to live with you. So, tell me now, who is the true renunciate; you or she?’

And Swamiji concluded:

'**Among men, only a few are true renunciates.** But among women, almost all are. Even in my path of renunciation, my wife's contribution was profound.'

In traditional Hindu weddings, when the groom holds the bride's hand, he chants a mantra. The meaning is deeply spiritual: 'In countless births, I have been born and have died, yet I have not attained fulfillment. Now that you have come into my life as my life partner, help me live righteously and bring this cycle of birth to a sacred end.'

This is not merely marriage; it is spiritual companionship, where the wife is not merely a partner in living, but a partner in liberation.

A woman who doesn't worship god, wakes up, worship

Her husband will have rain fall if she asks it to. *(Kural 55)*

At first glance, this verse seems to imply that **a wife who worships her husband instead of God** holds such power that **even the rain obeys her**.

But does this imply she ignores divinity and submits blindly to her husband? Wouldn't that interpretation reduce a woman to mere servitude?

The great commentator Parimelazhagar offers a profound explanation here. He clarifies that the phrase 'She does not worship god' does not mean she refuses divine worship altogether, but rather that her everyday service to her husband is done with a divine consciousness, as an expression of *duty rooted in dharma.* Let's understand it through the lens of **spiritual routine**: From 3 AM to 6 AM, known as Brahma Muhurtham, is the most sacred time for spiritual practices.

An ideal householder may rise during this time, **meditate or pray**, and begin their day with the awareness of God. But once the day begins, even the most virtuous man must engage in worldly duties, and especially when he is asleep, he is not remembering God. It is during these moments, even when the husband is unaware that the wife rises before him, offers prayers to the divine, and then begins her daily duties:

- Preparing for the family's needs
- Caring for her husband
- Nurturing the children
- Serving elders and managing the home
- All of this without complaint, like rainfall - quiet, continuous, and without expectation

And the crucial question arises: **When does she rest?** What is the end to this unceasing service?

This is the heart of reflection; not to glorify her burden, but to awaken a sense of reverence and responsibility toward women who live with such deep grace.

Even rain does not fall year-round; if it did, it would lead to flooding and destruction. It is like seasonal rain that falls without being told, simply because it is its time and nature to do so. Likewise, a noble wife performs all her daily duties with consistency, without complaint, and expectation, just like the gentle, nourishing rain. As Kannadasan profoundly said:

The greatest of all debts is the service of a good wife. When I reflect to repay it, many lifetimes are needed.

And he adds:

Mother's dowry, brother's vast wealth,

Is that enough, if they reached the mother-in-law's house?

Can wealth alone uphold the honor and tradition?

In Tamil culture, it is said that three debts can never be fully repaid:

1. **The debt of birth** (to one's mother)
2. **The debt of nurturing** (to one's father)
3. **The debt of education** (to those who teach us)

To these, Kannadasan adds a sacred debt: The silent, lifelong service of a good wife; a sacred debt no man can fully repay.

"True blessing is a virtuous wife, and her

Greater gift is children of noble worth." *(Kural 60)*

In the life of a virtuous couple, the greatest blessing that may arise is the birth of **noble children**. When the husband and wife unite, body and soul, the very **moment of conception** is imbued with **divinity**.

The qualities and destiny of the child are deeply shaped by the **mother's state of mind** during pregnancy.

In the **Mahabharata**, we read how **Abhimanyu** learned the secrets of warfare while still in the womb of **Subhadra**, as **Arjuna** explained them aloud; with the fetus listening and absorbing each word. Another striking tale from the **Dashavatara** is that of **Narasimha Avatar**. When **Hiranyakashipu's wife Renuka** became pregnant, he told her:

"You should not remain in the palace during your pregnancy. I have arranged a peaceful garden for you, and I'll send **Narada** to accompany and guide you. After childbirth, you may return to the palace."

During that sacred time, **Narada Muni** explained the greatness of God and the soul. The fetus, **Prahlada**, listened from the womb, and grew with unwavering faith. This prenatal devotion made him an unshakable devotee, firm even in the face of torment.

So, the period of pregnancy is not a time for casual indulgence but a sacred yajna. If the mother reveres her womb as a sanctified space for nine months, the virtues she holds during that time will become the innate character of the child and make it noble. As Thiruvalluvar said:

"When virtue is upheld in every birth,

Evil finds no place." *(Kural 62)*

Only a couple who live in accordance with righteous conduct and inner refinement can be truly blessed with children who carry such noble traits from birth.

A woman who lives with freedom and dignity gives birth to children with strength and excellence.

As the old Tamil proverb goes: 'When you feed a neighbor's child, your own child will grow well.'

This doesn't literally mean someone will feed your child in return. Rather, it reflects a deeper **natural law** - that when you lovingly care for your **daughter-in-law** (who is someone else's daughter), the child she bears in your home will be blessed with good qualities. In other words, **nurturing the wife** is nurturing your own future lineage.

As poet Poovai Senguttuvan said: Every child is born good on this earth; whether he becomes noble or wicked, that depends on how his mother raises him.

A mother's influence begins not just after birth, but from the moment of pregnancy. Her thoughts, emotions, lifestyle - all shape the child.

Even after birth, her role in shaping the child's personality, behavior, and future is **immeasurable**.

The father, in most homes, spends his time earning for the family's needs. The real joy of witnessing a child's divine smile is often missed by the **fathers** and often experienced only later, when they become grandfathers.

Even in **choosing life partners for their grown children**, it is often *the mother's instinct* that sees more clearly than the father's logic.

As Kannadasan beautifully said:

God gave the mind and placed memory within it.

He gave the wisdom to understand fellow humans.

Next, whether it is a grandson or granddaughter, the responsibility of raising the child lies with the elders on both sides of the family.

More than that, there are also **siblings** within the family, and often, while a brother might ignore or dismiss his sister, she forgives him every time, saying: "He's my little brother after all." This spirit of *sacrifice, compassion, and unconditional love* is found in abundance in sisters.

Even beyond the family, take a simple example: a woman who comes to help with household chores as a paid worker. Even there, *a woman supports another woman's family life.*

So, at every level of society, a woman's contribution is deeply interwoven; not just in service, but as a silent strength. This greatness must be recognized *by women themselves and by everyone else.*

Only then can **true freedom for women be protected** and respected. If we understand that a woman is a great treasure of Nature, then every home can experience complete, true happiness.

A woman's life is a multi-dimensional journey:

* A **daughter** to her parents

* A **sister** to her siblings

* A **wife** to her husband

* A **daughter-in-law** to his parents

* A **sister-in-law** to his siblings

* A **mother** to her children

* A **mother-in-law** to her children's spouses

* A **relative** to her extended family

* A **grandmother** to her grandchildren

* A responsible **citizen** in society

Through all her above roles, she embodies tolerance, sacrifice, and love, offering more than she receives, sustaining more than she displays.

She is the silent symbol of strength and sacrifice.

In modern times, when both husband and wife go to work, people often assume it's easier if elders are present to help. But beyond convenience, there is true beauty in welcoming one's in-laws; father-in-law and mother-in-law; with genuine love and acceptance.

Today, we see a positive shift: the **daughter-in-law is educated**, earning, and exposed to the wider world. She now stands with self-confidence, and from that arises courage.

Society must learn to accept and support this transformation. For this, every individual needs awareness of nature's justice, and an understanding of societal harmony.

Above all, **women themselves must realize their true worth**. Love and compassion are the hallmarks of motherhood. Nature has bestowed upon women the sacred quality of motherhood; a state of **divine consciousness** that arises effortlessly in them. But for men to attain such a state of godliness, they must take up intense spiritual effort. That is why Kavimani expressed that, to be born as a girl and naturally attain divine nurturing love, **one must have performed penance in a previous birth**.

Could it be that the world still survives because of the **boundless compassion of women**, who continue to forgive the injustices committed by men across generations?

Just as God is the foundation of the universe, a wife is the sustaining force of the household. *Poet Kannadasan beautifully honored this truth, saying: "Who else can understand my true needs? Only a divine being like you, my wife, can."*

WIFE'S APPRECIATION DAY:

On 30th August 1994, at Guduvancheri, Chennai, Tamil Nadu, India, Vedathiri Maharishi initiated a sacred celebration: Wife's Appreciation Day, in the presence of his own blessed consort and many other couples.

This was not just an event, but a spiritual recognition of womanhood. Through this, Maharishi highlighted the greatness of a woman, who carries out the sacred work of divine creation here on Earth, as a representative of the Creator.

Thus, was born Wife's Appreciation Day, a day to honor the dignity, sacrifice, and grace of wives.

Leaving behind parents, birth home, and native town,

She came with purpose, embracing duty and dharma,

Like a renunciate sage, taken up the family services,

On traditional basis, she accepted me as her husband,

By the merit of my past deeds, she became my life partner

A noble image of womanhood, with love and compassion

Serving even others with devotion, my virtuous one,

I revere my wife, bless her and rejoice! - *Maharishi*

Leaving behind her parents, her childhood home, and the town where she was born, a woman comes into a new family and fulfills her duties with grace and responsibility.

Recognizing this deep truth, Vedathiri Maharishi established "Wife's Appreciation Day" on August 30, the birthday of his own wife. He urged all husbands to honor and remember their wives' greatness every year on this day; not just ceremonially, but from the heart.

"I honor my wife, I rejoice in her, I salute my beloved wife!"

This should not be said just once a year but **lived every day** - with awareness and gratitude.

The **dignity of such a woman**, who supports and uplifts all those around her, is truly unmatched. Every man must realize that **his own wife is the noble one** in his life; her service, her heart, and her strength are priceless.

Therefore, it is essential that both families - the husband's and the wife's - develop **maturity and sensitivity** to protect her **emotions and freedom**.

3. MY WIFE BECAME MY MOTHER:

Maturity, Withdrawal, and Vanaprastha: In the third stage of life, one begins to slowly detach from material involvement. After experiencing the world through **youth** and **householder** responsibilities, this stage is about reflecting, guiding, and gracefully retiring from active desires.

It is a time to acknowledge:

- The partner who walked with you through life
- The woman who made your family flourish
- And the inner journey yet to be completed

With reverence, reflection, and inner peace, this final phase becomes a preparation for liberation with your life partner by your side, as a fellow traveler in both dharma and detachment.

At this stage of reflection, we must truly understand the depth of the Tamil proverb: ***'After mother, it is wife'.***

Only then will men realize the sacred responsibilities of womanhood, and that ***all good women are indeed karma yogis****, selfless in their duty.*

What, then, might a grateful husband say to such a woman?

Like aerial roots of banyan tree, you embrace every bond,

Like banana shoot lives in mother's shade, you made me live

Two bodies, two lives, but one heart. O my soul!

Alright, what does the proverb **"After mother, the wife"** really mean? Does it imply that after the bond with one's mother, the wife comes next?

If so, should a husband always give priority to what his mother says? If his wife's opinion differs, should he reject it outright?

Ah! This very question - What the proverb truly conveys - is indeed worth seeking.

Because only when a question arises does clarity follow. So, what is the essence of it?

'A temple that gives away the handful of food it has, without keeping any for itself. A living deity that sees a trembling soul and pulls it into her arms.' **This is motherhood.**

Then what about the wife? Is her virtue any lesser?

After feeding her husband and children, **whatever remains is all she eats**; she doesn't think of it as little, nor complain that it isn't enough.

*When someone in the home falls ill, **she serves without regard for her own sleep, fatigue, or even her own illness.***

Is this wife's sacrifice any less than that of the mother who gave birth to us? **Certainly not.**

*The wife who takes responsibility as a mother to the children throughout her life, **in old age becomes mother to her husband too.***

After marriage, as part of her duty, she shared in her husband's love and affection.

But later in life, she might choose to let go of that desire. Why? Puberty begins when the brain's hypothalamus triggers a hormonal chain reaction.

It signals the body to start producing sex hormones; testosterone in boys, estrogen and progesterone in girls, which bring about the changes of adolescence.

These hormones typically begin rising around age 10–14. In women, hormone levels remain active until around age 45–50, after which they **decline sharply** during menopause.

In men, testosterone levels remain steady through midlife and begin to **gradually decline from around age 40, though they tend to last into later years.**

Do you remember the lines I referred to on an earlier page?

Well, this is that secret of those lines, I reflect below:

In married life, woman's heart unites and

Woman's mind seeks motherhood each day,

The secret of life remains unknown.

There are wives who calmly explain themselves to husband's disgust. And there are also those who say nothing, bearing husband's disgust and everything in dignified silence.

This natural biological pattern should be part of universal education - for both genders. To carry a womb filled with divinity, to nurture creation is the sacred relationship the soul seeks in the form of **a wife**.

She becomes the partner to a man who offers his seed in this divine process of procreation. This is the **secret of creation**. ***Without such understanding, many couples experience emotional distance and conflict in midlife, mistaking***

biological changes for a loss of love or affection. While youth, attraction, and romance may be **hormonally driven**, the foundation of all relationships must still be **love and compassion**, and these never truly disappear.

They may change in expression or intensity; that's all. With **mature awareness**, we can manage the transitions gracefully. Thus, those who are **well-educated in the truths of life** can travel through all phases **without losing the sweetness.**

Womb to Tomb five sacred stations mark life's journey:

1. **The womb**
2. **The classroom**
3. **The bedroom**
4. **The retirement stage**
5. **The tomb**

Of the five stages of life, the middle three are ours **to live fully.** The fifth is carried out by others - **beyond our control,** yet a reflection of **how we lived.** The **womb** and the **tomb are not in our hands.**

But what lies between them reveals our true character.

- **The learning chamber**
- **The marital chamber**
- **The concluding chamber**

Of these, **the marital phase is the center of life**. Learning prepares us for it. Later, in retirement, one guides the next generation. But the essence of living - with love, challenge, and duty - lies in the **marital journey**, the central path. According to **divine justice**, the essential qualities for both husband and wife are:

- Tolerance
- Sacrifice
- Mutual understanding

Now you may ask: 'You've praised the wife so much; Isn't the husband's role equally worthy of honor?'

Absolutely.

Just as Kambar beautifully described Sita's virtues in many verses, at one point, he anticipates a doubt:

"Is Rama truly worthy of such a matchless Sita?"

And so, in one profound verse, he praises Rama:

His radiant form outshone the brilliance of the blazing sun,

He went with the slender-waisted wife, and young brother,

Was it eyeliner, emerald, raincloud, or the roaring ocean!

Alas, what a form is this - he is a beauty that never fades!

Likewise, for a husband who is:

- Responsible,
- Virtuous,
- Thoughtful,

- Honest, and
- A sincere hard worker; **there can be no equal.**

That's why Vedathiri Maharishi introduced a meaningful ritual: To exchange not just flowers and fruits, but to renew **awareness of mutual duty.**

The **husband gives a flower**, comparing his wife to a blossom, and says: ***"As I care for this flower, I will protect and cherish you."***

The **wife gives a fruit**, saying: ***"With this fruit, I offer sweetness and compassion to your life."***

She guards herself, and cares for him with strength;

She speaks with grace and never wearies. *(Kural 56)*

With gentle, harmonious, purposeful, and dignified words, with tireless effort and unwavering energy, I vow to serve my family with grace and responsibility.

This vow, taken in the spirit of **Wife's Appreciation Day**, must be **renewed each year**, a time to reaffirm gratitude, and to cherish the beautiful life gifted by God, living it fully, alongside one's life partner, and guided by the blessings of the Guru.

Maharishi, who firmly rejected the notion that women are unfit for spiritual attainment and instead empowered women with Brahma Jnana and established the **Women's International Spiritual Education Trust (WISE Trust)**, connecting it with the **World Community Service Centre.**

So, let us realize: To honor women, the embodiment of love and compassion; and to lead a life of daily spiritual practice, is the path to realize the Divine and uplift humanity.

I've realized the greatness of womanhood

All the people living in this vast world

Are the gift of womanhood, so what else

Greater glory could there be to praise?

A mother's heart never lets her children

Be raised by others nor let her spirit yield

Such sacrifice is essential for freedom

And for peace in the vast world. - *Vedathiri Maharishi*

Summary:

This chapter highlights that love, compassion, and justice are natural laws, while gender inequality is a man-made distortion. Peace in society can return only when humanity recognizes and honors the sacred role of women in every sphere of life.

Though women enrich the world as daughters, sisters, wives, mothers, and grandmothers, their contribution is often overlooked. Poets like Kannadasan and Bharathiyar lament this blindness. Vedathiri Maharishi affirms that women are not superior, inferior, or even equal to men - they are unique, with a divinity of their own.

From maidenhood to marriage, motherhood, and spiritual maturity, a woman's life is filled with silent sacrifices. Her strength is biological, emotional, moral, and spiritual. Freedom is not something to be 'given' to her; nature has already granted it - society must stop restricting it.

Kannika Danam is celebrated as the highest charity, and marriage is portrayed as a divine partnership in which the wife guides the family toward fulfillment.

Even the first night of union (Shanthi Muhurtham) is described as a sacred, cosmic alignment where life begins in harmony.

Vedathiri Maharishi notes that women are natural renunciates who give up comfort and personal identity to build families and nurture generations.

When spiritually awakened, a woman uplifts her husband and the entire household. As society drifted into materialism, women's dignity declined; true reform requires education, spiritual awareness, and rediscovering feminine divinity.

The chapter also introduces Wife's Appreciation Day (August 30), created by Maharishi to honor the selfless service of wives. Women are depicted as the spiritual foundation of homes, sustaining not just families but the world itself.

Drawing from scriptures, history, biology, and modern life, the chapter calls for a global awakening to the greatness of women - not as mere sentiment, but as a moral and spiritual necessity for humanity's peace and progress.

Plan Eight

Live by the Law of Divine Justice

Divine (God):

Is God the visible form revered in temples, or the formless divine realized through the experience of enlightened sages and siddhas? Which is the truth?

Divine Justice:

This refers to the consequences that arise from our actions; the natural law of cause and effect, often referred to as *dharma* or *fate*.

Path of Divine:

It refers to the way, the journey, the method, the rule, and reason. The symbolic meaning of Lord Shiva riding a bull (Rishabha Vahana) is that God, seated on the bull of Divine Justice, comes to grant results to each according to their karma.

Living:

Living means to act - to experience pleasure, pain, peace, and bliss. True living involves:

- Eliminating past suffering,
- Preventing future sufferings,
- Enjoying legitimate pleasures,
- Merging into inner peace,
- And rejoicing in supreme bliss.

To examine, understand, and act in harmony with these four principles is ***living in accordance with divine justice***. This is the real form of worship.

Worship is a matter of belief; ***living by divine justice is action of that belief.*** *Mere belief in God is not enough; this is the lesson that experience teaches us.*

Based on that lesson, my message to my descendants is this: ***Living in accordance with dharma is the path to a joyful and contented life.***

There is no need to fear God.

Instead, one must fear Divine Justice *and* ***Karma***. Align with them - and rewards are certain. Oppose them - and punishment is inevitable.

No ritual, offering, astrological remedy, money, or position or social status can save anyone from this law; this is the truth revealed by history.

So first, let us reflect: ***What is God? What truly qualifies as divine?***

If it's divine - then it's divine.

If it's a statue - then it's just a statue.

If it exists - it exists.

If not - then it doesn't. *- Kannadasan*

"To both those who disregard divine justice and to those who honor it, It is the total consciousness that grants wisdom;

It is Shiva - the divine, impartial force - who moves among all equally." - Vallalar.

Even if some deny it, and others accept it, The divine resides within both the dying human and the killing virus (like Corona). He is the **Primordial Shiva**, the **Formless Divine.**

As Kannadasan rightly said:

Of the stones that were broken, one becomes God,

One becomes temple, and one a doorstep.

In God's creation, all are the same essence,

Based on where they are placed, their roles differ.

All beings or materials may come from the same source, but their value and role change according to how they are used or where they end up.

It's a reflection on destiny, context, and perception; one stone may be worshipped, another stepped on.

"Birth is common to all living beings, but their greatness

Differ according to the deeds they perform." *(Kural 972)*

Though birth is common to all, the distinction or honor one receives in life is determined by one's conduct, effort, and character; not by birth alone.

Even the atheist does not deny the formless divine. *The real conflict often lies in* ***idol worship****.* **Theism and atheism are not two extreme poles**; there is a **bridge of harmony** that connects both – and that is the **true purpose behind temple**

worship. *A realized sage, who has experienced both the* ***form and the formless****, constructed temples and gave form to the divine; not for himself, but so that ordinary people could* ***approach the Supreme through accessible means****.*

But over time, the **original purpose was forgotten**. **Rituals replaced realization,** and the procedures of worship themselves came to be seen as "God". This has fostered blind beliefs and foolishness.

The way out is thoughtful reflection and disciplined noble practice of inner travel. *Today, this transformation is possible in the* ***Temples of Consciousness*** *established by Vethathiri Maharishi.*

To accept this shift, we must provide a **scientific and Vedathirian explanation** for the devotional path many have followed so far and being followed now.

After all, ***in God's creation, everything is made of the same essence; only its function and form differ by context****. How?*

A simple question: Can water be found in air?

- The common man or a blind believer might say, **'No'**.
- But science reveals otherwise. When you place an ice cube in a bowl, ***water droplets condense*** on its surface, showing how ***invisible laws of nature*** manifest visibly under the right conditions.

Scientific explanation: Due to differences in air pressure, oxygen and hydrogen molecules bond and form water. Likewise, based on conditions and context, anything can transform.

This ***universal substratum - divine space****, or* ***pure ether*** *- is the* ***state of God****.*

Next question: If God protects all, how?

As poet Kannadasan said:

In a hungry stomach, food is God;

In a desert, water is God;

In pouring rain, a roof is God;

In scorching sun, shade is God.

Here, ***whatever protects us becomes God****. This concept, that* ***Nature itself is divine*** *is accepted even by science and atheism.*

Then, has anyone seen God in an idol?

While devotees may claim 'Yes', ***Siddhas, sages, and realized beings have never claimed so.*** *Today,* ***devotion has been hijacked by those less realized than the sages*** *- the so-called religious authorities and loud believers.*

So, what verdict can we give?

Kannadasan said it best...

One who wandered in search said, 'I could not find it'.

The sage who clearly realized said, 'It is not, it is not'.

He who said 'It is not' - 'It is not'; what exactly is not?

He said, 'I never denied, there is some power within'.

The verdict:

Through idol worship, if the ***mind becomes focused****, and if one receives* ***initiation from a true noble Guru****, and engages in* ***intense spiritual practice (tapas)****, then one can realize the* ***truth of their birth and existence****.*

How?

Does a husband know the exact moment his wife conceives? Does the wife herself know it instantly? No. Only around the 45th day a doctor confirms the pregnancy.

Did the fertilized egg grow without being a true embryo? Of course not. If it was indeed an embryo from the beginning, why wasn't it known earlier?

Deep reflection reveals that the **union of life** during **sexual intimacy** is initially **formless**. That formless spark gradually develops into **form**.

And when the human being, who emerged from this invisible origin, dies, what is left behind for the world?

Once again - formlessness.

If both our ***birth and death*** *are wrapped in the* ***formless****, how can God alone be said to have* ***taken form*** *and* ***been born to someone****?*

A child has one father. But for **all of us**, the **true father** is **God**. He is the **father to all** and **has no father Himself**.

Whether we call Him **Parama Shiva**, **Parama Pitha (Holy Father)**, or **Allah,** the truth remains the same across all traditions. But instead of understanding this truth, **half-baked minds** planted **imaginary ideas** in our brains. This wisdom has been buried deep beneath layers of **rituals and dogma**.

We must clear away those false beliefs and strive to understand what the **realized sages** have experienced.

From the ***Vedha Vyasa*** *to* ***Vedathiri Maharishi****, many great souls have left behind guiding* ***philosophical insights****.*

Yet the **devotional stories**, **half-truths**, and **superstitions** spread through popular media have only nurtured **confusion and spiritual slavery**; not true freedom.

If God is ***formless****, can* ***Divine Justice*** *be seen by the eyes? No, it too is* ***formless****. And the* ***path to reach God*** *is also formless.*

Then what exactly is life? Is it the **body**? The **life-force**? The **mind**? Or **intelligence**?

Except the body, none of these can be seen with the eyes, measured with tools, or calculated. Can we say they do not exist just because we can't see them?

If we admit they exist - despite being unseen - then the ***life, mind, and intellect*** *within us, all of which have no form, proves that the* ***source of all - the Divine - must also be formless.***

Searching for God in form is like searching the **darkness** with a lamp in hand.

If someone asks, "Do you have intelligence?" we cannot show it. Similarly, even if God exists, we ***cannot show Him*** *- He can only be* ***experienced****, just like we experience* ***life****. And even then, only by those with a* ***mature and refined mind****.*

Thirumoolar said:

O ignorant ones who look only with outer eyes,

Bliss lies in the vision of the inner eye.

Was the great sage **Thirumoolar** inferior to today's **religious dogmatists** or **temple priests**? Was Thirumoolar a liar? **Devotees, think! Please!**

"Shall we cast aside the noble Siddhas and enlightened sages who realized the Primordial Truth, only to follow **costume-wearing pretenders**? **Is that not a tragic misstep?"**

He placed an egg inside a hen, and a hen inside the egg,

He placed a calf within a banana tree.

The name of that poor one in this world is God.

To those who have renounced all attachments,

He alone stands as their only kin.

Follow that One - and He is God.

Ruling the entire kingdom within nothingness,

He remains beyond understanding.

But if you realized Him, then He is truly God. - *Kannadasan*

It is not enough to see; one must understand. The eyes see, but it is the mind and intellect that comprehend.

"If you do not walk the path you begin, but merely stand afar, you'll never understand it." - *Poet Vali*

From Vedavyasa to Vedathiri Maharishi, many great sages have declared through direct experience that the formless Divine alone pervades everything.

Yet, this truth has not pierced deeply into the hearts of people. Even heads of religious institutions have not taken efforts to bring this understanding to light.

So, for many, even the initial explanation of Vedathiri Maharishi's philosophy may seem difficult to grasp.

That is why devotees must patiently and repeatedly study his teachings. Only then can this divine secret be truly understood.

The Divine as Creation, Preservation, and Dissolution:

*Our ancient sages symbolized the **divine state** through names like: **Aadhi Shiva, Brahma, Vishnu, and Rudra Shiva.***

In essence, it is (Aadhi Shiva) the pure space that expresses itself in three functions:

1. ***Creation** as **Brahma Shiva***
2. ***Sustenance** as **Vishnu Shiva***
3. ***Dissolution** as **Rudra Shiva***

When they named **Vishnu**, they referred to:

- The rotating disc (chakra) - symbolizing the rotational force of space (Sakthi - energy)
- And the conch (Sangu) - representing the sound vibration that arises from magnetic transformation

These symbols emphasize that the divine energy (Shakti) operates through:

- The **spiral motion of evolved space**, and
- The **sound born from vibration**

All those moves will eventually become still and return to pure Space, Shiva.

From a scientific perspective, we understand that: Electrons emerge from subtle energy, transform into protons and neutrons to form matter, and ultimately, under certain conditions, return to energy or formless space.

Similarly, in spiritual truth: Aadhi Shiva becomes Shakti, and expresses Brahma, Vishnu, and Rudra, and finally returns to Adhi Shiva.

Thus, science and spiritual wisdom both point to the same truth - A unified knowledge that bridges matter, motion, and divinity.

Brahman - The Ever-Expanding Force. The Sanskrit root **'Brah'** from **Brahman** means 'to expand'.

Science affirms: **The universe is an ever-expanding force.**

All cosmic functions operate under 4 fundamental parameters:

1. **Time**
2. **Distance**
3. **Mass/Density**
4. **Velocity**

These four are the very foundation of **mathematics**. That's why **Brahma** is symbolically represented with **four faces** - signifying mastery over these four dimensions - the structural base of all movement in the universe.

Vedas are not **Books - They are God particles.** In the Bhagavad Gita, Chapter 3, Verse 15, it is said:

"The Vedas arise from the Supreme Soul (Paramatma); Therefore, the all-pervading Veda is eternally rooted in dynamic action (Yajna)."

This affirms that Vedas are **embedded in creation itself** - not man-made.

From Formless God to Creation: The primordial formless divine - Aadhi Shiva, evolved itself as Shakti (force), which began rotating as space. From this rotation arose the five elements (Pancha Bhootas).

These elements gave rise to millions of star systems, including our solar system, within which lies Earth. Thanks to Earth's unique combination of waves, life evolved - from microbes to humans, with millions of species in between.

Creation is a Transformation of Divine State:

All forms, forces, and life are transformations of the Divine State, Pure Black Space. If the divine state were truly void or nothing, then nothing could have ever arisen.

But since creation exists, we must conclude that something must have already existed. As the **Upanishads** declare: 'That which does not exist can never come into being. That which exists can never cease to be.' This is the eternal truth of both **science** and **spirituality**.

Vedathiri Maharishi declared that Adhi Shiva is not void and possesses six intrinsic qualities: Kinematic, Quivering, Highly transparent, Mighty, Dark, and Fluid matter.

Kinematic refers to motion that occurs on its own, without any external force. This concept reflects the nature of Shiva. Shiva, having arisen by Himself, is thus called Easwaran (the Self-evolving Lord).

The direction in which the Sun rises by itself is called East. Jesus Christ was crucified and died on Good Friday, and the day His body resurrected on its own is celebrated as Easter Sunday. So, *Easwar, East, Easter.*

Quivering refers to subtle vibrations; the micro-movements known as *vibrations* and *cycles*. Vedathiri Maharishi described the secret of vibration as: ***"Time's finest length is the blink of an eye. The span between two vibrations is not measurable."***

When circular motions occur in close succession, they manifest as **frequent cycles**, known in science as *frequency*, *wave motion*, and *vibrational cycles*.

Highly Transparent means something that is both *permeable and penetrative*; this is the nature of the pure space. It gives room for all movements to occur, and at the same time, it penetrates and fulfills everything.

Mighty - *Mightiest of all is Almighty.* The structure supports us; the Earth supports the structure. The Earth floats and moves in the magnetic field of the Sun. The solar system is held by the

Milky Way galaxy. The Milky Way is upheld by the vast Universe. And the entire Universe is sustained by the pure, powerful void; **Primordial Shiva (Aadhi Sivam).**

If the formless pure black space has no power,

What else in the cosmos can be considered strong?

Between two objects that are just barely touching,

What is the formless presence that feels connected to,

In broad day light stars do not appear in the sky,

To those without vision they remain invisible forever.

Because it is not reachable by the (human) intellect,

Where then could nature's secret possibly hide? - Maharishi

One cannot deny the existence of God or Nature merely because they fail to understand what 'God' or 'Nature' truly means.

Darkness is the all-powerful pure black space - invisible or ungraspable by ordinary means. In Sanskrit and Tamil, the name **Krishna** or **Krishnam** itself means *darkness* or the **new moon** is also a symbolic representation of the unseen divine.

Fluid Matter - in English, the words **'fluid'** and **'liquid'** both refer to substances that flow. However, there is a subtle difference between them:

- If you place **pure honey** on a blotting paper, it stays where it is; this is called a **liquid**.

- But if you place a **drop of oil** on the same paper, it spreads in all directions; though honey and oil both are liquid, the inherent nature of spreading within the oil is called **fluid**.

Therefore, the vital sexual energy within a human, which originates from the root energy center and spreads throughout the body, is rightly called the **Sexual Vital Fluid** - a dynamic, life-generating essence.

Science of the Divine Force:

Pure black space is the primordial, formless state; the source of all origin. When the divine force compresses itself inward (**self-compressive force**), it results in **subtle quivering** (minute vibrations).

These two - *self-compression and quivering* - combine, break apart, and generate **countless micro-particles**. These particles are referred to as *"God Particles"*, for they are the first manifestations of divinity in 'invisible form'.

Since **Shiva**, the divine principle itself functions as this vibrating and compressive force, and since **these particles** arise from Shiva's own transformation, they are rightly named *God Particles, Divine Particles.*

These God Particles are continually held together and permeated by the pressure of **pure space**.

This *surrounding pressure of the divine field* never changes. As the self-compressive force concentrates on scattered particles, this surrounding divine pressure acts upon them, causing them to **accumulate**; thus, giving rise to the foundation of matter.

Scientific Parallels and Symbolic Alignment:

1. ***"Particles cluster and rotate to form structures"*** – Atoms and subatomic particles exhibit angular momentum and structured orbitals.

2. ***"From subtle particles arise more complex structures"*** – Early universe cosmology affirms that fundamental particles (like quarks, electrons) formed soon after the Big Bang and later combined into atom.

3. ***"Cycle of creation and dissolution"*** – This mirrors spiritual symbolism (Shiva → Brahma → Vishnu → Shiva) and aligns with cosmological theories like expansion, entropy, and transformation.

4. ***"Magnetism arises from particles"*** – Particularly from the spinning motion of charged particles like electrons.

As particles are emitted from a spinning body, its rotational velocity naturally decreases. Thus, we see the cycle: From the Divine Source, particles form → They become Electrons, then Protons, then Neutrons, and eventually revert back to subtle particles. This cycle mirrors the spiritual truth: Shiva → Brahma → Vishnu → back to Shiva.

What ancient philosophy spoke in metaphors, modern science now confirms with evidence. *In ancient times, lacking scientific tools, seers explained nature's secrets by giving them symbolic* ***forms****.*

Origin of Life on Earth:

For life to originate on Earth, three essential **divine conditions** were required:

1. ***Divine proportion and harmony of the five elements (Pancha Bhutas)***
2. ***Radiation from the Solar system***
3. ***Powerful cosmic energy influences from 27-star clusters (Nakshatras)***

The union of these three energies intensified Earth's field energy, giving rise to the **Bio-Magnetic Field**.

When **mild heat** and **moisture** combined with this field of bio-magnetism, **micro-bacteria** (early forms of microorganisms) emerged.

That is why, in all life forms, for reproduction to occur, two essential conditions are always required:

- **Fluidity (liquid essence)**
- **Heat (warmth)**

The process of ***sexual union*** *evolved precisely to fulfill these two conditions.*

All that arises up to the level of the five senses is known as *"sensory perception"*. Beyond this lies a sixth sense, called the truth-sensing faculty or intuition, which reveals hidden or subtle realities.

Entities like the soul, mind, intellect, and divinity are all invisible or subtle phenomena, not grasped by the five senses.

To understand where we came from and what we are living, we explored cosmic evolution and biological evolution.

God did not create life by placing humans onto Earth, nor do children descend from the heavens*. Rather, in every living being, the* ***experiences gathered over many births*** *continue as the* ***soul (Atma)*** *which carries forward life after life, adding imprints.*

The ***Bhagavad Gita****, in the chapter on* ***"Akshara Brahma Yoga"****, affirms that the soul is* ***imperishable****. The* ***soul keeps imprinting itself*** *again and again through successive bodies - grandfather to father, father to child, and so on.*

No matter how many times it is replicated, the soul remains untouched; The **child is born with its own soul**, evolved on the union of man and woman. Even after childbirth, the **parents retain their own souls**.

Just like ***a lamp's flame*** *can light many others without losing itself, the* ***soul*** *too can manifest in children* ***without dividing or diminishing****. Thus, even after multiple offspring, the* ***original soul remains intact*** *in the parents.*

The **formless divine state** transforms into **forms**, moves through **activity**, and at a point, dissolves again into the **formless**. During the phase of activity, there operates a law; a **law of nature** marked by **pattern, precision, and regularity**.

This same ***natural law****, when expressed in human life, becomes* ***karma*** *and* ***divine justice****.*

Therefore, ***worship of God*** *does not mean interfering with divine order, but rather* ***living in alignment with Dharma****, in harmony with the divine path.*

That is the essence of **divine justice**.

"Without knowing God, one cannot truly worship. The one who knows God needs no worship." "Once the wisdom of self-realization is attained, the self lives in a state of purification".

For example, what we see as a bean seed is not the actual **seed**. When split, the bean reveals two halves, and **at the center** - in the tiny, ***hollowed spot - lies the true seed: the magnetic essence – characterized bio-magnetic domain*** where the ***entire life experience of the mother plant*** has been compressed, and stored.

When planted in soil and watered, with the support of **sunlight and air**, everything hidden inside that essence begins to unfold over time; turning the seed into a sprout, the sprout into a plant, and then into a tree.

*Just as **a tree resides within a seed**, and **the seed resides within the tree**, likewise, **divinity resides within man**, and **man resides within divinity**.*

Understanding this natural secret is true wisdom (Jnana).

Until childbirth, a human being is governed entirely by the control of **nature**. But **death** is determined by each person's:

- Food, labor, rest, sexual conduct, and thoughts.

Pain, illness, obstacles, and death - these are what compel man to reflect, eventually making him realize that God is the underlying cause behind all. Those who grasp these hidden truths are the ones whom people honor as great souls.

"Though one may master many profound scriptures,

His true self-knowledge precedes." *(Kural 373)*

According to *Siddha and Ayurvedic medicine,* even though it is said that *disease arises from the divine state,* and healing too comes from the same divine source; for that healing to take place, a ***material medium*** (a physical agent or catalyst) is required.

*A result can arise **only through an action**. If there is **no action**, the result cannot manifest, even if the cause exists.*

There are some siddha physicians with deep knowledge of hundreds of herbs, yet they sometimes cannot diagnose a patient's illness.

Despite consulting many brilliant doctors, some patients' conditions still remain undiagnosed.

This is because the ***doctor's knowledge*** can only bring healing when the ***patient's karmic maturity*** allows the time for resolution.

*Only then will the physician **accurately recognize the cause** and prescribe the **right medicine**. And only then will the disease **heal easily and quickly**.*

Regardless of how advanced or intellectually gifted one may be in any field, and no matter how much intellectual brilliance or mastery over intricate knowledge one possesses, ***the workings of fate cannot be fully explained***.

*In the end, **it is destiny that stands, overshadowing all human skill and talent**.*

"What power is greater than fate? Whatever else

May intervene, fate will still prevail." *(Kural 380)*

There is ***no force stronger than fate, i.e. divine justice****. The hand of fate keeps writing; and once it has written, not even tears or prayers can erase a single letter.*

For example, a person may have excellent driving skills, but still, an ***unseen force decides the outcome****. Even when it seems like a crash is inevitable, sometimes* ***an invisible divine intervention*** *occurs and prevents the accident.*

Conversely, there are times when, on an almost empty road, a motorcycle may hit a small stone, skid and fall, and the rider ends up bedridden for eight months.

So why does God allow accidents to happen when there's no visible danger, yet prevent others when the situation seems much worse?

This is because ***if the person has no karmic debt requiring suffering at that time****, the* ***divine intelligence*** *intervenes and protects him.*

It is said: ***'Dharma will protect those who uphold it.'*** *But if the* ***time for a karmic effect has arrived****, even if the situation does not seem serious, a* ***tiny event*** *(like a small stone) can trigger a* ***major consequence****.*

Some may argue, "How can such **a small mistake cause so much suffering**? Isn't that unfair?" But let us consider this:

When using a ***balance scale****, even a* ***small amount*** *added at the end can tip the pointer into the perfect balance. This shows that a small weight has completed the whole. Similarly, even* ***a minor mistake*** *can activate the* ***deep karmic imprint*** *already stored. That is how a* ***small error*** *can result in* ***great suffering****.*

Seeing great suffering arise from a small mistake,

Some may claim that the law of karma seems unjust.

In a balance scale, when weights are placed on one side,

And an object is added to the other side for weighing,

Even a small amount, added to that, at the end,

Combine with all that came before to tip the scale

This reveals a profound truth: A long record of evil karma

May manifest through even a minor fault committed now.

- Vedathiri Maharishi

Whether or not the wealth we accumulate protects our descendants, the store of good karmic deeds we accumulate will certainly protect our children.

The words of great sages are words of divine truth. If we believe in them, we may progress; if we ignore them, we may suffer loss. But the loss is never for the sage.

Those who rise into life through unjust means will eventually be required to pay the price for it. *A person who sees only one side will view someone else's wealth, fame, or influence as accomplishments.*

But only when we also see the other side of their life can we understand that **God's judgment is truly accurate**.

The conscience within us - the inner moral compass - records all our actions. If our deeds align with dharma (righteousness), we will experience joy as the natural result. If our actions violate dharma, we will face life's difficulties and diseases as consequences.

What does a human being desire - suffering or joy? Success or failure? Every person naturally seeks happiness and goodness. Therefore, our actions must be worthy of that goal. ***This is the undeniable truth and divine verdict.***

A human must live a sincere and righteous life. One must live with reverence and fear of the Divine. If not, there is no escape from suffering.

Divine justice never forgets and never forgives. When suffering finally strikes and we cry, "Oh no! It has come to us," who can help us then?

What use is it to pray to God after having knowingly committed mistakes, when consequences are already manifesting as part of divine law?

Heaven, hell, sin, and virtue are nothing, but imaginative stories told by those who used human ignorance to either entice or threaten.

In truth, ***our own soul is our court of justice****. Heaven and hell are not elsewhere, they are* ***here, within us****.*

It is ***our own karma*** *that brings consequences to our actions. God does not sit elsewhere and dispense pleasure or pain to us. It is the* ***natural justice of our own deeds*** *that governs our fate.*

Heaven and hell are within us.

Let your heart listen to what I say.

May truth and righteousness prevail,

May this echo as the voice of motherhood. – *Kannadasan*

Sin, virtue, heaven, and hell - these are all natural laws embedded within human beings. No matter in which generation or at what point of time an action was performed, the appropriate consequence is determined and delivered at the right time by the soul, which serves as the ***divine court of justice within us.***

How does nature decide when, where, and in which of the seven generations a karmic record will surface? Without understanding this subtle mechanism, no explanation of karma and its effects is complete.

The great sage Thiruvalluvar was the first to express this profound idea by grasping the law of nature.

The five principles - ***object, instrument, time, action, and place*** *- determine the appropriate result for every deed.*

Therefore, we must act, speak, and think with careful awareness so as not to invite suffering.

The framework laid out by Valluvar is further elaborated by Vedathiri Maharishi, who clarifies that every deed aligns with five corresponding truths: **intention, skill, time, place, and action**.

According to these, the ***divine justice*** *functions through* ***magnetic transmission*** *within the soul.* The words *"nature's law"* refers to harmonious and orderly functioning - that is, ***divine justice operates through our own soul.***

The pleasures, sorrows, peace, and even the supreme bliss experienced by beings on earth arise from karma. According to these five principles, every karmic record exerts a specific **intensity** (force).

Furthermore, every action carries a **wave-like density**, which finds a matching **resonant point** within the magnetic field of the soul. When appropriate time comes, it surfaces naturally.

From all this, we can understand a great truth: ***Our soul is not just a witness, but the very engine of divine justice; recording, storing, and revealing each karmic imprint in perfect harmony with time and nature.***

The Divine, becoming energy, united with the laws of nature and unfolded into the universe. The Divine itself is what is referred to as the Supreme Soul in the cosmos.

The mechanism that ensures appropriate consequences for human actions is the **law of karma (Law of Nature)**, governed by the discerning intelligence of the Paramatma.

The natural law of the Divine has become the **law of cause and effect** in the universe.

The medium through which these laws operate is the magnetic field. The attractive force of magnetism draws and stores the experiences of pleasure and pain resulting from one's actions.

Its repulsive force, at the right time, releases these stored karmic impressions and compels the individual to act accordingly; thus, giving rise to the corresponding joys or sorrows. This magnetic center within each being is what we call the **soul (Atma).** At birth, through one's parents, one inherits accumulated karma from past lives, called **Sanchita Karma**.

After birth, starting from the age of three, the actions one performs begin to generate **Prarabdha Karma**, which is the karma set to bear fruit in this life.

Together, these two layers of karma give rise to a third: **Agami Karma**, the new karma being formed through present thoughts and actions.

When a negative thought arises that could lead to suffering, it must be consciously avoided. For this, **awareness and self-restraint are essential**. This discipline is what we call spiritual austerity, and hence, **meditation should become part of our daily life.**

Driven by desire, man strays into error and adharma (unrighteousness). The mind, the source of desire, cannot be controlled unless it is properly trained.

If the mind is not disciplined, it generates countless desires related to possessions and people. Achievable desires lead to ambition; unachievable ones lead to greed.

When one is overwhelmed by such intense craving, dharma is easily forgotten. As man matures, he often compromises integrity for the sake of desires, and adharma inevitably results in suffering.

Once we understand this, even a karmic force standing before us in the form of temptation (past karma) or about to arise in the form of destructive desires (future karma) will dissolve and lose its grip. By simply engaging in **righteous actions**, we can live a life of joy and peace.

Consequences never change; it is the inner drive (karma) that can be transformed. *Swami Vivekananda said: "Even God does not have the power to stop the good or bad results you are destined to receive."*

If we fail to understand this subtle truth, we can never truly grasp the God we worship, the laws it ordains, or the nature of destiny. Nor can we escape from meaningless rituals and rigid customs.

The images (idols) we worship are merely **mediums** to help us realize the **omnipresent Divine**, the vast Cosmic Space. But forgetting this essence, we shrink divinity into a visible form and continue worshipping blindly like children; never maturing in spiritual understanding.

Realizing the soul within oneself is Atma Darshan. Realizing the all-pervading Supreme Soul is Paramatma Darshan. Realizing the boundless, unconditioned Truth behind all, the Pure Space is Divine Darshan. *To experience these three levels, what is essential is the* ***Darshan of a true Guru.***

Living in accordance with divine justice is Karma Yoga. Karma refers to actions driven by the mind. Its results may bring either joy or suffering. But Karma Yoga is acting in union with the Divine Will.

When Divine Consciousness becomes our guiding wisdom, then our actions will be marked by discipline, dharma, and virtue. Hence, the result will be **only joy**.

In every action, whether for oneself or others, in the present or future, for the body or mind, if our thoughts, speech, and deeds are aligned to produce **only good**, then that is true **Karma Yoga**.

The great poet **Mahakavi Bharathiyar** places a heartfelt plea before the Divine Mother, *Parashakti*: "Oh, Mother Parashakti! You created all living beings; you created humankind. You blessed man with not only a noble body but a great and discerning mind; a sixth sense."

"What immense merit earned us this rare gift, Mother? You draw my intellect ever upwards, urging me to rise and merge with the Divine in supreme bliss."

"But my body, my tongue, my eyes, nose, and ears - my five senses, drag me downward into desires that are never satisfied."

"Trapped between this tug of war, like Trishanku suspended in mid-heaven, you have left me, Mother! Then why, oh why, did you give me this extraordinary gift called *intelligence*, if not to rise?"

Bharathiyar asks: "If a master craftsman in Thanjavur, having made a fine veena (musical instrument), casts it away in the dirt instead of playing it; what is the point of that craftsmanship?

In the same way, Mother, you have crafted me with the sixth sense of reason yet left me to live like a creature ruled by the five senses. ***So, what do I ask of you?*** Deliver me from the clutches of sensory temptations and let my full intellect be offered in service to this world, this nation!

O **Shiva Shakti**, will you let me waste away as a burden to the Earth without protecting me?" He laments:

Having crafted a fine Veena

Would anyone throw it in the dust, to rot?

Tell me, O Shiva Shakti! – you who

Have created me with radiant intellect!

Will you not grant me the strength

To live this life usefully and well?

Tell me, O Shiva Shakti!

Will you allow me to live

As a mere burden upon the earth?

With these words in mind, we are reminded: ***To live each day as Karma Yogi; living in accordance with Divine Justice.***

*Live with **awareness, integrity, and compassion**, guided by **Divine Grace and Guru's Blessings**, So that we may live fully and attain **liberation of the soul.***

Summary:

This chapter explores the essence of God not as a statue or image, but as the formless, all-pervading intelligence behind creation.

True divinity is not bound by rituals or religion but is experienced as divine justice; the law of cause and effect governing all actions.

Divine Justice is the unfailing moral law that ensures every action yields a corresponding consequence.

No offering, prayer, or ritual can erase karma. To live righteously, one must align with this invisible but exact law.

God is formless, like space - subtle, mighty, quivering, dark, and fluid. All creation evolves from this formless source (Aadhi Shiva) and returns to it.

This cosmic cycle - creation, preservation, and dissolution - is symbolized by Brahma, Vishnu, and Rudra.

Science and spirituality both affirm this unity of existence. The formless divine operates through the soul, which serves as the medium for storing and releasing karmic imprints.

The soul, governed by magnetic fields, records every thought, word, and deed, and dispenses appropriate joy or sorrow based on five key factors: intention, skill, time, place, and action.

Living by divine law means:

- Understanding karma,
- Accepting responsibility,
- Practicing self-restraint,
- Acting in harmony with dharma,
- And realizing the Divine within and around.

Idol worship, when used rightly, helps focus the mind. But clinging to rituals without inner transformation leads to spiritual stagnation. Temples were originally built by realized sages to guide people towards the formless Truth; not to trap them in form.

Vedathiri Maharishi and other sages affirm that divinity is the essence of space itself - pure consciousness that manifests matter, life, and intelligence.

Through deep reflection and meditation, one can realize this truth and live a meaningful life as a Karma Yogi; one whose actions are aligned with divine will.

The final message is clear: Heaven and hell are not otherworldly - they are states of mind shaped by our actions. The soul itself is our court of justice.

To live with awareness, integrity, and spiritual understanding is to live in the light of divine justice. This is the path to peace, fulfillment, and ultimate liberation.

Plan Nine

Avoiding the (Temple) Car-Festival

Where is the chariot, where the idol, where the festival?

When people have forgotten God Himself?

Where is the chariot, where the idol, where the festival?

When all humans begin to live like gods themselves?

– *Kannadasan*

Family celebrations like weddings, birthdays, puberty ceremonies, and baby showers are occasions of joy and union among relatives and friends.

A Divine Festival is a community celebration centered on temple worship. The Car-Festival is especially intended for devotees who are unable to visit the sanctum. During this event the main deity - represented in the form of a processional idol - is placed on a grand chariot and taken through the streets.

This allows people to receive the divine's grace and be reminded to live a righteous life based on dharma, the divine justice.

From the Vedas to Vedathiriam, all enlightened sages have declared that true spirituality is the union of two principles: divine consciousness and righteous conduct.

This alone helps eliminate physical, mental, and material suffering, allowing us to live in health, peace, and abundance. Nature's inherent energies can be harnessed only through the path of devotion and ethics. Most people believe in the existence of God.

Some ridicule this belief, calling those who invented God, fools. Others sit on the fence, unsure of whether God exists or not. Many participate in rituals and festivals without knowing their purpose or benefits.

As a result, confusion persists. There is no one in the world who can decisively declare what exactly *God* is. The divine truth is something that cannot be expressed in human language.

Even if described, it remains incomprehensible; a transcendental principle beyond action, sitting silently like a stone. Realizing this subtle truth is the core of *true realization.*

Just as we cannot trace the root of emotions that generate our feelings, so too the source of God cannot be comprehended through the senses.

Only through refined inner perception can we grasp it. Until that happens, confusion will persist.

Even those who claim *"Spirituality is life"* may not have truly attained divine awareness. If we observe their behavior and beliefs, we see that they are far from realization.

People worship saffron robes and spiritual costumes, mistaking appearances for inner truth. Many who pretend to be spiritual leaders are not divinely realized.

People end up offering their time, money, and even their dignity or chastity to false gurus, leading to suffering.

Wearing the mask of goodness with outward disguise,

Among such pretenders, God does not reside – (but)

One who lives with grace and follows true virtue,

Among such noble people God dwells.

In the realm of truth, in the noble path of harmony,

In the power of love, in the devotion of affection,

In the righteous path that reveals true equality

There alone the Divine abides. - *Poet Aathmanathan*

Not all who go to temples are theistic or devotional. 99% of devotees seek God for physical or material needs, bargaining like beggars.

Rare indeed is the true seeker who wants to realize the divine. People say, "If we worship God and save some money, our children will be fine."

Is it money or God that protects your child? What kind of faith is this?

A child may have one father,

For all of us, the Father is God.

Did you come, believing a man? - or

Did you come with faith in the Divine? *– Kannadasan*

We must think realistically and ask ourselves: what is true devotion? What does genuine faith in God mean? What benefit do we get by living accordingly?

Those who have understood these questions clearly and reformed themselves live as evidence - they are the *sages and saints* (*Siddhas* and *Jnanis*).

Some devotees injure their own bodies with knives and offer their blood to God, calling it devotion and claiming it doesn't hurt them.

But if we truly understand this, we will ask: does God need blood donations? And we'll realize clearly: ***No, He doesn't. What God seeks is love and compassion***, for that is His true nature.

Another belief says that during a temple festival with fire-walking, anyone who fails to observe strict austerities for 48 days will be burned by the fire. But if a person can walk barefoot on the scorching summer ground, why not choose that instead?

Why create fire and walk through it, to prove devotion? We must recognize this as ignorance. If God is pleased by torturing the body, how is He different from a villain?

In earlier times, such rituals may have helped people develop good habits; fasting for 48 days might help one restrain desires and avoid harming others.

But when we forget the symbolic meaning and continue performing them as rigid rituals, **truth is lost**. What we need is divine grace that shines through true love.

Through thousands of years of human history, none of these rituals have truly led to universal realization. If we understand the true purpose behind religion, rituals, and temple worship, we can use them wisely, and discard what is unnecessary.

Uncritical adherence to rituals causes poverty, due to wasted human labor and material resources. Through reflection, we must find proper explanations and release ourselves from suffering.

Long ago, a man rubbed two stones and saw sparks. Instead of teaching the action behind it, he used the fire to pretend he had magical powers, tricking people into bowing before him and offering him gifts. Thus began the art of earning without effort.

Normally, when we give someone something valuable, they fall at our feet in gratitude. But in religion, we are expected to fall at the feet of religious figures after giving them something!

The first man to discover fire turned it into a myth of superiority and posted as a *deceptive guru.* This cleverness later transformed into political strategy, business tactics, and false religious systems.

* *"Give me everything, I'll protect you from enemies"* – that's politics.

* *"If you give to me, God will bless you; I'll pray for you"* – that's religious manipulation.

* *"You give me one, I'll give you two"* – that's business logic.

All of these are different masks of human exploitation.

God does not have a human form. Hence, He cannot be shown directly. But by holding onto this *invisible truth*, many have launched thriving businesses.

Since people neither reflect on history nor experience God personally, it becomes a case of blind leading the blind. Many carry religion in their hands under the name of *spirituality*. This ignorance has become a profitable opportunity for some.

It gives them influence, power, status. Seeing this, others created new gods and minor deities, and religions multiplied like political parties.

Evolution of Religion:

The Tamil word *Samayam* comes from "Sama + Iyam", where *Iyam* means "explain." Religion is essentially an explanation that human beings are equal to their origin (God). **Philosophy**, in contrast, explains *why* we fail to realize that truth.

When did temples come into existence? Why? And who built them? Temples were born out of faith in a higher power. In ancient times, people worshipped shapeless stones, calling them *"Shiva lingam"*.

As rationality evolved, people began to question how a god without eyes or ears could see or hear. To address these questions, divine images were created with human-like features.

Two key philosophical ideas are embedded in idols.

- *Narasimha* depicts a human body with a lion's head.
- *Matsya avatar* features a fish body with a human head.

Every idol incorporates human elements, because only humans have the capacity to seek and realize the divine. No other creature on Earth searches for God.

To aid this journey, three tools evolved:

- **Yantra**: Sacred diagrams or symbols - believed to influence material life, prosperity, and sensory pleasure through thought concentration.
- **Mantra**: Sacred sounds - based on vibrational science and phonetics. Ancient scholars calculated the effects of syllables and their combinations.
- **Tantra**: Application of willpower - selecting a desire, converting it into mental intent (*Sankalp*), and using focused repetition to refine the mind and attain goals.

Worship practices were built around these three concepts. To inspire faith, myths and stories were composed to associate specific deities with specific outcomes.

Kings and rulers who had deep devotion funded temples, designed with the help of spiritual psychologists of the time.

Merchants, for profit, built markets around temples. Temples became forts; walls were reinforced, multi-tier towers (gopurams) were erected to detect enemies from afar.

Sculptures appealed to human aesthetics and kept devotees mentally immersed in divine contemplation. (Mandapams) Halls were created around sanctums for this purpose.

Through temple worship, the human mind gains some refinement and begins seeking inner truths. But **true realization** happens only when knowledge merges into the soul; this is *Aalayam* (temple), a training hall for the merging of consciousness. Until mind matures, symbolic worship remains necessary.

In every religion, there is a noble concept of God.

There are many ways of worship, each with reverence.

These serve to refine our senses and sharpen our intellect,

And help us gain some benefit suited to good living.

The speed of intellect refined through such practice

Rises higher to realize and unite with the Divine.

To use that intellect to attain peace and harmony

Come, turn inward and practice the true light of tapas!

– Vedathiri Maharishi

Every ritual is built upon the power of thought. By understanding its inner meaning, we must train the mind to grow strong.

Once one is established in self-discipline and inner realization, idol worship becomes optional. But for those unaware of this path, **at least idol worship provides a fear-based morality.**

For example, a person may wear a sacred thread or rosary and begin 48 days of penance. Even if they avoid wrongdoing for just 48 days out of 365, doesn't that still carry *some merit*?

However, only those truly capable of following such austerity should undertake it. Otherwise, wearing the thread in the morning and visiting the temple in the evening serves nothing.

Let us explore the scientific and symbolic wisdom behind temple worship.

According to the Agama scriptures, every temple built using sacred geometry has its own *Sthala Puranam* - a spiritual legend that inspires faith.

These stories are designed to instill belief in devotees that by worshipping a particular deity, specific benefits in life may be attained.

Additionally, sacred trees (*Sthala Vriksha*) such as neem, vilva, or peepal are associated with each temple.

The belief strengthens the devotee's thought energy, which in turn helps manifest the intended benefits. However, as faith varies, so do the outcomes.

The core **purpose of temple worship** is this: Its purpose is to guide humans from form to formless, from the known to the unknown.

This journey begins with image worship and gradually matures into the realization of the unmanifest. The ideal time for such spiritual practice is *Brahma Muhurta,* between 3 AM and sunrise.

Bathing at this hour and circumambulating the temple (*108 rounds*), while mentally focusing on the divine, aligns the body and mind for inner harmony.

Why this time? Scientifically, during the early pre-dawn hours, the part of Earth we live on begins facing the Sun. At this angle, the sunrays interact with Earth's moist atmosphere to produce **ozone**, - a life-nourishing gas. When a devotee walks briskly around the temple at this hour, the lungs expand and contract rhythmically, absorbing more of this vital ozone.

This process:

- Enhances **physical health** and **immunity**
- Cultivates **mental calmness**
- Aligns the mind with **divine justice**
- Strengthens **life-force**, aiding in healthy progeny

The sacred trees around the temple - neem, vilva, peepal - emit beneficial waves. These combine with ozone to purify both **body and mind**.

However, as sunlight becomes direct after 8 AM, the ozone disperses upward due to heat. So, worship performed later in the morning may lack these bio-energetic benefits.

Rituals are meant to carry truths that aid human evolution. But over time, **meaning is lost, and only the ritual remains**. When this happens, it becomes blind belief.

For example, the *Mariyamman* festival is celebrated with fervor, but what tangible benefit has society gained from it?

Behind such rituals, however, lies profound wisdom. The name *Mariyamman* comes from *Maari + Amman, meaning* "Mother who transforms".

Life is born through the mother. When we suffer from physical illness, mental distress, or karmic entanglements, our inner cry is:

"What wrong have I done? I was born without under-standing, and I don't know how to live. O Mother! If you stand near and explain it to me, won't I understand?" - (Kannadasan)

Mariyamman represents this compassionate force that frees us from confusion.

This body is but a swollen corpse, like a pot filled with salt.

There is no medicine for me to be born again, transformed.

If such a medicine for rebirth anew were found, would I not

Cast off this puffed-up corpse and unite with Your feet,

O my Kannamma! *Saint Azhagu Ani Siddhar*

"Unless you turn and become like little child, you will never enter the kingdom of heaven." - *Matthew 18:3*

This verse emphasizes **innocence, humility, and purity of heart** as essential qualities to attain the divine realm. The face of a child, who drinks milk and lies in peaceful bliss, that is the only *divine face* we can truly witness with our eyes.

But as life progresses, experience accumulates, and mind clings to illusion, the child's divinity fades, just like Rama moved away from Sita, who had fallen into illusion of the golden deer.

Mariyamman and the Kundalini:

– A Symbolic Path to Self-Realization:

The child and God are alike in nature

They forgive and forget with innocence.

But after maturity, confusion clouds the heart,

And the divine that once lived slowly fades. - *Kannadasan*

The **loss of this inner divinity** is what spiritual awakening seeks to reverse. It is the essence of being *born again,* not in body, but in consciousness.

Having become enslaved to the mind and lost in time, man is shown the path to redemption by the great sages. That is why, in Christian symbolism, **Mary (Mari)** is called the Mother, and **Jesus** the Redeemer.

In Indian yogic wisdom, this return to divinity is achieved through the **awakening of Kundalini**; the primal life energy that resides at the base chakra and rises to the crown chakra. This science is known as *Brahma Vidya.*

In the **Mariyamman temple rituals**, the act of *placing lotus in a water-filled pit (poo saattuthal)* represents the identification of the kundalini energy.

The next ritual, *"Kambam Saattuthal"*, placing fire atop a trident-shaped structure with three prongs, symbolizes the awakening of the Kundalini fire through the *third eye center*, situated between the eyebrows, known as the *Agna Chakra.*

At the feet of Mariyamman are **three demon heads**. These symbolize the **three major inner obstacles** one must overcome to reach the divine:

- **Ego (Ahamkara)**
- **Karma (Imprints)**
- **Illusion (Maya)**

To confront these enemies, the mind needs two key abilities:

1. **Wisdom** – to clearly understand these forces.
2. **Technique** – to overcome them, which includes learning philosophical insights and practicing meditation under the guidance of a qualified *Guru*.

Through philosophical understanding, **illusion is dispelled**. Through ethical and selfless actions aligned with divine justice, **karma is dissolved**.

But to destroy **ego** - the strongest of the three - requires deep spiritual maturity. This is symbolically expressed in the form of **Dandu Mari Amman** (Dandu – staff / spinal path).

In this context, *"Dandu"* refers to the path between two points - the *base of the spine* and the *crown (Sahasrara)*. The divine mother who travels this inner path and resides in *Sahasrara* is **Dandu Mari Amman**.

She represents the inner transformation of the ego-bound mind into the liberated soul. The **demon crushed beneath her feet** represents the ego that is subdued for union with the Absolute.

When the awakened Kundalini crosses each energy center - *Swadhistana, Manipura, Anahata, Vishuddhi*, and reaches *Agna Chakra*, the mind attains subtle purity.

Beyond this, in the **Third Eye**, self-awareness arises. And beyond even that lies the experience of **pure life-force**, felt at the **Sahasrara**, the crown.

A mind that reaches this peak, free from ego, merges with the source and becomes **Karumari Amman**. Unlike Dandu Mari, *Karumari* is often depicted as having only a **head** - no body. Why?

The body is the field of **emotion, desire, and suffering**; the flesh-tied existence of worldly bonds. When one transcends all this, the divine no longer needs a body.

Karumari symbolizes this transcendence - a state where the individual ego is dissolved and one lives in **Jeeva Samadhi**, the deathless bliss state achieved by realized Siddhas.

In this eternal union, **Adhi Shiva**, the Supreme Being, becomes the space in which all forms live, grow, and dissolve.

The intelligence that governs, preserves, and transforms this order at the right time is what we call ***Koniyamman*** from:

- *Ko* – king, ruler, wisdom, supreme governance
- *Ni* – you, stillness, subtle essence
- *Amman* – the divine feminine, the energy

Thus, Mariyamman is not merely a village goddess or ritual deity; she is ***Shakti*** herself. She represents the entire journey of the soul: From base ignorance → through inner struggle → to spiritual union → and finally, supreme liberation.

FROM DEVOTION TO LIBERATION:

Even after attaining spiritual heights, a single lapse in awareness can awaken ego and plunge one back into unrighteousness. This warning is symbolized by ***Vidhya Garva Asura***, the demon of intellectual arrogance, trampled beneath the feet of ***Koniyamman***.

Thus, the symbolic representations of ***Mariyamman, Dandu Mari Amman, Karumari Amman, and Koniyamman*** reflect different **states of human mental evolution and spiritual refinement**.

Temples (*Aalayam*) serve as sacred spaces for inner transformation, where the individual soul matures and merges with the universal soul. The very word "Aalayam" means "place where ego dissolves into supreme realization."

The goddesses ***Kamatchi, Meenatchi, and Visalatchi*** embody the guidance that devotion *(Bhakti)* must be supplemented by meditation and realization *(Jnana)*.

The awakening of Kundalini requires not just faith but a Guru's divine *initiation (Deeksha)* into inner stillness and self-mastery.

The *Ajna Chakra* (the command center) governs ***Kama***, or desire. This inner command over desire is the essence of the ***Kamatchi Devi*** principle.

Only with the Guru's *Agna Deeksha,* where the Kundalini is raised from *Mooladhar* and made to rest at the *Ajna* center between the eyebrows, can desires (Kama) be mastered.

In *Mariyamman temple rituals*, devotion points toward the rising of Kundalini from Mooladhar to the brow center, but only through Deeksha from a divine Guru can this be fully realized. Thus, ***Bhakti* represents the path**, and ***Jnana* is the gateway**.

During this journey, the brain's wave frequency shifts from **Beta (active desires)** to **Alpha (peaceful receptivity)**. This mental shift naturally weakens sensory cravings and immoral urges; *Kama* is conquered. This is the metaphysical power of **Kamatchi**, the goddess of desire-mastery.

Even if one conquers ***Maya*** and ***Karma***, the final demon, ***Ahamkara* (ego),** remains strongest. This can only be subdued by the Guru's direct energetic gaze, the ***Nayana Deeksha*** (initiation through sight), symbolized by ***Meenatchi*** (Fish shape Eyed Mother), just as a fish infuses life into its eggs by gaze alone.

In this tradition:

- ***Dandu Mari Amman*** symbolizes the spinal path — from base (Mooladhar) to crown (Sahasrara).
- The **Guru raises** the disciple's energy upward, as the fish raises life through vision.
- This upward movement, governed by *spinal channel*, is realigned through Guru's grace and inner instruction.

Once the mind stabilizes in the **eighth frequency**, **ego ceases to function**, bodily desires fade, and even the senses and intellect rest. This state is ***Karumari Amman*** - the head-only goddess, representing transcendence of physical form and union with life-force.

As the mind dissolves in this *state of stillness*, the soul merges with **cosmic intelligence**. Here, the delusion of viewing the body as everything vanishes.

The mind, once intoxicated by ego, now sees itself as a *speck in the cosmos*, amidst billions of humans, planets, stars, and galaxies.

This expansive awareness is ***Bhakti's vision in Koniyamman***, and the method to reach this realization is through

Thuriyatheetha Tapas, or ***Visalatchi Jnana Deeksha***, granted by Guru through subtle divine thought.

Just as fallen leaves become fertilizer for new seeds, Bhakti decomposes to feed the seed of Jnana. And the rare pearl that blossoms in this wisdom is ***Moksha*** – liberation.

In this **state of liberation *(Mukti)***, one attains:

- Physical well-being
- Mental fulfillment
- Abundance in wealth and family
- Virtuous offspring
- Deep spiritual satisfaction

*What more is required? Such a life is the **fulfillment of birth**.*

Even temple rituals like ***Abhisheka*** (ritual bathing of deities) contain embedded truths. Pouring tender coconut water, milk, curd, ghee, honey, sandalwood paste, sacred ash, Kumkum, and Panchamrit over the idol changes its appearance each time, yet the **form's core remains unchanged**.

This is the unspoken truth of *Abhisheka:* no matter how many forms, layers, or experiences we carry, the true Self beneath remains ever the same.

The Deeper Meaning Behind

TEMPLE RITUALS AND CAR FESTIVAL:

Though the formless **Adi Shiva** appears as countless manifestations across the cosmos, His **essential nature never**

changes. This is the profound truth illustrated through ***Abhisheka*** (ritual bathing).

During ***Deepa Aradhana*** (worship with lamps), the priest first offers:

- A **multi-faced lamp**
- Then a **five-faced lamp**
- Followed by **four-faced**, **three-faced**, **two-faced**, and finally, a **single flame**

This ritual represents: God manifests through many forms. Yet the basis for all are five elements - Earth, Water, Fire, Air, and Energy - and ultimately, all return to the One Light.

After this, **devotees are asked to close their eyes and bow.** Until now, devotees witnessed only the abhisheka and external worship. Now, they close their eyes and offer their prayers inwardly.

Maharishi says, "When you worship God, observe your thoughts with focus, for it is in your thoughts that God stands revealed."

Initially, the image (statue) we saw with open eyes is imprinted in our mind. But when we close our eyes and remain still, the image begins to **dissolve**, turning from form to formless.

At this point, the mind sheds its illusion (*maya*) and begins to perceive its own source: **pure intelligence**, which, like God, is formless. In ***Saiva Siddhanta***, this realization is called ***"Tatpurusha",*** that which is beyond form, yet immanent.

Why does this matter?

Because the **ever-desiring mind** finds peace in this realization. Just as all rivers find stillness in the ocean, the human mind chasing wealth, fame, status, sensory pleasures, etc. ultimately finds peace in the **Self-realization of Atma**.

This is why our ancestors declared: "*Worship at the temple is always a noble act.*" Because the **rituals**, if understood in spirit, offer **physical health, mental calmness**, and **spiritual clarity**.

Even Maharishi Vedathiri never rejected temple worship. He only warned against **meaningless festivals** and **wasteful grandeur** like the Temple Car Festival when conducted without inner awareness.

The *Amman* principles teach that divine truth can only be realized through the mind. But over time, middlemen and misinterpretations have distorted the original intent.

Similarly, temple Car-Festival, which once symbolized spiritual ascent, has become a cultural showpiece. Originally, **pulling the temple chariot** symbolized this:

* Devotees holding **one end of the rope** begin their journey.

* The **other end of the rope** leads to the **deity** on the chariot.

* Similarly, *within us*, the **spinal cord (Dandu Vadam)** links the **Mooladhar (base)** to **Sahasrara (crown)**.

* Through **meditation and inner discipline**, the mind travels this path and realizes **God at the crown center**.

The mind and God are opposite ends of the same inner rope. Pulling with sincerity, we reach the "Divine". But today, the Car-Festival often forgets this truth. As Kannadasan lamented:

He stands adorned like a saintly beggar - yet they

Deck him as a king and pull his chariot in splendor

To him, none are favored, none are rejected,

Though he dwells in the mind's shrine, no one truly sees.

The path of devotion, having forgotten this fundamental truth, refuses to reflect on the true benefit of conducting grand car festivals year after year.

In today's life, where the Divine is neither sought nor realized, such festivals become meaningless. Only when one seeks and realizes God through meditation, gaining inner clarity, does the need for such rituals naturally fade.

As a result, people may gradually withdraw from these festivals. This, in turn, prevents the waste of valuable time and resources, curbs religious hatred, and enhances social harmony. The economy will flourish as unnecessary expenses are avoided.

From temples centered around the Divine to various rituals, traditions, and festivals - all were originally intended to refine the mind and encourage mutual cooperation among people. But this noble truth has been lost.

In its place, arrogance has taken root, and leaders are revered, even deified, under the names of God, religion, caste, and race. If we realize that such practices are not conducive to the growth of true knowledge, we can begin to reflect on the greater good that may result.

With that humble request for deeper contemplation, I conclude this thought.

Summary:

This chapter critically examines the purpose and relevance of temple car festivals in the modern age, calling for a shift from ritualistic display to inner spiritual realization.

Originally, car festivals symbolized the movement of divine energy from temple sanctum to the streets, allowing all to receive grace. But today, they often lack true spiritual intent and become mere extravagant spectacles.

Vedathiri Maharishi and other sages emphasized that true worship lies not in grandeur, but in righteous living and meditation.

Temples were once spiritual centers for refining the mind and uplifting society. Now, many festivals focus more on cultural pride and social display than inner growth.

Kannadasan's verse reflects this concern: "What is the use of car, idol, or festival when humans have forgotten God?" Real spirituality involves transforming the ego-bound mind through love, meditation, and wisdom - not through elaborate rituals devoid of meaning.

The chapter explains the symbolic value of rituals like **Abhisheka**, **Deepa Aradhana**, and **Car-Festival** - all intended to help the seeker move from form to formless, from outer worship to inner realization. The chariot represents the spine, and the pulling of the rope symbolizes the inward spiritual ascent of the mind toward the crown center.

However, when such symbols are misunderstood, they lead to blind belief and wasted resources. Instead of guiding people to the Divine within, many modern festivals perpetuate superstition, economic burden, and religious division.

The chapter further explores the **Mariyamman** tradition and its connection to Kundalini awakening, showing how rituals once encoded deep yogic truths.

Through symbolic goddesses like **Dandu Mari**, **Karumari**, and **Koniyamman**, the path of inner transformation, from ego to liberation, is mapped.

When society returns to this **inner-centered devotion**, time, energy, and wealth can be redirected toward education, health, and harmony. Festivals need not be abolished, but their deeper meanings must be revived and practiced.

Plan Ten

Sports for Children Only

The human body is a sacred form that has evolved over billions of years in accordance with the laws of divine transformation.

It is a composite of three bodies - physical, life-force, and magnetic - joined in divine proportion. The physical form includes 12% bone and flesh, 72% blood, 4% heat, and 6% breath.

In addition, **6%** is composed of life-force and biomagnetism, while the remainder represents immeasurable intelligence or consciousness.

The purpose of such a superior human birth is to realize the Divine; the source of all five elements; and to immerse in supreme bliss.

However, for this goal to be fulfilled, the bodily functions governed by nature's laws must be balanced. The body appears stout due to bone and flesh, but it is life-force that drives their growth and renewal.

For the life-force derived from food to reach the entire body, the three flows - air (breath), heat, and blood - must remain unobstructed and stable.

This can be illustrated by well-known physical experiment: A lamp is placed facing a screen, with three cards in between, each with a hole. Only when all three holes are perfectly aligned in a straight line does the light pass through to the screen. If even one card is misaligned, the light does not reach.

Similarly, if there is an obstruction in any one of the flows, - air, heat, or blood - life-force will not reach the next tissue, leading to decay or death.

Therefore, bodily movement is essential to ensure these flows remain balanced. Maharishi classifies bodily movements into eight types: climbing, jumping, bending, swimming, running, throwing, lifting, and leaping. All other movements are essentially variations of these basic eight.

In ancient times, when survival required hunting, wandering, and farming, these movements occurred naturally, making additional physical training unnecessary.

Even today, those involved in labor-intensive fields like farming, construction, carpentry, or weaving naturally receive adequate physical activity and do not require extra exercise.

With the rise of science and technology, most people now work in sedentary jobs where physical activity is minimal.

As a result, in today's world, exercise has become essential for most people. Our ancestors recognized this long ago and incorporated structured physical exercises as early as the Vedic period.

For health and strength, especially for success in battles, people practiced wrestling, javelin throwing, horse riding, and other physical disciplines.

Historical records show that games like chess, dice, snakes and ladders, polo, judo, and karate originated in India and later spread to other parts of the world.

Chess was a popular game among the Kshatriyas, the warrior class responsible for protecting the nation and engaging in warfare.

That is why chess includes infantry, cavalry, elephants, a king, and a queen. Even in peacetime, chess was a way to retain the memory and strategy of war.

In the Ashtanga Yoga system structured by Sage Patanjali, the first four limbs are exercises for bodily health, and the next four are for mental refinement.

Yama, Niyama, Asana, and Pranayama are practices that strengthen physical wellness. Of these, "Asana" later came to be known as Yogāsanas. These Yogāsanas were designed for the hot climates of southern countries.

However, colder western countries required faster and more intense movements to suit their climate. Thus, they developed sports based on running, jumping, and leaping.

History notes that the Olympic Games were formalized in Greece around 3000 years ago, though various games existed even earlier.

Up to the age of 15 is the prime period for physical growth; after that, only lateral growth continues, while height ceases.

But intellectual development has no limit. The phase of life meant for nurturing one's potential in food, play, sleep, education, and positive thinking is called *Learning Discipline*.

The foundation of education lies in the teaching of good habits and moral conduct. In developed countries like America, the very first lesson taught in schools is how to maintain cleanliness after using the toilet.

From the beginning, students are taught both self-interest and social responsibility. The school provides the restroom as a facility to meet the student's personal needs.

At the same time, it instills the duty to keep it clean for the next user; thus, promoting public consciousness alongside personal care.

Next comes instruction about nature and the divine. Only after these foundations are built do they begin to teach literacy and vocational skills.

A society filled with children raised on the foundation of moral discipline would resemble the divine world we only imagine.

Therefore, it is the responsibility of parents to raise children who are healthy, capable, strong, thoughtful, and ethical. And it is the duty of the government and society to provide the necessary facilities to support this noble upbringing.

Study when you wake in the morning

Then sing sweet, gentle songs.

Play through the whole evening

Make this your daily habit, dear child.

Run and play, dear child; Never stay idle. - *Bharathiyar*

Study upon waking up – Rising early is a noble and excellent habit. The early hours are when the ozone-rich air is closest to the earth. This vital air enhances both physical health and mental clarity. The ideas planted in the mind during these alert morning hours get deeply imprinted in the subconscious mind and remain beneficial throughout life. That is why one should start reading and studying as soon as one wake up.

Then, a sweet and gentle song – Music has the power to focus the mind easily. Melody is a talent not only for singing but also for dancing. Songs that include references to the divine contribute to inner purification. That is why gentle and soulful music is important for children.

Play throughout the evening – The rays of the sun during evening hours are soothing to the human body. The sunlight provides Vitamin D freely; an essential energy that strengthens bones.

The importance of strong bones becomes clear during old age. This is why, even today, people living in colder countries sunbathe wearing minimal clothing during sunny seasons to absorb the sun's health benefits.

Between **5 p.m. and 7 p.m.**, one should devote at least an hour to physical activity through play. The most basic and essential forms of exercise are **walking, running, and hopping**. These should be practiced daily without laziness.

If this habit continues throughout life, the risk of pain and illness will be significantly reduced. Health, contentment, and a joyful life can be achieved, without any cost.

"*Every evening, let us gather with skill and joy, to dance with delight and refresh body and mind alike.*"

Recreation Clubs – After office hours, friends gathering to play indoor games like carrom or table tennis helps relieve the fatigue of the day's work.

Even if some conflict occurred during the day, this play acts as a stress-reliever. It helps return home with joy and nurtures harmony within the family.

So, every evening, let us come together with talent and cheer,
To revive our body and mind through joyful movement.

When the body is trained to move in ***multiple directions****, it develops* ***discipline, unity, character, and broad-mindedness****.*

Games cultivate ***professional skills, memory improvement, and noble virtues****.*

While running and playing - bending, stretching, twisting in various angles - the muscles get strengthened thoroughly. Therefore, one avoids sprains and injuries common in other activities.

Proper flow of **air, heat, and blood** is ensured, preserving health and strengthening internal organs.

For this reason, let us gather skillfully every evening, to dance with joy and nourish both body and mind.

When children engage in movement across multiple directions, it nurtures ***character, unity, discipline, and a broad-minded outlook****.*

Through play, children develop ***professional skills, improved memory, and virtuous behavior****.*

Character, unity, discipline, and broad-mindedness:

Children are like soft clay. They can either dry out into waste or be molded into beautiful dolls. Just as land must be cultivated for agriculture, children must be refined for life. That's what character and culture are about.

Unity is the ability to live cooperatively with tolerance and compromise - essential for social cohesion.

Discipline is the consistency of thought, word, and deed aligned with goodness.

Broad-mindedness – Two six-year-old kids were playing chess. One child won five consecutive games. During the sixth game, the losing child's elder brother gave him a few tips, and with that help, he won the game that time.

The previously winning child started crying. The new winner gently told him, "Arjun, don't cry. You really won this game too. If my brother hadn't helped me, you would've won."

Now ask - who is the better child? The one who wants to win at all costs, or the one who consoles a crying friend and values fairness?

This is the kind of character all children must be taught.

In this way, sports help cultivate noble qualities in children; not only in games but also in group activities.

Tolerance, acceptance, compromise, grace in victory and defeat, appreciation of others, a spirit of helpfulness, and time discipline *are all fostered through regular playing.*

Professional skills and memory enhancement:

Everyone must pursue a profession in life. For that, the body must be strong and flexible. Physical training prepares one for this.

And it's easiest to train the body in childhood. As the proverb says: *"What doesn't bend at five, won't bend at fifty."*

Bodily coordination improves functional ability. A refreshed mind improves memory. Though one may learn a skill, how well it is done depends on one's thinking ability and experience - both of which are supported by memory and physical strength.

"We see the wellness and virtues of life through games." Just as we say, *"By His grace, we bow at His feet,"* in the same way, we can train the mind in noble habits without strain, through joyful play.

Virtues learned in childhood guide a successful life. A body trained through play remains strong even in old age.

The body and mind need rest periodically. While fine arts can relax the mind, **games rejuvenate both body and mind together**.

As Swami Vivekananda said, *"Playing football is better than meditation"*- if it builds discipline.

Games eliminate anger and strengthen the body,

They come in eight kinds for children,

Climbing, jumping, bending, swimming, running,

Throwing, lifting, leaping – so says! - *Maharishi*

Games eliminate anger and strengthen the body – Desires, anger, and irritability are natural tendencies. But training and maturity can refine them, that's what we call culture.

Play is a simple, accessible form of such training. Though these habits may arise from past conditioning, with continued practice, the mind transforms easily, preserving health.

Just as a plant grows toward ripeness, the student phase is a time to cultivate **strength, maturity, and functional skills**.

Though physical training is an individual task, group games highlight it silently. Play is crucial in childhood and student years. Even watching play for a short time is refreshing.

Examples of traditional games:

* **For physical health and strength**: hopscotch (*Nondi*), kabaddi, skipping rope, mountain climbing, swimming, running, weightlifting, shot put, football, handball, basketball, wrestling.

** *Nondi* strengthens legs through hopping on one leg.

** *Kabaddi* develops lung strength by holding breath.

** *Skipping* boosts stamina and breath control.

**These games improve appetite, digestion, and metabolism.

* **Games for developing patience, acceptance, and compromise**:

** *Pallankuzhi* teaches the difference between desire and reality.

** *Snakes and Ladders* teaches that luck and misfortune can drastically alter our position, developing resilience.

** *Carrom and chess* promote strategic thinking, while also reminding us that there's always someone more skilled, teaching humility.

* **Games for nurturing friendship**: Hide and seek, swing.

* **Games for focus, strategy, and thinking skills**: Gilli, hide and seek, spinning top (*pambaram*), marbles, carrom, chess.

Harmful Games:

Video games, gambling, boxing, kickboxing, and all **commercialized sports**. In commercial games, **fame and money** are the driving force.

Competitions foster jealousy in children. Once jealousy arises, it destroys peace and satisfaction and leads to moral downfall.

When children play, it should be for the joy of playing; not for commercial gain. That's why event organizers don't focus on child sports; it doesn't bring profit.

But when adults play, **pride in winning** drives them. Fans too develop **egoistic attachment** to their favorite players. What are the consequences?

- Some earn enormous wealth without effort.
- They use that influence to elect corrupt politicians.

- They push inferior products through advertising, making fans waste money and health.
- They destroy peace.
- If the promoted product is food, health will be seriously affected.

"Boost is the Secret of My Energy" – What Are the Hidden Dangers Behind Such Advertisements?

The consequences of such promotional campaigns are far-reaching.

Health Hazards of Boost: Side effects include constipation, muscle cramps, respiratory issues, and heart problems. It's like inviting ruin with your own money.

The result? Unnecessary medical expenses lead to financial strain.

If the product is a luxury item, it creates economic stress in the family, disturbs domestic peace, mental well-being, and even affects relationships.

Cultural Degradation:

The minds of viewers watching seductive dance performances are corrupted, resulting in moral decay. Women's safety is also compromised.

Through entry ticket pricing, individuals are drained financially. The question arises - why is the ticket price even higher than a movie ticket? If movie ticket prices are already considered theft, this is **daylight robbery**.

Economic Implications:

When workers skip work to watch games, productivity declines, causing shortages and rising prices of goods. A worker's income drops while spending on tickets rises, affecting household finances. People may even take loans due to lack of money for essential needs.

Social Disruption:

If one's favorite player loses, anger and frustration spill into the home, affecting **domestic harmony**. Society too suffers unrest - arguments, conflicts, and enmity rise. Sometimes even **violence breaks out in stadiums**.

People start developing **hostile sentiments** toward other nations. Take, India vs. Pakistan cricket matches, for example - when asked who should win, the immediate answer is "India."

Why not say, "Let the better-performing team win"? Because sports are no longer seen as sport; it is viewed as **national pride**.

Health & Time Loss:

Watching foreign games broadcast late at night disrupts sleep, affects work the next day, and damages health.

Corruption in Sports:

Bribery, favoritism, and nepotism lead to underqualified athletes being sent abroad. Sometimes, athletes return without even a bronze medal. But when P.T. Usha won four gold medals, the nation celebrated everywhere. Match outcomes are sometimes predetermined for the sake of betting and gambling.

Youth are the biggest victims:

Commercial sports distract during their study years, losing focus and clarity, they ruin their futures. Yet, no media platform covers their stories. They don't get advertised.

Exploitation of Talent:

Even those who train hard and rise with dedication face bribes and politics when trying to enter national teams. Their **hopes get crushed**, leading to depression and family distress - again, ignored by media and society.

Idle Talk and GDP Impact:

Criticizing matches with friends wastes precious time. If arguments arise, friendships break. Unproductive chatter during work hours lowers output, hurting the nation's GDP. Personal productivity and **per capita income** fall.

Consumer Exploitation:

Overpriced fast food at stadiums, sports magazines, merchandise - all lead to **wasted money** and **poor health**.

The Athletes Themselves Suffer:

Due to constant travel, climate change, and food incompatibility, strange illnesses emerge. In old age, unrelaxed muscles cause **debilitating pain**. They suffer from mental health issues, broken families, strained relationships.

Many players become **puppets of sports authorities and sponsors**, unable to express their talent due to behind-the-scenes manipulation.

This causes inner conflicts, relationship breakdowns, and **social alienation**.

The Root Problem:

Commercialization of Sports

- Promoting sports through adult athletes and glamorous advertising **hypnotizes** the masses.
- Including seductive dances before or during games **triggers sexual arousal** in youth, leading to **cultural and societal degradation**.

Conclusion:
Commercialized sports must be abolished.

True play must serve physical health, moral growth, and societal harmony; not profit, pride, or perversion.

Summary:

A Path to Physical Health, Moral Character, and Social Harmony. Human life is the result of divine evolution; a union of body, life-force, biomagnetism, and consciousness.

To fulfill the higher purpose of life, realizing the Divine, bodily systems must remain balanced through regular movement and physical activity.

Why Children Must Play?

* Proper flow of air, heat, and blood sustains health.

* Maharishi identifies 8 core movements: climbing, jumping, bending, swimming, running, throwing, lifting, leaping.

* In ancient times, physical activity was part of life; today, we must reintroduce it intentionally, especially for children.

The Foundation Years

* Childhood (up to age 15) is the ideal phase for physical and moral development.

* Education must begin with hygiene, nature, God, and ethics, then literacy and skills.

* Play enhances strength, intelligence, and emotional balance.

"Study in the morning, sing gently, and play in the evening." – Bharathiyar

Evening Playtime: A Must

* Evening sun offers Vitamin D for free.

* Playing daily (5–7 p.m.) improves bones, circulation, digestion, memory, and mood.

* Games like hopscotch, kabaddi, swimming, and skipping build resilience and joy.

Building Values Through Play

* Games develop unity, discipline, tolerance, helpfulness, and time management.

* Example: A child consoling another after a chess match shows noble character.

* Physical training in early life supports professional strength and memory.

Beware of Commercial Sports

* Ads like "**Boost is the secret of my energy**" hide health risks and create false needs.

* Obsession with commercial sports causes family stress, economic strain, and social division.

* Fans waste money on tickets, and junk food, harming health and peace.

Wider Harms

* Youth get distracted, lose focus, and suffer long-term failures ignored by media.

* Talented players face corruption and politics.

* Athletes suffer injuries, stress, broken families, and mental health issues.

True play builds the body, trains the mind, and nurtures values. **Commercialized sports, driven by profit, pride, and lust must be rejected.**

Let children play for **joy, health, and virtue**, not for glamour or gain.

Plan Eleven

Education to Realize Cause and Effect

To people who tremble in confusion unaware of the Divine,

I gave Brahma Jnana to awaken clear God-consciousness

To realize the law of cause and effect and live accordingly

I present this book as the philosophy of Cause and Effect

Realize the use of five senses and divinize six evil characters

Let all people of the world live in peace and harmony.

Esteem this book that guides you to live with enlightenment,

As a supreme philosophy and derive its benefit. - *Maharishi*

The essence of Maharishi's book, "Philosophy of Cause and Effect" is captured in this verse. One of the key themes addressed earlier is ***"Living by Divine Justice".***

Only through realizing God can one comprehend Divine Justice, and by following this justice, world peace can be attained. Hence, Maharishi offered Brahma Jnana as a means to realize the Divine.

He also presented this book to explain the secret of cause and effect, emphasizing that Divine Justice is rooted in the law of consequences, and it is this law that determines the pleasure and pain experienced by human beings.

Though the mind becomes entangled in the allure of the five senses and deteriorates due to six dominant vices - beginning with desire - the vision of the Divine transforms this experience. The senses and the mind, like lamps that dispel darkness, become instruments leading one to supreme bliss.

The means to help all understand this is education -specifically, education that instills awareness of cause and effect. True education is when the realized guides the unrealized. Its purpose is to impart an understanding of life, where every action produces its own consequence.

The root of education is language; the root of language is letters, both written and spoken. The root of form is the dot; the root of sound is silence and solitude.

The all-powerful Divine State manifests itself as all things. Even before humans appeared or language invented, the four dimensions - mass, speed, distance, and time - already existed.

It was to quantify and explain these dimensions that language developed, with mathematics as its foundation. *The verb "to speak" gave rise to the noun "language".*

Thus, mathematics became the first branch of education, and language the second. It was Valluvar who proclaimed this truth to the world, showing that education is the key to understanding nature and its laws.

"What is named mathematics along with the other one named

Language - these are like eyes for human life." *(Kural 392)*

Understanding nature and moral law, and explaining them to those unaware, is the purpose of ***literacy***, ***philosophical knowledge***, *and* ***ethical education***. Those who understand the techniques of converting natural resources into usable facilities should share that knowledge with others; that is ***vocational education***.

Thus, the four foundational components of education are:

1. Literacy
2. Vocational skills
3. Philosophical understanding of nature
4. Ethical practice and discipline.

Once a person understands the disciplines of living in tune with the Supreme (Brahmam), the next step is transition from **Gurukul life** to **household life**.

In the household stage (Grihastha), one engages in work, earns wealth through righteousness, shares life with a partner, enjoys worldly pleasures in moderation, and ultimately reaches liberation (*Moksha*). This path of virtuous family life is the core message of the **Kural** way of living.

The four progressive stages of human life are –

Brahmacharya *(celibacy/student),*

Grihastha *(householder),*

Vanaprastha *(detachment), and*

Sannyasa *(renunciation)*

The traditional ***Gurukul system*** refined the individual, awakening a partially aware being into a fully evolved human. That was the true path of ***inner evolution***. But when the British colonized India, they imposed ***Macaulay's education system*** -

a poisonous seed that took deep root. Even today, it remains firmly entrenched, seldom ***recognized for its harm***, and continues to erode the very foundation of life.

In this system, ***literacy and vocational training were emphasized,*** *while* ***natural wisdom and moral discipline*** *were sidelined. The result?*

We multiplied conveniences yet lost the essence of life.

Amid material abundance, peace remains distant. Surrounded by excess, our true needs and troubles have only grown. Compared to the days of our grandparents and great-grandparents, we possess more facilities - yet face far more conflicts: legal battles, police interventions, and social unrest.

Just as the ideal of *Brahmacharya* has been distorted, the very meaning of 'education' has also been misunderstood. Today, countless scholars earn doctorates studying Thiruvalluvar's Kural, even though Valluvar himself never stepped into a school.

Similarly, degrees are awarded for studying **Newton's laws**, even though Newton lived without modern academia.

Science managed to convey Newton's Law to the world accurately - but scholars of language failed to bring Thiruvalluvar's moral wisdom to the masses. *As a result,* ***virtue (Aram) has faded into obscurity****.*

It is the government's duty - honored as the *sovereign power* - to establish and support institutions that teach virtue *(Aram).* Yet, a sovereignty lacking dharma has made adharma appear as dharma. People, though they have ***eyes, see not; though they***

have ears, hear no; though they have hearts, fail to feel; and they do not turn their minds inward.

They ignore the guidance of enlightened sages, ***nourishing only the body and mind***.

Yet, the ***Guru lineage continues by the grace of God***, and the fortunate one listens to the Guru's words.

"Learn thoroughly, without flaw the things that are worth

Learning; then live steadfastly according to that." (Kural 391)

He did not say *"learn everything"*. Saying *"even learn to steal and then unlearn it"* is the careless talk of someone who lacks a clear path.

What is learned must never be forgotten, so one should only learn what is truly worth learning with clarity, certainty, and without distortion.

The true measure of learning is not to boast, *"I know everything,"* but to ask, ***"What inner transformation has occurred within me?"***

When one lives by what is learned, gains fulfillment, and becomes an example for others, only then does learning bear its true fruit.

In today's education system, after a bachelor's and master's degree, we have the ***Ph.D. (Doctor of Philosophy)***.

But there's a subtle irony here - ***no matter the field of study, the word 'philosophy' remains in the degree***, even if there is no true philosophy being taught. That alone speaks volumes.

The reason is this: **Ph.D. stands for *Doctor of Philosophy*.** In truth, *Philosophy* is the pinnacle of human inquiry.

When one understands nature, *Divine Justice becomes clear*, and with it naturally arises *moral discipline*.

The purpose of a Doctor of Philosophy, according to higher educational standards abroad, is this: "***Philosophy should help one attain the Love of Wisdom.***"

Indeed, Philosophy leads to destiny, and ultimately to divinity; this is the true spirit of the Ph.D.

"What is the worth of a man who never seeks knowledge

Nor learns till the end of his life?" *(Kural 397)*

If a person, until the very end of life, does not seek a true Guru, does not attain wisdom, does not realize divine philosophy, does not understand the principles of righteous living, and does not strive to correct himself accordingly - then what is the use of such an unrefined heart?

What is the point of being born with a form that does not even feel remorse for the wrongs committed? If one's birth, life, and death leave behind no meaningful trace, then society simply forgets that person ever existed.

Yet, there are great souls who lived long ago - we may not know their faces or addresses, but even today we remember them with reverence.

Why? Because their ***life had meaning***, their ***existence had purpose***, and their life **benefit generations even today**. That's why we remember them; **they left behind a legacy**.

"Education pursued with concentration becomes

A lasting treasure for seven generations." *(Kural 398)*

When the mind is deeply concentrated and directed toward understanding God and Divine Justice, one gains profound insight into the laws of nature.

This divine understanding brings inner restraint even in darkness, and the child born through such awareness becomes a sacred offspring. Such an experience has lasting influence; not just in this life, but across seven births.

Even though many possess doctoral degrees today, the decline in society's moral fabric continues. Why?

Because most sought degrees merely for jobs, not for the ideal they represent - Philosophy, the love of wisdom, and the pursuit of divinity.

As a result, the number of the educated has increased, but the number of the wise has not. Consequently, education that helps people realize and teach the law of cause and effect has faded from society.

People often accept success easily, but when hardship comes, they collapse. They ask, 'What sin did I commit to face this suffering?'

If they had truly searched for the answer, they would have understood natural law. God does not assign suffering for no reason.

As Newton's law says: "For every action, there is an equal and opposite reaction."

But 'reaction' does not necessarily mean suffering. There is no intrinsic sin or merit in the action itself.

Only when the resulting impact is unbearable physically or unacceptable mentally does it feel like suffering. If the body can bear it, and the mind accepts it, the same experience may be felt as joy.

In human life, which consists of food, labor, rest, sex, and thought, when desire exceeds physical capacity and the mind pressures the body, it results in pain, illness, or complications.

These are self-inflicted consequences - a kind of personal karma. Such experiences imprint themselves on the soul and manifest their effects at appropriate times.

All experiences up to childbirth are recorded as Sanchita Karma in the fetus. After the age of three, Prarabdha Karma begins to form through personal experiences.

In this way, the actions, their nature, and consequences are all stored in the magnetic field, which is what we call the soul. The human soul is nothing but a characterized bio-magnetic domain - a microcosmic sample of the entire universe. Since these experiences (karma – ancestral and self) are stored within, they do not immediately cause suffering.

But when they reflect outward again in the form of **thoughts,** such as **desire, anger, worry, jealousy, hatred, pride, or unnecessary fear,** they manifest as pain.

On the other hand, if they manifest as **positive traits** like love, compassion, mercy, and sacrifice, they yield **beneficial results** without suffering.

*Therefore, using one's **intelligence**, one's **experiences**, and **spiritual practices**, one must understand the **law of nature**.*

When we realize this is how Divine Justice works, then that understanding matures into moral conduct rooted in wisdom.

Whether in thought, speech, or action - in any situation - one develops the maturity to live with respect for Divine Justice, this is what is truly meant by Sannyasa and Karma Yoga.

The soul (Ātma) consists of subtle waves whose density varies depending on our actions.

- The imprint of **good deeds** is called merit.
- The imprint of **bad deeds** is called sin.

When meritorious waves emerge, they bring success, happiness, profit, and healing. When **sinful waves surface**, they bring disease, pain, loss, and complications. Thus, one must act with **discernment and balance**.

"Resource, instrument, time, work, and place

Reflect on these five and act to dispel suffering." *(Kural 675)*

According to action, skill, purpose, time, and place,

Divine law flows through the magnetic path to yield results

People experience joy, sorrow, peace, and divine bliss,

Let us realize these truths and live in that awareness.

– Vedathiri Maharishi

Every thought, word, and action are stored in the soul based on its purpose, ability, timing, and place. When those stored waves resurface, they express results either as pleasure or pain, based on the environment.

If one calculates wrong and expects a certain result,

Can it ever align with the law of nature?

Nature gives exact outcomes at the right time

Who suffer constantly do not understand this. – *Maharishi*

The Bhagavad Gita (2.47) says: *"You are entitled to action, but never to the fruits of action." That is,* ***do your duty****, but* ***do not demand a specific outcome****.*

But is it really possible to act without expecting results?

We work 30 days believing we will get our salary on the 1st of the month. Parents educate their children from preschool to Ph.D. with the hope they'll have a better life.

So, **expecting a result is not wrong**. The point is this: One must consider **ability, opportunity, timing, environment, and eligibility**, and then plan and act methodically.

When success comes **through this awareness and effort**, it brings true inner satisfaction. For example, imagine someone planting a **spinach seed** and then praying like this:

"Krishna! I am your most devoted follower, your dear friend, your brother-in-law; please remember that. Let this spinach seed grow into coconut tree and bear fruit in heavy clusters!"

Can that ever happen? Yet, this is exactly what many people are doing in life. *They* ***do not pause to reflect****: Do I have the* ***qualification****? Do I possess the* ***required talent****? Do I have the* ***accumulated merit (Purva Karma Punya)*** *for it?*

None of these questions are considered. They simply say, ***"I want this. Which God should I pray to? In what way can I get it? Should I change my religion, if needed? No problem."***

All they care about is **getting what they desire**.

But ask this: Isn't it only the **one with intense desire** who changes their religion? Can anyone change the religion of a person who has **no desire**?

In the new religion they converted to, did **everyone** there get **everything** they desire? Can that be **proven**?

People must learn to think.

In today's India, the new mantra seems to be:

"Whether we deserve it or not, we demand it."

How many people, in how many ways, pray to God for favors - as though asking to pass an examination without attending school, studying the lesson, or writing the examination?

For example, someone **buys a dollhouse for ₹50**, ties it to a temple tree, and **prays for a real house worth ₹50 lakhs**! How is God supposed to grant that?

What the Divine actually says is: "*You perform your duty. You don't even have to ask for the result. At the right time, without error, I will give you exactly what you deserve.* ***But if you***

demand a specific result for a specific action, I cannot give. *"*
Devotees often complain: *"I'm not asking for Indra Loka! Just some basic needs. Can't God who created me at least give me that?"*

If you had the ***punya karma*** **(merit)** to receive it, He **would have already given it**. Without the necessary karmic credit, **how can He give it?**

If you plant a **spinach seed**, how can you expect a **coconut tree** to grow? In fact, if you plant one type of spinach and expect a different variety, **even that cannot be granted**.

This principle - **cause and effect** - is what Divine Justice is built upon. Without understanding this, **pestering God like a child** yields no benefit.

Take a child, for example: when they repeatedly nag for something, we might sometimes buy it, sometimes we don't, sometimes we explain, sometimes we scold, and occasionally, even punish. Now imagine the child asking: *"Why didn't you give me what I asked for? Is that fair?"*

What would we say?

- There's no money right now.
- You don't really need it.
- It was too expensive.
- You're not mature enough to handle it.

We have countless reasons.

In the same way, to God, we are all children.

"A child has one father. For all of us, that father is God."

*So, whether we **ask** or **don't ask**, whether we **pray** or **don't**, God **carefully decides**, based on our **karma**, what we should or should not receive.*

Teaching this secret is what we call the 'Science of the Cause-and-Effect System'.

Desires constantly chase us in pursuit of comforts. To ensure that these desires do not lead us away from dharma, and to instill fear and devotion in the mind, temple worship was originally established.

But when this system is turned into an institution that simply fulfills devotees' material wishes, who then takes pride in misleading them?

Those responsible for teaching dharma, when they preach that any sin can be forgiven through rituals, who bears the blame for turning devotees toward sin rather than away from it?

Among those who believe in God, the majority are devotees, not seekers of wisdom. To help devotees respect the righteous teachings of great saints and free themselves from the ignorance taught by dogmatists, the importance of understanding the law of cause and effect is emphasized.

The foundation of this education is simple: ***whatever you do, do it with awareness.*** With the sixth sense (reasoning), one must live with ***Trikala Jnana,*** i.e., awareness of past experiences, present conditions, and future consequences. Everyone has this Trikala Jnana. For example, even a doctor has experienced stomach pain from overeating. So, when a patient comes in with stomach pain, he diagnoses based on location and prescribes the right medicine.

The purpose of this "cause-effect education" is to ***remind us to use this awareness consciously.***

Take today - you attend a feast. Various dishes are served. If you eat moderately, no problem. But if you overeat, trouble is certain.

Here, the ***past experience (stomach pain),*** *the* ***present situation (feast),*** *and the* ***future consequence (well-being or illness)*** *must be weighed before acting. That is wisdom. Is that difficult?*

But instead, people eat driven by desire, then later suffer illness and circle the temple of Vaitheeswaran (God of healing) - what is the use?

When divine order exists within every action and its result, What's the point in violating it and then begging God for a remedy?

Every action yields a precise result based on five factors: **intention (purpose), instrument (means), time, deed, and place.**

Imagine holding a glass tumbler in your hand. You alone can choose whether or not to drop it. But once dropped, the result is inevitable.

Even if we release a tumbler from our hand, expecting it not to break depends on the environment. On the moon, it may not break due to low gravity but on Earth, it will. If it falls on a cushion, it rolls. On a normal surface, it breaks into pieces. On granite, it shatters completely.

The ***action is the same****, but the* ***result varies depending on the conditions.*** *This understanding is what the* ***science of cause and effect*** *aims to teach.*

Take the example of a lamp:

- One person writes the *Thirukkural* using its light is a great virtue.
- Another who writes a forged document is a great sin. The lamp is not at fault. Nor is the act of writing inherently sinful or virtuous. **It is the outcome that determines the moral value of an action.**

Even in modern medicine, many drug names end with **'mycin'** - sounding like ***"my sin"***. Look at the names of medicines discovered by science – Anacin, Terramycin, Crocin, Tetramycin, Erythromycin, – all ending "my sin, my sin."

It seems to say, "Because of my sin, I now suffer from this disease and must swallow this medicine."

Even scientists say, "This disease came because of your wrongdoing; take this medicine to cure it." Philosophy also explains that the cause of disease is sin.

To avoid this suffering, one must ***recognize the laws of nature and live ethically***. When you go to a doctor, they ask about your parents or grandparents. Why? Because diseases like **diabetes, cancer, and BP** are hereditary.

Just as **material wealth** is inherited, so are **the karmic imprints (sins or virtues)** of our ancestors.

You cannot separate fragrance from a rose, or smell from a fish; **likewise, you cannot separate the karmic essence from inherited wealth.**

If wealth is earned by cheating and harming others, the sorrow and curses of the victims stay attached to that wealth, and manifest as problems, misfortunes, or inner suffering.

Modern society, by ignoring this law, has become obsessed with **momentary opportunity**, saying: "Grab what you can, we'll worry later." This attitude has created a **world of theft, deceit, and ignorance**.

Those who carry the burden of suffering no longer seek wisdom or listen to the words of enlightened souls. This **ignorance of dharma, truth, and justice** continues throughout lifetimes.

To be liberated from this delusion, we need **spiritual training to realize true knowledge.**

Jnana Yoga (Path of Knowledge) is about recognizing the Source of all creation, the Power guiding all actions, and living with reverence for that Divine Force and its Justice, thereby enjoying nature's pleasures in a fulfilled way.

Bhagavad Gita – Chapter 4, Verses 1-3: Krishna says he taught this imperishable yoga first to the Sun God *(Vivasvan)*, who passed it to *Manu,* then to *Ikshvaku.* Over time, this **ancient yoga was lost**, and Krishna is now imparting it again to Arjuna.

The karma of ancestors lies recorded in the gene

All your past actions are imprinted in the brain

The deeds you do now are driven by the five senses

Along with habits formed from past experiences – All

These three must be gradually erased through penance

To transform the karmic imprints embedded within,

Wealth or influence is of no use, realize this! *– Maharishi*

"One who tries to cover fire with cotton is a madman

One who offers money to erase sin is a complete fool!"

- Kannadasan

A farmer, using his knowledge and the resources of nature, can feed many. He plants just a grain of rice yet reaps an abundant harvest.

God has provided us with such immense natural wealth, and also the intelligence to harness it effectively.

But when that intelligence is misused, turned toward selfish gain by harming others; the temporary pleasure gained is recorded as **sinful karma** within one's bio-magnetic field.

This imprint ripens over time and returns as suffering in later life. Valluvar said, "All diseases come from the one who caused them." Kanian Poongundranar echoed: "Good and evil do not come from others."

Tears turning to laughter, laughter turning to tears - these are not random events. They are the sharp and just fruits of one's own karma.

When we change our address, postal mail that cannot reach us is returned to the sender.

But divine justice never fails in delivery. There is no "return to sender" in God's karma system; **every action is delivered back** precisely at its **maturity date**, no matter where you are, be it America or Ireland.

There may be good or bad things in it. The mail may carry joyful news or sorrowful news. But the postman is not responsible for its content.

God is a marvelous, impeccable, honest, and unfailing postman; one **who knows the GPS of karma.** You cannot escape saying, "I'm not the person you're looking for." **He is a postman who can identify you without an ID card.**

When *punya karma* (virtuous deeds) ripen, unexpected gains and successes arrive. Even without merit or skill, one may receive great opportunities and comforts. Not everyone who succeeds is truly intelligent.

Another person may possess all the skills and qualifications but may not get the opportunity he deserves. Hard work may not always receive just reward. In both cases, the results are determined by the individual's karma.

God, being perfect and fully blossomed in all ways, is pure. But in us, both purity and impurity are mixed. Where did these impurities come from?

Water from the ocean evaporates and becomes pure clouds drifting through the sky. When they thicken and cool, they rain down. Until it touches the ground, rainwater is pure.

If it falls into the Ganges, it is holy water; if it falls into a gutter, it becomes dirty slush. It is the place where it falls that determines its value; one becomes sacred, the other dirty.

Likewise, the Holy Spirit (pure divine energy) becomes particles of God, transforms into the five elements (pancha Bhutas), and becomes the Earth - inhabited by subtle beings, plants, and more. Everything in creation is originally pure.

Plants, creepers, trees - grow both upward and downward.

This dual nature symbolizes that in human beings, both good and evil thoughts arise. Evil leads downward, virtue uplifts.

The *Garuda Purana* explains that for every sin, there is a corresponding punishment.

If one has done good deeds while living, they are invited to heaven; if one has committed sins, they are thrown into hell.

But ask yourself; has anyone ever gone to heaven, drunk a cocktail, and come back after meeting *Rambha, Urvashi, or Tilottama* (Ever youth dancers of heaven)?

You cannot get one's life back by loud cries

You will not win by going to the court;

Once one enters that fort, there is no return.

Only if someone returned from the dead could they say:

"I went to that world, drank ambrosia, saw Indra, and heard about all this." – Kannadasan.

The **purpose of the *Garuda Purana*** is to guide humans to live virtuously. Good and evil are not things we encounter somewhere else.

We or our descendants will face them right here in this world. Valluvar said: "Let not lie what your conscience knows; for if it does, your own conscience will burn you."

The **Bible** says: *"He who speaks against the Holy Spirit shall not be forgiven neither in this world nor in the world to come."*

When the consequences of one's father's actions emerge, they manifest in the same lineage, bringing joy or suffering as the karmic imprint ripens.

We call the all-pervasive supreme power as Brahma, the God

Those who realize it and live by the way of divine law,

The sages who have let go of arrogance and Brahma Jnanis,

As declared by the enlightened ancients with perfect clarity

In our life by uprooting evils from the Genetic imprints

Transcending animalistic deed through scientific inquiry,

All people of the world live with supreme consciousness

Let us welcome and celebrate that glorious day!" - Maharishi

Uprooting evil from karmic imprints is God's hidden compassion. How so? To satisfy a child's hunger, a mother offers breast milk, that is **nurturing compassion**. But when the child is sick, she forces medicine upon it, even if the child resists. This is **tough compassion**, meant for healing.

In the same way, when divine justice grants good results for virtuous deeds, it is **open compassion**. When it brings suffering appropriate to sin, it is **hidden compassion**. Once sin is cleansed and righteousness begins to flourish, that too is **compassion**.

If people come to understand and accept *that the true path of spiritual evolution lies in recognizing the inner truths hidden in worship, temple festivals, astrology, epics, and* ***Vedathiriam*** *is the essence and culmination of that legacy - a genuine spiritual training united with ethical living,* ***then that day will be hailed as the dawn of world peace.***

Summary:

To restore peace and justice in the world, education must be redefined; not merely as literacy or job training, but as the cultivation of wisdom to understand life's most fundamental law: **Cause and Effect System of Divine Law**.

Vedathiri Maharishi calls this the "Philosophy of Divine Justice," where every action inevitably yields a proportionate result based on intent, means, time, deed, and place. Maharishi offered **Brahma Jnana** to awaken humanity to God-consciousness, not as blind devotion but as clear realization of the universal law that governs all joy and suffering.

Just as Newton said, "Every action has an equal and opposite reaction," this principle applies morally, biologically, and spiritually. Even ancestral karma, encoded in one's genes and bio-magnetic field, ripens into effects that shape our lives. *True education must thus include:*

1. **Literacy** – to communicate truth
2. **Vocational training** – to harness nature responsibly
3. **Philosophical insight** – to understand Divine Law
4. **Ethical discipline** – to live with inner refinement

When desire overrules discipline, and society worships convenience over conscience, we suffer multiple times. But when man uses his reasoning to align with Divine Law, the same senses that trap the mind become tools for liberation.

True transformation happens not by ritual, fear, or emotional prayer, but by understanding and correcting one's own karmic imprints.

God, like a postman, delivers every result without error or delay, whether joy or pain. ***No prayer can bypass Divine Order.*** *Every soul bears its own record and that is the life.* Therefore, education that instills this awareness is the key to individual evolution, sorrow free life, and global peace.

If people come to understand that **Vedathiriam** is not a new religion, but **scientific essence of all spiritual traditions** uniting worship, epics, festivals, and astrology into a path of inner awakening; then we shall witness the dawn of a harmonious world.

Let us therefore celebrate and propagate this eternal wisdom and welcome the great glorious day when all humanity lives with all comforts in peace, awareness, and divine alignment.

Plan Twelve

Explanation of the Bio-Magnetic Principle

Magnetism is a Fundamental Divine Force. It is known by many names - Pranav, Divine Grace, Sacred Energy, Cosmic or Universal magnetism, and Bio-Magnetism. To live a complete and fulfilled life, one must have a clear understanding of magnetism.

Science explains that magnetic rocks exist on Earth, and that the North and South Poles are formed due to their magnetic force.

Without a clear understanding of the philosophy of magnetism,

- One cannot grasp the nature of the mind,
- The cause-and-effect logic behind pleasure and pain,
- Or the fundamental secrets of nature.

Can one know God without knowing about magnetism?

Can one attain wisdom without knowing the genetic field?

For anyone living virtuously with dignified noble qualities

There is no other path either in philosophy or in science!

– Vedathiri Maharishi

What is the relationship between God and magnetism?

When we merely look at a bitter gourd, we have no reaction. But once it touches the tongue, we sense bitterness. Why? Because our **bio-magnetism undergoes a transformation** in response to the gourd's chemical nature. ***Fine. But why does a feeling of aversion arise on my face the moment I taste bitterness?***

The secret is this: ***Magnetism undergoes transformation in two ways****.*

* *The* ***bio-magnetism in the tongue*** *transforms into* ***bitterness****.*

* *The* ***bio-magnetism in the brain*** *transforms to express* ***aversion****.*

The bitterness I feel cannot be known by others. Without facial expression, even my inner aversion remains unknown to others.

Bitterness and aversion are entirely personal experiences.

In the same way, God can only be realized through one's own experience; there is no other path.

Without understanding the genetic field, one cannot attain true wisdom. Why?

Because the very idea of a "center" is intertwined with the divine seed, which has been compressed into God particles.

This compression gives rise to evolution and what delivers outcomes is super consciousness.

Consciousness is the eternal link between dynamism and the result of magnetism. Every joy and sorrow a human experience are the result of the Consciousness that gives appropriate consequences for each action.

Therefore, **Consciousness is divine**.

When a person realizes that **everything within and around them is Consciousness**, and lives without deviating from that awareness, **that person is a walking embodiment of God**.

"One who perceives truth within himself without doubt

Is to be regarded as equal to God." (Kural 702)

Among those who live as human beings, who is nobler than one who lives as a walking embodiment of the Divine? What other life form, apart from the human being, is capable of this realization?

There is no alternative - neither in philosophy nor in science.

One must explore and understand the **magnetism within**. Its source is the unique, pure space of Supreme **Consciousness**. This truth can only be known through **knowledge itself**. Is there any other way? Where is it? Who has spoken of it? Who knows it?

One must realize that consciousness is the supreme reality, and with a mind in equilibrium, continuously chisel away unnecessary attachments. This is the state of *awakened vigilance - says Vedathiri Maharishi.*

The force of attraction, also called compression or self-contraction, is the basis of all motion. It is the power that contracts itself inward.

When the four -

- **Void (Existence without form)**,
- **Infinite Energy**,

- **Supreme Consciousness**, and
- **Time**

  merge together, they become the **vast divine space**.

From this self-contraction arises *subtle vibration.* And this *vibrational event* marks the *condensation of the divine state,* leading to the *emergence of God particles.*

When boson particles begin to spin, the Divine Space exerts ***pressure*** on them. This pressure causes them to penetrate inward. As these spinning divine particles repel that pressure, they cause it to deflect; this is ***refraction***.

Even though it refracts, the Divine Space continues to exert force toward the center; this is ***penetration***. As the center becomes denser and the force rebounds outward, it is known as ***reflection***.

When it merges with the surrounding pressure force, it transforms into magnetism through their ***interaction***.

These five phenomena - ***Clash, Refraction, Penetration, Reflection, and Interaction*** *- form the essence of* ***wave motion technology****,* which evolved later into specialized fields such as sound wave technology, light wave technology, and mind wave technology.

A divine particle is a wave spinning upon itself. Its spinning speed is just enough to be sufficient for its own motion but not strong enough to repel another divine particle.

Therefore, it lacks repulsive force. Due to the surrounding pressure of the Divine Space, these particles gather, interlink, and begin to move in spherical waves forming *matter*.

As atoms move under the ***constant surrounding pressure of pure space***, divine particles ejected from whirling force, interact with the surrounding medium, giving rise to two phenomena:

1. **Attractive Force** - the pre-existing inward compression of Divine Space.
2. **Repulsive Force** - arising from the outward burst of boson particles.

The inward pull is due to the self-compressing energy of the divine state. As particles burst outward and interact with the surroundings, **two types of interaction** occur:

Type 1: Repulsive Interaction

Here, the direction of the attractive wave reverses because of the whirling nature of the boson particle, transforming as repelling force. For example, pressing a sharp knife on a whirling tire breaks it down into carbon dust because of an interaction between pressure and the tire's surface.

This can be defined as:

Pressure + Refraction + Interaction = Magnetism

Type 2: Penetrative Reflection Interaction

Here, Divine Space penetrates through the movement of matter, reaches the center, becomes dense, and then rebounds, dissolving at the boundary.

For example, a car caught in a whirlwind gets lifted, hits the dense ground at the center, and is flung outward again.

This interaction is defined as:

Pressure +Penetration +Reflection +Interaction = Magnetism

Thus, the rotation of matter becomes magnetic fields. ***There is no isolated space for repulsion to exist by itself.*** Even if we differentiate between static, dynamic, and magnetic fields, the *conversion of motion into magnetism* is a seamless continuum.

This uninterrupted sequence is what we call ***'Time'.***

This is the ***'micro-unit' of time.***

The 'very first emergence' of time *from the stillness of pure space.*

The History of Matter:

- The divine state of consciousness gives rise to divine boson particles.
- Under the surrounding pressure of the divine state, they accumulate and begin to self-organize and rotate at extreme speed, which is the formation of the **electron** → ***'The birth of the Electron'.***
- When external pressure increases, some of these rotating particles break off and dissolve into the surroundings, transforming into magnetism. Thus, forming magnetic fields around the core.
- As the electron dissolves, its speed decreases → it becomes a **proton**, a partial electron. As it continues dissolving, its speed further reduces → it becomes a **neutron**, the nucleus.

- Without repulsive force, it can only sustain minimal self-movement. Eventually, as motion ceases entirely, it returns to its original state of divine particles → "***The death of electron*".**
- When it transforms back into the formless state, it transcends the universe and merges with the Infinite Divine.
- ***This is the life history of a particle of matter.***

The formation of matter and its transformation into magnetism is what we call cosmic magnetism.

These magnetic waves are continuously generated and spread out as they merge with the outer field.

Thus, the entire cosmos operates as dynamic energy fields and magnetic zones.

When matter becomes magnetized, it relinquishes its state of *pressure*, completing its transformation.

"An electron is a stable subatomic particle that carries energy and can exist for billions of years."

Hence, the source referred to in various ways as *Pure Space*, *Oneness*, *Unity*, *Being*, or *Self-compression* begins its transformation into divine particles, thereby initiating motion.

This leads to dual aspects: **space and motion**.

When the electron is formed, due to its immense speed, **no particle can approach another**, each repels the other, giving rise to **distance**.

From the birth of the electron to its dissolution, ***the duration becomes segmented as past, present, and future.***

Kaalan (the god of death) is Yama, who acts under Lord Shiva's will. *Kaali* is the manifest form of divine Shakti.

But the **Divine itself has neither past nor future**. What we call *duration* spans from the smallest microsecond (Pico second) to the longest unit like a light year.

"Can fate overtake intelligence?" I asked. "Time itself is the tool of consciousness," she replied. – Bharathiyar.

Here, consciousness refers to the human capacity for reason and logic. But even consciousness is bound by *fate*, which itself is governed by the **universal consciousness**. That universal consciousness is, in turn, subject to **Time**.

When divine particles gather to form matter, the **journey of time begins**. Alongside this, the **law governing motion** (cosmic order) also begins.

Thus, people often equate *time* and *fate* as one and the same in society. They say, "his fate" or "the time of his birth" = the **law of time** ultimately.

- The **fate** of time
- The **intelligence** governed by fate
- The **life** governed by intelligence
- The **experiences** governed by life. All of these are enclosed within **the law of fate**.

Has anyone ever escaped this circle? Is there truly anything beyond fate?

The supreme manifestation of magnetism is the mind. *The **universal magnetic field**, which pervades the entire domain of motion, is what Maharishi calls the **Mind of God**.*

*The **magnetic force operating within each soul** is what he calls the **Mind of Man**.*

*All **communication and remote connectivity** are made possible by this **cosmic magnetic field**.*

*The very presence of magnetic waves throughout the cosmos is why it's aptly termed: **Mega + Net = Magnet***

This cosmic magnetic principle was hinted at in Mahabharat. When Dron Acharya was astonished to see that Ekalavya had mastered archery techniques he had taught Arjuna, he asked: "Who is your teacher?"

Ekalavya replied: "I considered you my mental Guru and learned all this through inner concentration."

Dron Acharya taught Arjuna the *Astras* (divine weapons) by reciting sacred chants directly into his ears, in another place. How could Ekalavya, who was deep in the forest, possibly have heard this?

Each *Astra,* like the *Agni Astra* (fire), *Mohini Astra* (illusion), *Vayu Astra* (wind), etc., had to be invoked by installing the corresponding energy into an arrow using precise mantras.

That is, when Drona began to teach the mantras to Arjuna, those vibrations were absorbed into the **cosmic magnetic field**.

"The place where thought arises is a point; but the field where it completes its action is the boundless cosmos; the Universal Field." – Maharishi.

Reflecting on this, it becomes clear: Sage ***Vyasa had realized the cosmic magnetic principle even back then.***

As soon as a thought arises, it merges with the **cosmic magnetic field**. From that field, one can retrieve knowledge; this is what we today call the **Internet**.

Thus, the **first used internet-like potential** was **Ekalavya**. Vyasa understood this subtle technique, though he had no scientific language in those days to explain it.

Maharishi beautifully elaborates this in verse:

That one which is once understood; from God to the life

Can reveal and make one realize all, that is the magnetism

The ancient seers realized it through deep meditation

But for lack of analogy, struggled to express it fully

Now that science has advanced - the same truth

Through dynamic electricity, can be explained to all

Both the supreme spiritual wisdom and atomic science

To understand and uplift the life's path; like a bridge,

From life to liberation is none other than Magnetism.

Today, we can **demonstrate through electricity** what was once accessible only through inner spiritual experience.

Electricity is nothing but the ***continuous motion of invisible electrons****.*

The magnetic nature arising from that flow manifests as ***rotation, sound, light, heat, or coolness*** *- depending on the conditions.* ***It is pressure differences that cause a single magnetic energy to appear in many forms.***

Not just that —

- **Atomic energy** (from atoms),
- **Wind energy** (from wind),
- **Solar energy** (from sunlight),
- **Hydro energy** (from water), and
- **Thermal energy** (from coal/heat)

All these are different sources, but the electric energy extracted from them is of the same quality.

The creative knowledge that acts as a bridge to uplift and liberate life by uniting supreme spiritual wisdom with atomic science - that is Magnetism. **How?**

It is magnetism that enables us to understand both *spiritual truth* and *scientific knowledge*. From the origin of magnetism in divine particles, all the way to the bio-magnetic imprint of human actions, known as the **Bio-magnetic domain**: its journey is uninterrupted and unhindered by anything.

Cosmic magnetism governs the motion of celestial bodies, spreading as magnetic waves across the entire universe, acting as the **medium of informative transmission**.

*Let us now explore how this **divine cosmic magnetism** transforms into **individual bio-magnetism**.*

If one forgets noble celestial magnetism and bio-magnetism

There is no other way to realize God and consciousness

Because the Supreme Truth is the all-pervading vast space

Into which cosmic waves of rotation integrate and settle

Bio-magnetism manifests as the soul and governs the body

No doubt, the energy is life, and its nature is swirling waves

The noble consciousness of the space centered within life

Truly wondrous, its expansive state is the mind itself."

- Vedathiri Maharishi

Maharishi bridges both forms of magnetism - celestial and bio-magnetism. Life cannot arise from celestial magnetism alone. Only on planets where a bio-magnetic field develop can living beings emerge. For evolution of bio-magnetism, three basic principles must be present:

1. The wave vibrations of the 27 constellations
2. The wave vibrations of the nine planets
3. The vibrations caused by the combination of the five elements on Earth, arriving in divine proportions.

Body, life-force, bio-magnetism, genetic center, brain,

Conscious, mind, and the senses; sum of the eight is soul

For beings that live in the sea, the land, and the sky,

If even one of these eight functions ceases to operate,

They no longer deserve to be called 'life' – thereafter

By another name to call it, as inert substance, is just

With blossomed wisdom like a fully unfolded flower,

Let the people of the earth live free from delusion. - Maharishi

The first of the eight components is the **physical body**.

We accept that life exists within the body. Without life, the body cannot grow. There was a time when it was believed that life enters the fetus in the seventh month.

This belief arose due to the lack of scientific and intellectual development. When a mother felt the baby breathe, it was said that life had entered.

But **life is not merely breath**. Life **existed even before breath** and **exists as breath**. The father's and mother's life-forces unite, evolve, and form a body that is born into the world.

*The **genetic center** becomes the core of the body, of life-force, and of magnetic action. It is the center for the body, the center for life, and the center for magnetism.*

*When experiences are added to this core, it becomes **the soul (Ātma)**. Even the tiniest micro-organism possesses a genetic center. When its movements and experiences combine with it, **that becomes the soul**.*

Genetic Center + Characterization = Soul

Today, in any living being, we can no longer distinctly separate the terms *genetic center* and *soul*. Therefore, both terms - **genetic center** and **soul** - now refer to the same concept.

It is the **characterized magnetic domain**: a field of bio-magnetism imprinted with life's experiences.

Next is the **brain**. When we sleep, the brain's activity changes. While conscious thought subsides, vital centers associated with the autonomic nervous system remain active to maintain essential life functions.

The senses operate through the brain. Philosophers refer to *buddhi* (intellect), *Chittam* (mind-substance), and *ahamkaram* (ego). ***Chit*** refers to the intermediate mind.

Since sensory functions are executed through the brain, no perception is possible without it.

The ***five sense organs and five working organs*** *along with* ***mind's activities*** *all pass through the brain as a monitor and are recorded in the shell of the* ***genetic center****.*

Thus, ***the human being is a cosmic computer designed by the Almighty.***

Next is the **Inner Consciousness**. The divine particles present in every living cell are referred to in various ways: as heart, genetic center, and soul.

Next comes the **mind**. Through instruments like **EEG (Electro Encephalo Gram)**, the activity of the mind is categorized into brainwave frequencies:

- Delta (1–3 Hz),

- Theta (4–7 Hz),
- Alpha (8–13 Hz),
- Beta (14–40 Hz).

But these devices can only measure the **brain, not the mind**. Measurements like time, distance, density, and speed correspond only to **brain vibrations**, not to the **mind**, as Vedathiri Maharishi said: **'There exists no instrument to measure the mind, nor can it be measured'.**

The **mind** is a **field of characterized bio-magnetism** that stores experiences and operates through the senses. Hence, no mechanical device can measure it.

The waves of thought arise from the **genetic center**, and are received by the brain cells, which categorize them as time, space, mass, and speed.

All calculations and measurable thoughts processed through the brain are ultimately of mental origin.

Next, the **senses**. Humans have invented thousands of tools for convenience, but all are extensions of the **five action-oriented organs**.

Many machines now perform functions once done by our body; vehicles from bicycles to airplanes extend the function of our **legs**, doing in minutes what once took hours on foot.

Similarly, countless machines in industries replicate the work of our **hands**, completing in minutes what would take months manually.

We have also invented devices to **record music and speech** extensions of our **ears and mouth**.

But the stomach is irreplaceable. *No invention can substitute it. The body must* ***consume food*** *directly to nourish itself.*

Another irreplaceable function is reproduction. *Even in the case of test-tube babies, it is still the* ***man's sperm*** *that initiates life, and it must still* ***grow in the mother's womb****. There is no alternative to these two functions.*

The Integration of Eight Aspects: The Essence of Life:

Body, life-force, bio-magnetism, genetic center, brain, inner conscious, mind, and senses. The dynamic integration of these eight aspects forms what we call **life**.

Among the five elements (*Pancha Bhootas*), creatures living in sea, land, and sky rely on those eight aspects (*Body, life-force, etc.)*. If even one of these components ceases to function, the being loses its distinct status as *life*.

From ***space (void)*** *to the* ***human body****; From* ***divine particles*** *to the* ***individual soul****, the entire journey is the* ***unfolding of divine evolution:*** *the very path of knowledge.*

Bharathiyar poem: **The Flood of Supreme Shiva**: Explains:

1. "All that exists within and without - is none but That itself."

All that exists is : Pure magnetism

Within : Soul

Without : Body

Is none but That itself : There is nothing else beyond that.

2. "A single flood exists - the Vedic sages call it God."

It is the single pure black vast space without limits; the enlightened sages named it God.

3. "What I see in the heart, what I conceive inwardly..."

What I see : Transformation of that Space in everything

In the heart : In my Soul, the same space.

What I conceive inwardly : All experiences are characterized

4. "All that I cherish is born from that same flood."

All thoughts reflected in me are nothing, but the outcomes of the experiences recorded and preserved as Soul, which is a characterized bio-magnetic domain.

5. "It is boundless and indivisible and holds no attachment to anything."

That pure space of consciousness has evolved into everything in and as the universe. So, it is boundless and indivisible. In humans or anything else in the universe, the Supreme has no attachments or bondages. Whether people live happily or suffer heavily, the God has no attachments or involvement in either. God does not interfere.

6. "Still, the learned endlessly fall into delusion debating its existence."

Even great scholars fall into delusion, questioning whether god exists. The debate continues endlessly. If we see gold, the ornament disappears; if we see the ornament, we forget the gold. But noble sages clarified: the ornament is only a form - the substance is gold. Similarly, everything is shape and the content is god.

7. *"It is pure, vast consciousness - empty space - and it emits various powers..."*

The pure space contains consciousness, and from it evolved all - from boson particles to humans. All types of energy particles evolved from that pure vast consciousness.

8. *"Like a pouring cloud, it assembles and disperses atoms."*

Hydrogen and Oxygen particles unite to form water, and water evaporate back into Hydrogen and Oxygen. Like-wise, association of particles forms mass and dissociation of mass returns to particles. The pure space showers like cosmic rain.

9. *"It becomes gross matter, subtle essence, and subtler than the subtle..."*

In humans it is the body, it is the life-force, and it is the bio-magnetic energy. In the universe some forms are visible to the naked eyes; some others to electronic eyes; and yet there are so many things we can perceive only through intellect, wisdom, or pure consciousness.

10. *"It becomes finer than all, manifesting every characteristic itself."*

Nothing is finer than the space and that alone has evolved into everything, and also holds experiences, characterized as soul.

11. *"Yet, it remains without a single trait, as one eternal entity..."*

All manifestations and characterizations are the outcome of so many transformations with frequencies ranging from 1 to 40 Hz. Since the space is nothing, nothing in the universe can penetrate and disturb or define the purity.

12. *"And at the same time, holds many traits and stands as all multiplicity."*

Though it remains pure, it permits all traits to manifest and coexist - just like even in the dirty water, hydrogen and oxygen remain pure.

Vedathiri Maharishi explains as:

Through the five senses, when life's energy is drained,

Believing that decaying to be joyful pleasure, is delusion.

When thoughts ascend to higher states, the bio-magnetism

That scattering is perceived as five types of sensual pleasures

As the kundalini rises step by step to the brow center

The power of supreme wisdom that flows from within

By self-effort let us explore and understand the life,

And align the speech, thought, and action in harmony.

Sweetness does not inherently exist in sugar, nor within us. Pleasure arises only when both meet and transform into bio-magnetic experience.

No matter how many ways the cups may be designed,

The liquor poured into them tastes the same.

It is only the mind that imagines a difference

There is no difference in the drink itself. - *Kannadasan*

Unless **thought, speech, and action** are aligned in harmony, one cannot increase the reserve of **bio-magnetic energy**, nor experience the **supreme bliss** it brings.

To attain this, Maharishi prescribed the discipline of the **Five-Sense meditation -** an extraordinary method to subdue the dominance of the sense organs.

If one understands the **origin, transformation, experiences, presence, and benefits** of bio-magnetic energy, one can enjoy the pleasures of body, mind, and intellect **in a refined way** and live with deeper fulfillment.

No matter how advanced science becomes, **a rocket cannot reach pure consciousness**. Nor can religious rituals help one reach God.

Only by understanding the mind and the bio-magnetism underlying it, can one realize that the transformation of this magnetic energy is what becomes sensual pleasure, joy, and sorrow.

*By maintaining balance in **material protection, management, and desire**, and allocating **time and energy** to transcend them towards **intellectual refinement**, one can make the mind realize its **source - the eternal, complete Divine.***

If the philosophy of **celestial magnetism and bio-magnetism** is thoroughly understood, one will realize that the entire universe is filled with **magnetic-waves** that govern all the movements. These same **cosmic waves**, manifesting on Earth as **bio-magnetic fields**, have evolved from micro-organisms up to human beings.

This journey makes it possible for us to rise beyond sensory pleasures, to perceive subtle truths, and attain **supreme bliss**.

The supreme intelligence of the Divine has descended into humans as discriminative intellect. It is only through this rational intelligence that we can touch, know, and realize the supreme wisdom, thus fulfilling the purpose of human birth.

Vinayaka, who symbolizes the five elements (Pancha Bhootas), does not possess the nature of direct perception. ***Perception*** *- the ability to feel and know - belongs only to* ***magnetism****, the living, conscious force.*

Those who are rooted in the inertial nature of the five elements require the knowledge and wisdom of magnetism to transcend their limitations.

Murugan, on the other hand, has already realized and experienced the truth of magnetism; he requires no further knowledge. Since the operation of the five elements is based on ***expansion****, Vinayaka could not grasp the infinite expansion of the universe.*

Yet, because he recognized ***Shiva*** *as the center - the source of all actions and elements - and grasped this truth through inner clarity,* ***Ganapati*** *attained victory as a Siddhant: one who perceives the Source at the center of all.*

*Murugan, who realized the all-pervading **cosmic magnetism**, understood that the **Vedas** and the **divine particles** are the very foundation of existence.*

*He perceived **Vedanayaka** - the Lord who is the inner essence of these divine particles - and through that realization, Murugan triumphed as a Vedhant.*

*These two philosophical standpoints were later crystallized by **Vyasa** in the great declarations of the Vedas:*

- ***"Aham Brahmasmi"** – I am Brahman – the human soul recognizing its origin is the voice of **Siddhanta**.*
- ***"Tat Tvam Asi"** – That Supreme has evolved into everything – is the voice of **Vedanta**.*

When one perceives the whereabout of magnetism, within

God and the Mind appear as a silent, sacred unseen dance

In humans touch, sound, smell, light, taste, mind, and also

Pleasure and pain, all are the effects of invisible magnetism

In a calm subtle mind, if one observes without disturbance

Your consciousness testifies, free from doubt and confusion

This is common to kings, sages, and merchants; in the vast

Consciousness to realize God, I explained after realization.

- Maharishi

Ancient imaginative beliefs, crashing like relentless waves, occupy the minds of people and prevent clear thinking. But once **wisdom of magnetism** is attained, this confusion vanishes like a mirage.

In **magnetism**, there is **existence**, **attraction**, and **repulsion**. Is there anything else in the universe beyond these three?

All the forms we see, all living beings, all experiences of pleasure and pain are but transformations of magnetism, mere scenes in the grand **illusory cosmic dance**.

One cannot perceive this truth amidst the turbulence of emotion. Only in a tranquil and steady mind, when one reflects without disturbance, does clarity arise without doubt; truth becomes self-evident.

Whether guiding as *sages,* governing as *rulers,* or managing as *merchants,* only those who possess both **knowledge and experience of magnetism** can truly serve the people's well-being. It is with such a realization that God entrusts them with responsibility.

But when **those who lack divine awareness** take up the role of teaching **dharma**, righteousness becomes distorted, and confusion multiplies.

For the mind to expand and evolve into true wisdom, one must receive **initiation** *(Deeksha)* from a realized **Guru**, undergo penance, and attain the truth through experience.

"Taste, light, touch, sound, and smell – who discern their

Nature, to him alone, the world is revealed." *(Kural 27)*

Bio-magnetism transforms through the five senses - taste, smell, sight, sound, and touch. Through this transformation, living beings experience **pleasure and pain**. The transformation of bio-magnetism gives rise to the **mind**. No human exists without a mind, yet few truly **understand how it functions**.

Only who knows the mind can rise through intellect, perceive subtle truths, and unite with Divine; the path to realization.

Five physical elements, five senses, and five kinds of pleasures - this is how the fivefold awareness arises. Exploring how pleasure and pain emerge from these is **rational inquiry**.

Tracing the **history of the primal force** behind all of this is **true discernment**.

Why do the **eyes, ears, nose, and tongue** exist? Why are they all located in the **head**? Asking such questions and investigating deeply leads to understanding of spiritual evolution and its connection to higher intelligence.

The one who realizes the **secret of divine evolutionary force -** built over **millions of years** - is truly the conqueror of the world.

Worldly objects, pleasures, praise, or blame no longer affect him. Such a person lives with perfect **equanimity**, organizing his life in the path of **righteousness**, experiencing **pure joy untouched by sorrow**, and sharing that blissful way of life with others.

Some among the people accept his teachings, follow them, and in that supreme joy, become realized beings themselves. Thus, the world recognizes and reveres such a Divine soul.

Summary:

Magnetism is identified as the **fundamental divine force**, known variously as Pranavam, Divine Grace, Cosmic Energy, Celestial magnetism, and Bio-Magnetism. It is the bridge between **formless divinity** and the **manifest universe**.

To live a fulfilled life and realize God, one must deeply understand this force. Vedathiri Maharishi asserts that **pleasure, pain, mind, and consciousness** are all outcomes of magnetism's transformation.

All human experiences - from taste and emotion to thought and spiritual awakening - are governed by **bio-magnetic dynamics**. Misunderstanding these leads to delusion; realization dissolves it.

Magnetism transforms into five ways - **clash, refraction, penetration, reflection, and interaction** - forming the foundation of wave motion and all physical phenomena.

From the birth of electrons to the evolution of protons and neutrons, matter's life-history is a process of magnetism under pressure. When matter dissolves, it merges back into pure divine space; a process that parallels the soul's journey.

This uninterrupted magnetic flow across space is what we call **Time**, and its flow governs **karma**, **consciousness**, and **destiny**. Fate, time, and life are all part of this divine magnetic law.

Maharishi identifies the **mind of God** as the universal magnetic field, and the **mind of man** as the individual's bio-magnetic response to it.

All teachings, spiritual transmissions, and divine wisdom - as symbolized in ancient epics like the Mahabharata - are transmitted via this **cosmic magnetic net (Mega + Net = Magnet)**. Maharishi equates this to the modern *Internet*, where thought vibrations travel and can be received by purified minds.

Scientific energy systems (atomic, solar, wind, thermal, hydro) and spiritual practices (like Kundalini Yoga and five-sense regulation) are both expressions of the same **magnetic principle**.

The transformation from divine particles to human soul, from universal consciousness to individual awareness, all operate within the **Bio magnetic Domain**.

The **eightfold structure of life** - body, life-force, bio-magnetism, genetic center, brain, consciousness, mind, and senses - enables the soul to experience life. When even one aspect fails, the being loses its identity as "life."

Bharathiyar poetically echoed this:

"All that exists within and without is none but That itself - the single flood of energy the Vedic sages call God."

*Vedathiri Maharishi concludes that the **supreme bliss** and **divine realization** can be attained not through rituals or religion, but by **understanding and aligning the mind, body, and magnetism**.*

True Divine Justice lies in this inner clarity and lived in harmony with Divine Magnetism.

Plan Thirteen

Globalization of Food and Water

Let seasonal rains fall in harmony across the world

Let all farmers joyfully multiply their harvests

Let various laborers flourish with comfortable living

Let rationality and collective wisdom uplift culture.

- *Vedathiri Maharishi*

Human culture is rooted in and based on agriculture. Rational thinking leads to fragmented awareness, while integrated consciousness arises from a deep unity with universal intelligence.

To perceive the analytical awareness of 8.2 billion people and the intelligence operating throughout the universe is one - that is integrated perception.

The feeling of, "Seeing the withered crop, I too withered," is an expression of integrated perception. Because integrated perception sees everything as one, it fosters a life of mutual help and harmony.

Regardless of the stage of world civilization, this perception uplifts and leads to the highest potential.

For example, when a beloved child asks for our favorite food, we share it with love and joyfully watch the child eat it; this is ***analytical empathy***. When we buy sweets and notice a poor child looking longingly at them, we offer a portion and feel joy in their happiness; this is ***integrated empathy***.

The nature of considering others as oneself is essential.

To develop that nature, compassion must arise in the heart.

If one possesses a noble heart, there is no greater wealth.

No deity greater than the one who understands this!

- Kannadasan

Hence, let analytical empathy evolve into integrated empathy, and let it uplift culture. Let humanity rise. However, today the dominant thought is: *"Why should I share my wealth or the resources of my country with others?"*

A man thinks: "I will raise my son, educate him, and get him a job." Meanwhile, another raises a daughter, educates her, gets her a job, and also spends a fortune on her wedding and gold dowry.

Despite all this, she is expected to enter her husband's household, manage a job, take care of household duties, and show utmost respect to in-laws. How can people with such expectations ever be willing to share their wealth with others?

What would happen if a farmer too began to think like this? If he said, "I will not share the produce I cultivate with anyone else," the world would descend into chaos and conflict.

Every person must develop the awareness: ***"I am not just an individual, but a representative of the universe."*** *"There is certainly a share for you and a share for me in this world.*

Through the labor of each individual, the world attains prosperity." – Poovai Senguttuvan

We are all born on this earth called the world.

The life-sustaining air we breathe is the same for all.

The sun that shines across the globe is one and the same.

The ocean evaporates into vapor and rains down is one.

No one in this world has done anything at all about this.

Every one of us is born, lives, and dies in turn.

If one section of the world accepts killing another is justice,

Then only the murderers would remain in this world.

- *Maharishi*

Killing is not limited to taking a life; it also includes **economic murder**, **denial of rights**, and more.

Consider the price of petrol: ₹100. Out of this, ₹35 goes to central government tax, ₹35 to state tax, ₹20 to other costs, and only ₹10 is the actual base price. A natural resource, given freely by nature, ends up costing ₹100.

If someone has already paid ₹70 in taxes, is it still fair to say they must perform charity?

This is how **rights are murdered**. If someone buys a school seat with money, does that not rob a deserving, talented student of their rightful place?

If it is a Clay hut, will the gentle breeze refuse to enter?

Will the evening moonlight deny its glow to the poor?

Just for you only, and just for me else, God has never given.

Whatever He gave, for whom He gave?

For a single person? No, He gave it for all. - *Poet Vaali*

Let this bitter truth awaken us and let the flower of compassion bloom to relieve the suffering of others. When **food and water** become common for all on this Earth, it is a noble sign that ***humanity has matured.***

The clouds, like a father, shed tears of rain.

Here plants rose like children, each in their own way.

Crawling in the lap of Mother Earth, they grew.

Even for the ailing and sorrowful, they gave medicine.

- *Kannadasan*

From Bharathiyar's powerful declaration: ***"If even a single person goes hungry, let us destroy the entire world"*** - we understand the essential need for food.

Over a century ago, Bharathi urged: *"Let the excess water flowing in Bengal be used to irrigate the lands in the central regions."*

We celebrated Bharathi's centenary grandly, but we have not implemented his principles.

It's time to think deeply. ***Without water, the world cannot function. Without food, life cannot exist.***

The boundless water and land were given by God;

Why did the thought arise that they are one's property?

Even God Himself does not understand this;

He cannot comprehend the principles of man. - *Kannadasan*

Let seasonal rain fall uniformly across the world. Let people develop the wisdom to understand the **value of water** and use it wisely. Let us recognize that the Earth has never truly lacked water, and realize the **abundance that nature offers**.

Yes, at times, rain may not fall where it is most needed. But if we think scientifically, we will understand that seawater evaporates day and night. That vapor must **return to the Earth** and somewhere, it must rain again to restore balance.

In hilly regions, **tall trees** help bring rainfall naturally. Rain falls in the mountains and flows down as rivers across the plains.

Though removing sand may increase a river's depth temporarily, it weakens the banks, disrupts natural absorption, accelerates water flow, and causes erosion. Over time, this leads to higher flood risk during heavy rains.

"If heavy dark clouds withhold the rain, even the

Vast ocean's water level will decrease." *(Kural 17)*

Sea water evaporates due to the sun's heat and floats like clouds. As these clouds condense, they turn into dark rain clouds and fall back to Earth as raindrops. They then flow like waterfalls, streams, and rivers, eventually merging back into the ocean. ***If the water taken from the sea does not return to it as rain, the sea itself will dry up.***

Similarly, all of a human being's needs are drawn from society. If nothing is given back, the **wealth of society** will eventually **dry up**.

Let us forget the spring water; Let us excavate the hills,

Gather the rainwater that falls on the surface, and

Increase the river's flow and let us store that water

And meet our needs throughout the year.

Let us enrich the wetland crops as much as we can.

Whatever the nation may be,

Let us erase the term "foreign lands" and establish

Wise, unified governance across the world. - *Maharishi*

Even the great Thiruvalluvar, in the chapter(2) ***"The Excellence of Rain"***, does not mention springs or seas directly in all ten couplets, he praises **rainfall** alone.

Why? *Because the* ***immense heat rising from Earth's core*** *can only be balanced by* ***spring water sources*** *which act as natural regulators of heat.*

Due to the excessive use of ***deep bore wells****, most natural* ***spring sources*** *have dried up. As the* ***unrelenting heat from within the Earth*** *rises,* ***plant roots dry out****, and vegetation withers.*

Global warming *increases and torments humanity. At least now, we must respect the* ***wisdom of sages****, honor* ***nature****, and lead a harmonious life.*

"Farmers can not till their fields, if the

Floods bestowed by storms diminish." *(Kural 14)*

Meteorologists now say: *"The water we get from seasonal rains is not enough. Only during cyclones do we receive sufficient water."* ***Thiruvalluvar had already said this 2,050 years ago***.

Only through cyclonic storms can we receive abundant water, enabling farmers to plow, sow, irrigate, and reap rich harvests.

Cyclones are nature's blessing, not a curse.

It is **ignorance** to believe headlines like: *"Floods enter homes along stormwater paths."* Building houses or huts on public land and natural water flow paths and then claiming **"floodwaters have entered homes" is utter foolishness.** Asking for cyclone flood relief in such cases is a claim without any rightful basis.

They blame the cyclone instead of acknowledging human error. People have been made to **hate cyclones** by repeatedly portraying them as nature's wrath upon people.

But ***the areas struck by the cyclone****, especially along the* ***coastal belt****, are* ***not meant for human habitation****. Violating this natural boundary is* ***an encroachment upon nature****. When nature reclaims its space, it is* ***not injustice****; it is* ***justice itself****.*

Even human death in such cases is **not unfair**; it is a consequence of violating nature's law.

"Charity and penance cannot endure in this vast world,

If the sky withholds its rain." *(Kural 19)*

The most fundamental need of a living being is food. Only after hunger is removed can the mind move to higher thoughts.

Charity is doing good for others. **Penance** is the effort to seek and realize the self within.

But without water, - the foundation for moral life, duty, and compassion - there can be ***no charity to help the poor*** *and* ***no penance to elevate divine consciousness****.*

If we calculate the amount of rainwater that mixes with the ocean and compare it to human needs, we will realize that ***many times more water flows into the sea than we actually require****.*

Using water economically according to our needs is our right but using it beyond our needs or wasting it is theft.

Rain enables plants to grow and become food for living beings. Other natural resources, when combined with water, are transformed into comforts and goods for use.

We must respect the needs of others, regulate our own desires, and live by sharing **equitably and fairly** with all.

To realize that ***all natural resources belong to everyone****, we must develop* ***awareness of divinity and divine justice****.* If **virtue is absent in action**, then the benefits of nature will be hoarded by a few - by certain individuals, states, or nations - while those truly in need will be left without.

If one forgets that the wealth they acquired came from the **intellect gifted by God**, their **own physical labor**, and the **cooperation of fellow humans**, then the greatness they have attained **cannot be sustained**.

This idea has been handled very accurately by the English language. If we explore the meaning of the word **"Godown,"** we can understand a deeper truth. A **godown** is a place where goods produced using **natural resources** and **human resources** (given by God) are stored.

The term **Godown** itself can be read as **"God + own,"** implying: *"All these goods ultimately belong to God."*

One who realizes this truth and **upholds righteousness** will never fall or be disgraced. But one who thinks, *"This is mine,"* will not only face downfall but eventually **go + down** as history has shown many times over.

"If farmers' hands lie idle, even saints who've renounced

All desires must renounce life itself." *(Kural 1036)*

If the farmer does not till the land, even a hermit who claims to have renounced everything - no desires, no attachments - will eventually have to renounce his life itself.

In devotion, what is placed to God is called ***'offering'***, and once it is shared with everyone, it becomes ***'divine grace'***.

To truly feel the pangs of hunger, **fasting** was introduced into religious practice. The month-long **Ramadan fast** is based on this principle: "Feeling the pain of hunger during the day and then cooking food after sunset and ***sharing it with others*** before eating."

The core idea behind this practice is to cultivate **a culture of shared nourishment** throughout the world.

Natural resources are not evenly distributed across all regions. Due to the atomic structure of Earth's layers, each location differs in what it possesses. Since humanity is spread across all lands, there must be a balance between resources and needs.

If needs grow while resources diminish, **scarcity** will arise. If that scarcity remains unaddressed while the population grows, **poverty and deprivation** will follow.

Therefore, we must establish fair systems to ***share and enjoy resources collectively****. As Maharishi said: "Science has helped us multiply goods; Let us now restrain money and live by* ***sharing****."*

Through science, we have power to increase production and send surplus goods to where they are needed most.

The cause of today's poverty is not lack of goods, but the ***improper handling of resources by a few***, which prevents them from reaching those truly in need.

Man has failed to acquire the wisdom to ***use nature's gifts wisely***. Even when told, many lack the maturity to accept it.

Every living being has the right to enjoy natural resources. *At the same time,* ***no one has the right to waste even a tiny fraction of it****.*

If every individual - from common citizen to world leader - accepts and lives by this truth, we will find that ***Mother Earth provides far more than enough*** for the needs of all beings.

The word **"Resource"** itself means **having more than what is needed; surplus**. If resources are shared wisely through knowledge, everyone can live with fulfillment, **poverty would vanish**.

Even when we understand how deeply poverty can affect life, we often remain indifferent. After rising from hunger to comfort, we forget what it was like to have nothing, and waste food just to match our lifestyle. This must be avoided.

"If one asks what the greatest misery of poverty is,

It is that poverty itself is misery." *(Kural 1041)*

If one does not have the means to meet basic needs, life becomes a form of hell. People struggling even for fundamental necessities are suffering the worst of all.

What is crueler than such poverty? ***"Some don't even have rice gruel to drink,"*** *said Bharathiyar.*

They don't even understand the causes of their condition.

When people who cannot feed themselves give birth to children, they are unknowingly ***imposing a life sentence on their own child****.*

This is the **cruelest outcome of intellectual poverty** - lack of awareness of one's own condition. Once **ignorance is removed**, material poverty will disappear on its own.

"Poverty is such a sinner that it comes deprived of

both this life and the next." *(Kural 1042)*

It is ***poverty that gives one the courage to commit sin****. When the stomach aches with hunger, both* ***conscience and justice become irrelevant****.*

Sinful acts arise primarily from ***material poverty****, and from* ***the envy born of ignorance****. Who can ignore the fact that* ***poverty not only affects those alive today but also inflict suffering on future generations****? Shouldn't we act?*

The **Bhagavad Gita** says that the best form of charity is ***"Nidhaan"*** (deliberate giving with care). ***Ni+Dhan= Nidhaan.***

- *Dhan* means giving.
- *Nidhaan* means giving with mindfulness; **not squandering but preserving**. Don't exhaust everything you have. Leave something behind for the future generations; this is true ***Nidhan***.

"Protecting the Earth and passing it on to future generations is our duty." - Maharishi

"When poverty comes without virtue, even one's own

Mother will look upon him as a stranger." *(Kural 1047)*

The first day when intelligence awakened to remove others' suffering, Dharm (righteousness) was born. Living in a way that causes suffering neither to oneself nor to others is Dharm. That is why Dharm and poverty cannot coexist. If poverty arises without righteousness, it is as if a mother rejects her child. Likewise, when people disrupt the balance of nature out of selfishness and greed, Mother Nature turns away from them. As a result, humanity faces losses, suffering, and poverty.

From plants to humans, night is nature's designated time for rest and recovery. Rest is the time when lost energy is regained; it is a law of nature. It is the period of metabolic restoration and transformation.

So, night also symbolizes the elimination of deficiency and the pursuit of growth. In the same way, when someone shares their abundance with another, the receiver's deficiency is fulfilled. This too is a form of growth-transformation; a metabolic exchange of matter and well-being.

The energy for the electron's orbit comes from the nucleus itself. If the Supreme Force does not offer its gravitational pull, the planets cannot rotate in space. Hence, giving and receiving is the law of nature. Lack and abundance are two sides of the same truth.

*Night comes; day comes - **the world is one**.*

*Poverty comes; prosperity comes - **life is one**.*

*Friendship comes; enmity comes - **the heart is one**.*

*Loneliness comes; companionship comes - **journey is one.***

- Kannadasan

Therefore, considering it a matter of pride to give to others, in accordance with natural law, is actually a misconception of human dignity.

The Prophet said: *"No one truly benefits another. The good deed done today will return as a reward - either to this person or to their descendants."*

So, what we call a good deed today is not a charity, but a spiritual investment. Only God is the true giver. Human prosperity comes from the effort of the body, the power of intellect, and nature's system of mutual growth.

Everyone is eager to **receive**, eat comfortably, and rest peacefully, if there's someone willing to give. But if giving is involved, people hesitate to work.

Thus, it is better to be in a position of **giving to others** rather than **depending on others**. The wise have said, *"Better to die than to live by begging."*

Whether something comes unsought or only by asking, whatever the case, we must strive to live.

Those with even a little love or compassion will respect others' needs and come forward to help. Only when this attitude spreads globally will food and water become common for all.

One who gives with the compassion that says, *"Let the other's pain be removed"* -their wealth will never diminish like Karna.

We are only ahead or behind each other based on our own karmic records, but all of us come from the same source and are journeying back to that same source.

We came yesterday. We live today; we leave tomorrow. Whatever happened here is just a completed play upon this world's stage." - Kannadasan.

When the wisdom that *all beings are equal* is truly realized, the notions of 'giving' and 'receiving' themselves will disappear.

Maharishi said, *"What kind of debt accounting is this? The one who had surplus gave, and the one who had nothing, received and ate. That's all."*

If this simple truth is understood, society will experience abundance in food, in resources, in everything. But for this, **a shift in mindset is essential**.

Food and water are fundamental needs for the survival of all living beings. Even today, when purchasing land for a house, the first question is: *Is there water access?*

From ancient times, people settled only where water was available for living and for farming. Politics originated as a system to protect agricultural produce, but to this day, it has turned into a machinery of **resource exploitation** across the globe.

Though the **United Nations** was formed to change this, it is yet to function in alignment with its ideals.

Nature's law dictates that the population must match the available natural resources. This spiritual truth is most clearly conveyed in the **Ramayana**; yet, people have not understood its message, only developed superficial devotion.

Rama married at the age of sixteen, lived in the household for twelve years, then went to the forest for fourteen years. After that came his coronation, and only the following year were the twin sons Lava and Kusha born.

Why were there no children during all the married years?

The **philosophy of progeny** that Ramayana teaches is this:

Only after *Seetha (the soul)*, who had been imprisoned by *Ravana (ego/arrogance)*, is liberated through the grace of the *Guru (Hanuman),* and *Rama (Supreme)* can the *liberated soul* unite with the divine and bring forth the *next generation.*

If people had understood and approached childbirth with this ***spiritual awareness****, world peace would have already been achieved, and* ***Maharishi's avatar might not have been needed****.*

Therefore, even now, we must realize that population must be proportionate to natural resources. At the very least, we must start living economically and responsibly.

A lack of frugality increases scarcity. **Conflicts over food and water will never end**. Every year, water disputes between Tamil Nadu, Karnataka, and Kerala never cease.

If we barely have enough water for ourselves, and our neighbor asks, will we share it? Then how can one law apply to us, and a different one to states?

In this land, one's own wealth is private, but another's wealth is considered common property. - Kannadasan.

We must eradicate such **ignorance** and **declare food and water as common property** of the world. Pattukottai Kalyanasundaram said:

"If everything is placed in common, there's no need for hoarding or rationing."

A council of wise thinkers must come together, discuss openly, and create systems to share resources fairly with all. The right to live belongs to everyone, but only the wise will live meaningfully.

For the light of justice to shine, we need a mind that considers others as oneself, and that heart must be filled with compassion. Let us all embrace the love-filled truth of Kaniyan Poongundranar: 'All places are one; all people are kin.'

Communism is defined as forcibly being taken from those who have and give to those who don't, equalizing wealth through redistribution.

Maharishi*, instead, called for* **'Come-unism'**; *"Come, let us unite." If we truly unite, it marks the* ***dawn of one world governance****. Rather than only making* ***property common****, a deeper solution is to cultivate* ***human beings as a shared global source****.*

To make humanity universal, a system where **children are raised by the state** must be implemented. It is inherited property and family lineage that push people away from dharma and toward adharma. Maharishi says:

Just as the furious rush of floodwaters in a river

Is harnessed by building a dam and put to use

Let us harness the strength of noble humans,

Whose senses are refined, and unify their sharp

Intellect and skills through cooperation.

Let us elevate the world through wisdom, hygiene,

Economy, and righteous governance and join hands

To help humanity live on Earth with love, joy, and peace!

Summary:

Vedathiri Maharishi's vision emphasizes that **food and water must be recognized as common resources** for all humanity. This chapter advocates for a cultural, spiritual, and policy-based transformation to achieve global equity and sustainability.

1. Integrated Empathy – The Foundation for Equality

Human civilization must shift from **analytical empathy** (helping with reason) to **integrated empathy** (feeling one with others). When we see others' hunger and suffering as our own, mutual compassion arises, fostering a world of cooperation and dignity.

2. The Illusion of Ownership

Natural resources like air, water, and land are **freely given by nature or God**, yet modern society treats them as **private assets**. Such thinking leads to injustice, exploitation, and imbalance. As Kannadasan said: "Even God cannot comprehend the greed of man."

3. Rain – The Equalizer and Sustainer

Rain is the most **universal and impartial provider**. Thiruvalluvar emphasized that without rain, even charity and penance are impossible. Maharishi and classical Tamil wisdom teach us to **respect water**, harness it wisely (via hills, rivers, and flood management), and use it sustainably.

4. Poverty – The Root of Sin and Suffering

Thirukkural and Bharathiyar highlight that **poverty**, especially when divorced from righteousness, leads to moral downfall and generational suffering. Once **intellectual and spiritual poverty** is removed, material poverty will vanish.

5. Justice in Sharing Resources

Today's scarcity is not due to lack of goods, but due to hoarding, misuse, and improper distribution. Maharishi calls for scientific production, wise use of resources, and voluntary sharing rather than forced redistribution.

6. Spiritual Insight from Ramayana

Ramayana teaches that only after ego (Ravana) is destroyed and the soul (Seetha) is liberated by guru (Hanuman), should the next generation be created. This allegory reminds us that procreation must align with awareness and responsibility, not mere tradition or desire.

7. From Communism to "Come-unism"

Instead of forced redistribution (communism), Maharishi promotes **"Come-unism"** - an invitation to unite through compassion and collective consciousness. Human beings, not just goods, must be treated as **common property of the world**, cultivated through shared responsibility and spiritual maturity.

8. Global Governance and Ethical Living

Real justice lies in recognizing **no nation, caste, or individual holds exclusive rights** over food and water. Wise governance must be founded on:

- **Scientific knowledge**
- **Hygiene and health**
- **Economic equity**
- **Moral leadership**

9. Call to Action

Let all nations:

- **Abandon the term "foreign lands"**
- **Establish universal systems for sharing**
- **Embrace one-world governance based on love, wisdom, and justice**

As Kannadasan and Poongundranar beautifully stated: 'All places are one; all people are kin.' 'Poverty comes; prosperity comes; life is one.'

Closing Vision

'Just as floodwaters are harnessed by dams, let us harness the strength of noble minds, unite intellect, compassion, and governance, and build a world where all live with love, joy, and peace.' - Vedathiri Maharishi

Plan Fourteen

Abolishing the Practice of
'Many Religions – Many Gods'
and Discern the Single Truth

He saw the bird and built the airplane.

He saw the leaping fish and created the boat.

He heard the echo and invented the radio.

But what did he see to create religions? *- Kannadasan*

Today, there are:

- 2.1 billion Christians
- 1.3 billion Muslims
- 900 million Hindus
- 380 million Buddhists
- 190 million Jews
- 30 million Sikhs
- 1.7 billion people of other religions
- 1.1 billion people with no religious affiliation

*These **1.1 billion non-religious individuals**, who respect societal law and live peacefully, reflect the ideal that aligns with **Maharishi's vision** of universal harmony.*

There are over **4,300 religions** in the world today.

But how many gods?

- **Christianity** teaches **one God in three persons**: the Father, the Son, and the Holy Spirit.
- **Islam** affirms **one God** (Allah), with **99 beautiful** names *(Asma'ul Husna)* reflecting divine attributes.
- **Hinduism** refers to **33 crore (330 million) deities** but generally centers around five principal deities in major traditions: **Shiva, Shakti, Ganesha, Karthikeya, and Vishnu**.
- The term **"Hinduism"** was **coined by British colonialists** roughly **400 years ago** to categorize the diverse spiritual practices of India.

Before that, spiritual life in India was known as **Sanatana Dharma** - the eternal way of living in harmony with nature's laws.

The *first tradition* to teach God to humanity was *Saivam,* followed by *Saaktham, Gaanapatyam, Kaumaram, Souram and Vaishnavam* - each focusing on different aspects or levels of divine evolution.

The *ancient worship of the Sun* was also accepted and elevated into *Souram* (solar tradition).

The first spiritual quest for God in human history arose in India. And it was here that a way of life called Sanatana Dharma was developed - a path that emphasizes living in alignment with nature's eternal laws.

***Sanatana Dharma**, in later times, came to be understood as* ***Henotheism** the worship of one God without denying the worship of other gods.*

*To explain the **one supreme, omnipotent divine force**, the **Vedas** emerged in India over **3,000 to 3,400 years ago** (traditionally dated around 1500–1200 BCE or earlier).*

*Following them came the **Upanishads** (approx. 800–500 BCE), which elaborated on the spiritual and philosophical meanings of the Vedas.*

Later came the **epics *(Itihasa)***:

- **The Ramayana** (traditionally attributed to Valmiki, dated roughly 500 BCE to 100 BCE)
- **The Mahabharata** (attributed to Vyasa, dated approximately 400 BCE to 400 CE)
- **The Kumarasambhavam** (a classical Sanskrit poem by **Kalidasa**, not part of the **Skanda Purana**, but inspired by it; composed around 5th century CE)

Note: Kumarasambhavam is a poetic work, while Skanda Purana is one of the major Puranas focused on Lord Muruga (Skanda). They are related in theme but are not the same.

Around the **same ancient period** (traditionally about 1200–1000 BCE), in **Israel**, the **earliest parts** of the **Hebrew Bible (Old Testament)** began to be written.

These texts reflect the philosophical and moral foundations of **Judaism**.

The teachings of **Jesus Christ** were compiled in the **New Testament**, which dates back to around **1st century CE** (approx. 2,000 years ago).

Later, around **610 CE**, the **Qur'an** was revealed in **Arabic** to **Prophet Muhammad** and completed around **632 CE** — making it about **1,390 years old** today.

These scriptures - Vedas, epics, and Puranas - were written by *enlightened sages:*

- To establish **righteous principles** for living in harmony with nature,
- To warn against **destructive traits and behaviors** when such principles are ignored,
- And to **prevent suffering, disease, and moral decay** in human society.

However, the *unfortunate truth* today is that very few read the Vedas, Upanishads, Bhagavad Gita, Ramayan, or Mahabharat in depth.

A small number engage with these texts merely to prepare for lectures or discourses, rather than for self-transformation.

Moreover, even among those who give spiritual discourses, most do not practice meditation. Only when thoughts are expressed from a state of tapas, do they carry life and inner essence.

When words are merely translated from Sanskrit into another language, we may get the literal meaning, but we miss the core, the spirit, and the deeper insight embedded within.

According to researchers who have studied world religions, **India stands unique among all worship traditions**. Why?

Because here, **God is intertwined with economics.** Is this something to **celebrate with pride**? Or should we **grieve it as a distortion**?

If the body never experienced **pain or illness**, and money came in abundance whenever we desired it, **what would then be the role of God**?

If the exact hour of death were known,

would man still remember and revere God?

I asked all these only because I believe You exist.

If it is concluded You don't exist, I will not cry. *- Kannadasan*

Across the world, there are *1.1 billion people who hold no belief in God.* And among the *devotees* who live under the *banner of religions responsible for defining God, none have ever actually seen God; this is a plain reality.*

Why? Because, as the **Bhagavad Gita** says: 'Among millions who seek Me, only a few strive to know Me truly. And among those rare seekers, hardly one truly knows Me as I am.' - Chapter 7, Verse 3.

The reason is this: The *soul (Jivatma),* which gives rise to the human body, has been *buried for generations* under the weight of *ego (ahankara), karma, and illusion (maya).*

Only when one's **mind becomes purified**, can they **truly realize the Supreme**. Therefore, it is only **one among millions** who attain this rare maturity. And the *spiritual truths* taught by such a *realized being* to the masses - those are what we now call **divine principles** or **spiritual philosophies**.

So, regardless of the religion, ***if a person becomes mature and righteous, that alone is enough.***

"Whatever be your religion, strive for self-perfection". This is the universal truth taught by true spiritual masters, who guided people to make this their way of life.

But over time, the ***sacred traditions established by the noble enlightened sages*** *for inner refinement have become* ***cluttered with rituals*** *added by* ***false representatives****.*

Many who merely learn the *external rituals, end up implicitly declaring themselves as representatives of God,* misguiding the masses.

A personal reflection: Two months ago, I visited Tirupati. There, I encountered strict rules:

- Only the dhoti is allowed; no other attire for gents.
- Shirts or even undershirts are not permitted.
- Women must wear a sari or at least a dupatta over their dress.
- No electronic devices like cell phones are allowed.
- Even after standing in queues for hours, you cannot bring water bottles or food.
- Cameras are prohibited.

But there's one thing ***no temple ever forbids****:* ***Bringing money.***

No one seems to realize that these restrictions ***indirectly foster a sense of slavery among devotees***. In temples, those working under religious institutions behave like ***intellectual elites,*** while devotees are often treated as ***ignorant inferiors***.

This creates a ***social power dynamic*** that suppresses the independent thinkers, and sadly, no one questions it.

The **rise of ritualism** is due to **two main causes**:

1. Blind obedience
2. Lack of awareness.

What do the Tirupati temple rules ***actually signify***?

Those who come to the temple should shed their ***attachments, bonds, and identities*** and enter the presence of the Divine with an ***open and pure heart***.

For example: Woman without a dupatta might unintentionally cause distraction due to ***bodily allure***, which may agitate a man's mind. To prevent this and ***maintain spiritual focus***, women are required to wear an upper cloth.

Likewise, ***phones and money*** - conveniences that bind the mind to the outer world, are asked to be left aside so that ***inner silence*** may be achieved.

In truth, ***everything apart from the body, life-force, mind, and intellect*** such as relationships, friendships, comforts, wealth, status, etc., all belong to the ***external world***.

But by ***mentally carrying their imprints***, and due to the ***desire to gain more*** *or the* ***fear of losing what we have****, we are tossed* *around by* ***restlessness and anxiety****.* Therefore, as **Bhagavad Gita** states: *"Leave what belongs to the external world, outside. Do not carry the unnecessary burden into your soul." - (Chapter 5, Verse 27)*

It is the duty of Gurus and spiritual leaders to explain the inner meaning of ***temple traditions and rituals****.*

Since ***religious authorities*** failed in this duty, people have come to ***worship idols themselves as God****,* without ever ***seeking the true Divine****,* nor desiring to understand or follow ***divine justice****.*

Man, who cannot fence the wind or cover the ocean, has somehow ***locked the infinite, all-pervading Supreme Being*** *within a tiny shrine and convinced the masses, '****This is God****'.*

What do we call such a clever feat of social hypnosis?

Another irony that few observe: As long as the statue is in the sanctum, it's called a ***deity****.*

If it is stolen, it becomes just 'idol theft' in the news.

Thus, ***what cannot be stolen is the formless God****. But neither the temple authorities nor the devotees seem to search for a* ***God who is beyond form and within form.***

As ***Thirumoolar*** *says: 'O blind ones, who look with your eyes! True bliss is seen only with the eye within.'*

The ***Gita*** *also declares: "Unintelligent people do not know Me in My immutable, supreme nature. Because I appear with form, they assume I am merely that visible form." - (Chapter 7, Verse 24)*

"Veiled by Yogamaya, I am not perceived by all. Though I am unborn and imperishable, this ignorant world does not know Me as the Supreme Being." - (Chapter 7, Verses 25–26)

Neither **rituals** nor **traditions** have led anyone to see God or attain lasting peace; this truth is made clear by both the **Gita** and real-life **experiences**.

Only those who conquer the mind through **meditation** and **penance (tapas)** have been able to realize the Divine.

*And it's clear beyond doubt that **temple worship that does not threaten or control** through fear is the one that most effectively helps one progress toward the divine realization.*

*Originally, **religions were created to elevate humans toward the Divine.** But in practice, they have done the opposite; **they've brought God down to human levels.***

A business built around an ***invisible God*** has continued for ages, where a few individuals enjoy great wealth and prestige, while the masses are emotionally enslaved.

*This must be **questioned.***

*We must seek **true spirituality**, which brings us closer to the **Divine through rightful practice and tireless effort.***

The result of realizing God is:

- A **healthy body**
- A **fulfilled mind**
- A **prosperous life**

- A **harmonious family**
- **Balanced relationships**, and
- **Sixteen types of blessings: (Given below)**

The sixteen values of a glorious life are: divine awareness, righteousness, education, wealth, grain, youthfulness, strength, courage, noble progeny, wise friendships, loving nature, inner penance, beauty, fame, moral conduct, and forbearance.

What more could one ask for?

But so far how many people have received all these blessings **through rituals and traditions**?

*Only those who have realized God through **sincere penance** and **spiritual discipline**.*

Let us go back in time...

One early human, while rubbing two stones, discovered **fire**. But instead of revealing this discovery openly, he **pretended to possess divine powers**, fooling others and making them **bow at his feet**, thus learning to **eat without labor**.

His **cleverness** in discovering fire turned into **a claim of divine birth**, and he was elevated as someone **favored by God**. This gave rise to **ego** and **boastful pride**.

And this very **ego** has spread ever since.

It has made people:

- **Compete to appear superior**
- **Beautify themselves to feel superior**

- **Pursue degrees to be called intellectuals**
- **Pretend to have moral excellence**
- **Chase fame**
- **Ignore dharma in pursuit of wealth**

and finally, it has turned the world into one filled with competition and envy.

The Atheist View of God's Nature:

The life of the human race can broadly be divided into two types:

1. ***Living only for bodily needs*** *- survival, comfort, consumption.*
2. ***Living with only basic physical necessities, while dedicating the rest of one's time and effort*** *to exploring nature and seeking the self within.*

The Tamil terms **"Astikam"** (believer) and **"Nastikam"** (non-believer) have lost their original clarity in practical use.

The Tamil term **"Ikam"** refers to a way of life.

- **Astikam** originally referred to a material-oriented life-style: acquiring property, land, field, gold ornaments, money; enjoying and safeguarding them; and eventually bequeathing them to the next generation.
- ***Nastikam****, by contrast, refers to a* ***non-materialistic lifestyle****, as exemplified by the* ***Siddhas****, who lived with detachment and realized the* ***formless Divine through undoubted experience****.*

There are also those who say: "Whether God exists or not is irrelevant to our practical lives." Surveys show that around 1.1 billion people globally fall under this view; those with no specific religious belief.

Even ***before the concept of God emerged****, humans lived their lives. And* ***even today****, amid debates and conflicts over religious beliefs, people continue to live.*

So, the question arises: **'Does God really exist?'**

There still exists a minority of people who firmly believe that God does not exist. And among those who do believe in God, how many in this age have actually seen or realized God?

If asked, "You've been worshiping for years. Will you see God before you die?"

Can we find a single devotee who confidently says, 'Yes, I will'?

Most would say: "Oh no, that's too great a thing. Even great saints struggled for it. We ordinary people don't have such fortune."

In truth, isn't it ***atheistic*** *to believe that* ***God can never be seen*** *and yet to* ***go in circles around temples without conviction****?*

One says, "There is no God." The other says, "God cannot be seen." Aren't both essentially the same?

Moreover, the ***Islamic rejection of idol worship*** *and the* ***atheist denial of anthropomorphic gods*** *are* ***philosophically similar****.*

Both declare: 'God is not in forms, idols, or statues'.

The God Revealed in the Ramayan:

The protagonist of the Ramayan, Ram, is known by ten glorious names; each rich with deep symbolic meaning.

Ram's life represents ***threefold evolution of human existence****:*

- Survival of life,
- Experience of worldly pleasures,
- Maturation of the mind leads to divine realization.

The Ten Divine Names of Ram:

1. **Siva Ram** – He is Siva Ram because the primordial energy called Sivam has evolved into everything that exists. Ram embodies that source.
2. **Dasaratha Ram** – Son of Dasaratha, who overcame the ten negative tendencies: greed, anger, lust, pride, jealousy, hatred, deceit, egotism, attachment, and intoxication with power.
3. **Kausalya Ram** – The son of Queen Kausalya, who possessed a purified mind and realized Divine Justice (Dharma).
4. **Sita Ram** – The Supreme Consciousness who accompanied Sita, Jivatma (human soul) that never wavered from divine contemplation even for a blink.
5. **Kodanda Ram** –
    - Ko = King, Intellect, Consciousness.

- Danda = Axis, central channel (like the spinal cord)
- Am = Aum, the vibrational energy. The Kodanda bow symbolizes raising the Kundalini energy from the root chakra (Mooladhar) to the crown (Sahasrara) and merging it into the Turiyatita (state beyond consciousness).
- The bow resting in horizontal position, symbolizes the spine; the arrow in vertical position, symbolizes the mind; the target is the formless divine realm. Thus, **Kodanda Ram** is one elevating awareness to enlightenment.

6. **Raghu Ram** – A spiritual lesson: only after overcoming ego and achieving fullness in knowledge should one propagate a lineage. Ram demonstrated this truth as a descendant of the Raghu clan.
7. **Ayodhya Ram** – Ruler of the unconquerable Ayodhya, symbolic of the invincible inner state. He is both the Shiva (absolute source) and the Jiva (individual soul) and is undefeated by anything(Ego).
8. **Setu Ram** – All creation is one continuous evolution:
    - Subtle space becomes galaxies,
    - They become five elements,
    - Elements become micro-life,
    - Micro-life becomes organisms,

- And finally culminates in humans. Ram, who built the Setu (bridge), represents the **interconnected journey of consciousness**.

One evolves within the other. One exists because of the other. Can one exist without the other? – Kannadasan

9. **Raja Ram** – As Divinity governs everything, Rama, being its divine embodiment, is **Raja Ram**, the King of the Cosmos.

10. **Anantha Ram** – Since all manifestations in this infinite universe are forms of God, Rama is **Anantha Ram**, the limitless one, countless one. "As an idol, He is Sriram. As the Infinite, He is Anantha Ram." – Kannadasan

Realization Through the Self: "Without understanding the soul within you, you cannot know Me, the Supreme. Sit alone, fix your mind on the point between your brows, and meditate upon Me." – Bhagavad Gita. ***The Gita does not say that seeing God is possible just by visiting temples.***

"When you pray, enter your inner chamber, shut the door, and speak to your Father in secret." "Whoever knows Me knows the Father; one who doesn't know Me shall never reach the Father." – Jesus Christ

Jesus emphasized that Jivatma and Paramatma are one. Without realizing the individual soul, God cannot be known. People deified Jesus and even his mother, Mary.

- Protestants revere the Cross and worship God through Jesus Christ.

- Catholics worship Jesus and Mary as the Mother of God.

• Pentecostals emphasize Spirit-filled worship, focusing on the presence of the Holy Spirit.

The Prophet Muhammad later declared: "Worshiping the all-powerful God in form is ignorance. To define God with limits is a disrespect."

"Fools think of Me as having taken human form and under-estimate Me, not realizing that I am the Supreme and the Lord of all beings." – Bhagavad Gita, Chapter 9, Verse 11

"To counter idol worship, the Prophet initiated reform through Jihad and social service - not to destroy, but to reaffirm the boundless and formless nature of God."

'God is All-Loving and infinitely Compassionate.' – Islam

'Anbe Sivam (Love is God).' – Hinduism

'Love is God.' – Christianity

The essence of all religions is ***oneness****. When people truly understand the teachings of great sages, inner transformation occurs.*

Then, ***religious conversion becomes unnecessary;*** *only* ***mental and spiritual conversion*** *is required.*

Sadly, the world is still caught in the battle of superiority:

"My religion is superior; yours is inferior."

In all religious riots, ***not a single religious leader has died****, only innocent people.* More people have died in religious conflicts than in natural disasters or political wars.

In the name of a God who protects all, more people have been killed *- does that mean God failed to protect them?*

Destruction is against God's nature. *No religion supports the killing of life.*

All religions aim to teach Divine Awareness and Righteous Living.

Every religion rest on two pillars:

- God-consciousness (Iman)
- Righteous conduct (Deen)

Islam upholds monotheism (Tawhid) and adherence to prophetic teachings (Risalah). We must honor all enlightened beings who revealed divine truths and strive to follow their path toward spiritual realization.

This principle is also present in Christianity and Hinduism. Let us understand the **true meaning** of the words of great masters, rather than blaming them for the formation of sects.

We must ***practice their teachings properly and consistently****, and through* ***true spiritual discipline****,* ***realize the Divine state****.*

Particularly in Islam, moral codes for daily living are deeply emphasized. In Christianity, acts of charity, such as offering food, clothing, and education are highly encouraged. Hinduism focuses on virtues, love, compassion, patience, and tolerance.

As people worshipped different deities and entered into marriages within those devotional groups, over time these affiliations evolved into what we now call religion, caste, etc.

Valluvar's View of God:

The sage Valluvar avoided sectarian or ritualistic terminology when speaking of God. Instead, he used scientifically meaningful expressions.

He referred to God as Bhagavan, derived from the first letters of creation (pa), protection (ka), and destruction (a) - the three divine functions, combined with a grammatical suffix.

"As alphabets begin with A, so as

Pure space unfolds God." *(Kural 1)*

"Those who surrender at the feet of Divine, that evolved

As flower, live secure for ever." *(Kural 3)*

The divine force that existed at the beginning, emerged as power, expanded as the cosmos, and bloomed as life; Sat, Chit, and Ananda (Consciousness, Existence, Bliss).

"At His peerless feet the soul must bow,

Else the mind's deep sorrows never end." *(Kural 7)*

Whether one calls **Him Allah or "the Incomparable One,"** the meaning remains the same. Unless one understands and aligns with the laws of the Divine, escaping worldly and self-inflicted suffering is difficult.

"Who hold the Divine Law will cross the ocean of birth

Who turn away shall never be free." *(Kural 10)*

Just as rivers originate in different places yet reach completion in the ocean, so too can only those who attain God's feet transcend the endless cycle of birth.

In the six Kural of the "Invocation to God" section of the Thirukkural, Valluvar poetically explains the formless, eternal, and cosmic nature of God, who is the origin, the sustainer, and the end of all that exists.

In the remaining four Kural, he emphasizes that it is only through an enlightened Guru, one who has realized this divine truth, that others can also attain this realization.

The God Revealed by Science:

Science began by transforming Earth's natural resources into tools for human convenience. In this exploration, it discovered a precise order and regularity in all material forms, marked by three dimensions:

Pattern, precision, and motion with regularity.

Upon deeper analysis, it is revealed that all matter is formed by associations of energy particles, and when broken down, matter reverts into energy again.

Thus, science declared that the universe is composed of energy waves – interactions of attraction and repulsion. The fundamental origin of the atom is subtle energy waves.

One scientist defined an atom as "that which cannot be divided further." Later, another broke the atom to find subatomic particles. Continued research identified that an atom consists of three core elements: ***electron, proton, and neutron***.

In recent decades, science reached the pinnacle of atomic research. On **July 4, 2012**, the discovery of the **Higgs Boson (God Particle)** indicated that this particle itself could not be directly seen or measured; only its presence could be inferred through faint trace, like **a wisp of smoke**.

At this frontier, **only spiritual wisdom (Jnana)** can grasp the essence of these divine particles and the concept of God, says **Bhagavan Vedathiri Maharishi**.

Where scientists once described ***gravitational pull*** *as "force of attraction," it is now being refined as* ***"surrounding pressure force."*** *Science further proves that every physical object functions through four dimensions:*

1. **Volume** – the space required for an electron to orbit;
2. **Velocity** – the rate of spin or movement;
3. **Distance** – the repulsion that prevents one wave from colliding into another;
4. **Time** – the continuity from the formation of energy particles to their transformation into matter and back.

But in the **God Particle**, these last two - distance and time - do not exist. The particles move too closely for measurable space, and they are timeless.

Thus, only ***spin (velocity)*** *and* ***space for spin (volume)*** *exist. The unified force driving them is called* ***binding energy*** *or* ***integrating force*** *in science.*

Bhagavan Vedathiri Maharishi *uniquely united both scientific and spiritual perspectives, explaining that from the* ***pure space***

called the Primordial Source *arose all divine particles, and from them emerged the entire evolution, from atom to human.*

The God Explained by Vedathiri Maharishi:

Our ancient sages described the Divine as Aadhi Sivan, Brahma, Vishnu, and Rudra-Sivan, representing creation, preservation, and dissolution.

Maharishi Vedathiri interpreted this scientifically: **Shivam** (pure space) is the primordial source, a self-compressive force or gravitational pressure.

From Shivam arises **Shakti** (energy), which is the base for the **five elements (pancha bhootas)**.

The overlord of these elements and their magnetic fields is **Ganesha (Vinayaka)**.

Their five sensory transformations combine with analytical intelligence (from the Supreme Wisdom), evolving into **six manifestations** - known symbolically as **Arumugam** (six-faced).

Vishnu represents the spinning motion (wheel) and the sound (Conch shell) generated from this energy, both born from the rotating field of space.

The chakra and Sankha are symbols of energy and rhythm. When the motion completes, they all return to **Shivam**.

The electron, one of the fundamental particles in an atom, is a high-speed entity characterized by constant motion.

According to Vedathiri Maharishi's interpretation, under the influence of surrounding pressure (akin to gravitational or cosmic compressive forces), this motion gradually slows down. Symbolically:

- When its motion reduces significantly (not scientifically quantified as exactly 25%), it transitions to a more massive and slower particle, likened to a **proton**.
- With further reduction (symbolically 50%), it becomes a **neutron**, which is heavier and charge-neutral.
- When all motion ceases entirely, it metaphorically collapses into a **point of singularity** or **black dot**, representing the **God Particle** - a state of absolute stillness or unified energy.

Scientific note: In physics, electrons do **not** transform into protons or neutrons by simply slowing down. These are different particles with distinct properties.

However, in **spiritual-scientific metaphor**, Maharishi uses this imagery to illustrate the progressive densification of energy into mass and eventual return to formlessness.

Thus, what emerged from pure space as **electron**, later becomes **proton** and **neutron**, and finally reverts back to formless space. *Shivam is the source, Shakti, Brahma, Vishnu, and Shivam again.*

The word **Brahmam** derives from "Brah" meaning **expansion**. Science echoes this: "The universe is ever-expanding and eternal."

From the Divine Space (Shivam), came force (Shakti), then the five elements, which combined into countless **galaxies**. Among them, our **solar system** emerged, and Earth, with its unique features, gave rise to life, from micro-organisms to human beings.

Scriptures speak of God's attributes, but not **how God became everything.** Vedathiri Maharishi fills this gap. If God were truly **nothing**, then nothing would exist.

Yet everything exists; therefore, God cannot be non-existence.

This aligns with the **Upanishadic truth**: "What is, cannot become nothing; and what is not, cannot come into being."

According to Maharishi, God is:

- **Kinematic** – Moves by its own impulse, without external force.
- **Quivering** – Subtle vibrations, creating time and rhythm.
- **Highly Transparent** – All-pervasive, allowing everything to move through it.
- **Mighty** – The strongest force holding the universe together.
- **Dark** – Invisible to the naked eye, like "Krishna" (meaning dark or unknown).
- **Fluid** – Like a vital fluid, it spreads and flows without limit.

This **pure space** compresses itself (self-compression) → causes vibrations (quivering) → breaks into **countless particles** called **God Particles**.

Vedathiri Maharishi anticipated the scientific discovery of the **Higgs Boson** (God Particle), long before it was identified.

He affirmed: "God Particles cannot be measured by science; they must be realized through divine wisdom."

*To know the Divine, **divine wisdom is the only path**. Since **God transformed into all**, only through God can we realize God.*

*God as **consciousness and energy** manifests as **human evolution**, and man is the final refined product of that transformation.*

*The **brain** is only a medium. **Intelligence** is God within. Hence, man is not separate from God; he is **God evolved into self-awareness**.*

*God doesn't create from afar. Children don't fall from the sky. Every soul carries forward its past life's experiences; this is the **law of karma** and the soul's journey.*

"Birth is common to all living beings, but their greatness

Differ according to the deeds they perform." *(Kural 972)*

There are no differences at birth; only variations in the karmic imprints each soul brings. Understanding this helps us see all as equal. When one realizes that God exists within every living being and protects them from within, the anxiety to store excessively for the future will naturally disappear.

Let Us Seek God:

We now understand that God is formless, pure space. But how do we realize that divine state? Without experiencing divine bliss, one cannot truly break free from the boundaries of religion, caste, clan, or creed.

Nor can one consistently follow Dharma in daily life. ***"To be relieved from all boundaries(regions) is religion."***

The way to realize God is through **meditation** (Dive + in = Divine): focusing and settling the mind inwardly, toward the soul. It's the process of reversing the mind's outward flow back inward; to dive into the Divine.

Taqwa, as in Islamic teachings, is living in alignment with divine justice. The Qur'an too speaks of evolution.

Today, it is easy for people to accept the idea that God is Consciousness.

If religious leaders renounce their egos and their insistence that everyone accept only their religion's name, and instead propose a universal term, then the idea of "one God, as pure space," will become the true universal religion.

If we accept that ***God is Consciousness***, then we realize that one omnipresent Consciousness exists everywhere; active as existence, movement, sensation, and magnetic force.

When the world recognizes that ***God is Consciousness***, all religious divisions and idol worship will dissolve.

The Universal Way:

To cultivate the inner realization that all life is one

Let us make it possible for everyone to learn

Then every day, many wise ones meet in Satsang

Will fulfill the duty of explaining spiritual philosophy.

Founded by many great sages from ancient times.

They will explain the pure San Marga path

All the religions that have spread until today

Will unite in this state, free from all differences. - *Maharishi*

When karmic differences are removed, we realize all life originates from the same divine source.

To support this realization, the **World Community Service Society** provides access to meditation training.

Enlightened individuals who have realized Brahma Jnana will teach the secrets of the universe's evolution through daily meditation practice.

Through this, people will understand that the spiritual path underlying all religions is one and the same.

Summary:

This chapter begins by questioning the origin of religion with poet Kannadasan's quote, asking what inspired humans to create religions.

While billions follow different religions, the text highlights that over a billion people live peacefully without any religious affiliation, aligning with Vedathiri Maharishi's vision of a spiritually aware humanity beyond religious boundaries.

It traces the history of religion from the Sanatana Dharma of India to the Vedas, Upanishads, Ramayana, and Mahabharata. These scriptures aimed not to create rituals but to guide humanity in harmony with nature and inner truth.

However, today, rituals and priestly control have distorted these teachings.

The chapter critiques blind ritualism, idol worship, and sectarian conflicts, calling instead for spiritual maturity through meditation and inner transformation.

The story of Tirupati illustrates how religious customs often enforce discipline without explaining their spiritual essence. Rules should serve spiritual elevation, not submission to dogma.

Vedathiri Maharishi's scientific-spiritual philosophy is introduced. He describes God as pure space (Shivam), which becomes energy (Shakti), then transforms into matter.

Using atomic science as a metaphor, Maharishi explains the transformation of energy to mass and back, aligning ancient metaphysical ideas with modern discoveries like the God Particle (Higgs Boson).

The text explains how every religious tradition originally taught divine consciousness and righteous living. Whether in Islam (Tawhid and Deen), Christianity (love and charity), or Hinduism (virtue and karma), all religions share the same essence.

Religious divisions, caste, and idol worship arose later through misinterpretation and ego.

The ten names of Rama in the Ramayana are interpreted symbolically as steps in human spiritual evolution - from survival to enlightenment. The importance of meditation, Guru guidance, and realization of the soul is emphasized across Gita, Bible, and Qur'an.

Finally, the chapter urges the reader to transcend sectarian identities and realize God as formless consciousness, accessible through inner practice and spiritual wisdom.

Maharishi's vision of a universal religion rooted in self-awareness, divine justice, and unity of all life is proposed as the only lasting path to peace.

Vedathiri Maharishi's prayerful call:

Let the whole world live well, preserving the goodness of life

Let true intellect grow, in the bliss of enlightened living.

The quest for Supreme Truth arises in all people worldwide

Let our hearts elevate further in harmony and oneness!

Long Live the World!

Live with Prosperity!

www.ingramcontent.com/pod-product-compliance
Lightning Source LLC
LaVergne TN
LVHW090307210926
848480LV00001B/164